BUT WHAT IF
I DON'T WANT
TO GO
TO COLLEGE?

REVISED EDITION

BUT WHAT IF I DON'T WANT TO GO TO COLLEGE?

REVISED EDITION

A Guide to Success Through
Alternative Education

Harlow G. Unger

™ **Checkmark Books**
An imprint of Facts On File, Inc.

*T*o my good friends
Liz and Howard

But What If I Don't Want to Go to College? A Guide to Success Through
Alternative Education, Revised Edition

Checkmark Books
An imprint of Facts On File, Inc.
11 Penn Plaza
New York NY 10001

Library of Congress Cataloging-in-Publication Data

Unger, Harlow G., 1931–
    But what if I don't want to go to college? : a guide to success
through alternative education / Harlow G. Unger.
      p. cm.
    Includes index.
    ISBN 0-8160-3793-0 (hc). — ISBN 0-8160-3861-9 (pbk)
      1. Occupational training—United States. 2. Vocational education—
United States. 3. Alternative education—United States.
4. Vocational guidance—United States. I. Title.
HD5715.2.U53 1998
374'.013—dc21   97-50278

Text design by Grace Ferrara
Cover design by Cathy Rincon

Printed in the United States of America

MP FOF 10 9 8 7 6 5 4 3 2 1
   (pbk) 10 9 8 7 6 5 4 3 2 1

This book is printed on acid-free paper.

Contents

About the Author

In addition to many newspaper and magazine articles, Harlow G. Unger has written four books on education for Facts On File: *School Choice—How to Select the Best Schools for Your Children; How to Pick a Private School; A Student's Guide to College Admissions—Everything Your Guidance Counselor Has No Time to Tell You* and the three-volume *Encyclopedia of American Education*, which can be found in all major libraries. Unger is a graduate of Yale University and holds a master's degree from California State University.

*Upon the education of the people of this country
the fate of this country depends.*

—Benjamin Disraeli

Part I Career Education— Alternative Routes to Success

1 College Isn't for Everyone

Nurses, computer operators, chefs, plumbers, air traffic controllers, actors, mechanics, barbers, glaziers, security guards, bank tellers, firefighters, clerks, telephone operators, carpenters, postal workers, railroad engineers, masons, police officers, telephone and electric company linepeople, meat cutters, travel agents, dental technicians . . .

How could our towns, cities and nation—how could our world—get along without the talents and skills of the brilliant men and women who fill these and hundreds of other jobs? The answer is we couldn't, and all who are thinking of joining these important professions should be proud of the vital contributions they'll make to our world.

Aside from their essential nature, all of these jobs have something else in common: None requires a four-year college or university degree. Some don't even require any schooling after high school—even at a two-year community college. That doesn't mean any of these jobs is easy. No important job ever is. All require hard work, dedication, knowledge, intelligence and on-the-job training. But, as in most occupations, success not only yields a sense of professional pride and accomplishment, it can yield considerable financial rewards—again, without ever going to college.

Anyone who wants to can go to college, but not everyone wants to, and not everyone should go—certainly not for four years. There are about 1,200 two-year and 2,200 four-year colleges in the United States, and the vast majority admits almost everybody who applies. So, it's easy to get into college. But nearly one-fourth of students at four-year colleges and universities quit without ever graduating, and more than half of all college seniors fail tests that measure basic knowledge of history, literature and foreign languages. So not everyone who goes to college belongs there.

The fact is millions of students all over the world are not suited for and have no interest in traditional academic schooling—which is why alternative career education was developed: to teach students the skills they need to get a good job. Most European and Japanese schools automatically test all 14-year-olds to determine their aptitudes. Such tests let the academically skilled continue traditional schooling, while students with other talents move into alternative forms of education—career education that refines those talents and ensures their becoming successful, respected artisans and craftspeople.

Many U.S. schools offer the same choice, but a lot of students automatically reject alternative education because well-meaning, but often misguided, friends, teachers, counselors and parents pressure them to stick to traditional academics and go to four-year colleges to get a "good" job. The truth is that a four-year college is only one route to a good job. There are many other routes that can lead to the same or even greater success and personal fulfillment than jobs requiring college degrees. In fact, according to recent U.S. Department of Labor statistics, more than 28 percent of all full-time workers *without college degrees* earn *more* than the average worker *with* a bachelor's degree from college. The Department of Labor reports that the median, or middle, income for *all* full-time, year-round workers in America in 1996—including college grads as well as those without any college—was $557 a week. Appendix C at the back of the book lists the median weekly pay for 600 of the most common jobs.

The median income for full-time workers with a bachelor's degree was $716 a week, or about $37,200 a year. In the same year, about 9.3 million workers *without* four-year college degrees earned $700 or more a week. In a few occupations, as you can see in Table 1 below, more than 10 percent of the workers without college degrees earned more than $800 a week.

Table 1.   The *minimum weekly* earnings of the top 10 percent of workers *without four-year college degrees* in eight high-paying jobs.

Mining, manufacturing and wholesale sales representatives	$1,051
Production occupation supervisors	1,000
Registered nurses	961
Police and detectives	889
Administrative support occupations, supervisors	888
Engineering and related technologists and technicians	856
Carpenters	801
Truck drivers	800

Table 2. Occupations of workers with *less than* a bachelor's degree and the percentage earning $700 or more a week.

Occupation	Number of Workers	Percent
Assemblers	845,000	96
Automobile mechanics	480,000	96
Bus, truck and stationary engine mechanics	274,000	98
Carpenters	606,000	93
Computer operators	367,000	82
Correctional institution officers	261,000	91
Designers	154,000	53
Electrical and electronic equipment repairers (except telephone)	271,000	87
Electrical and electronic technicians	212,000	83
Electrical power installers and repairers	101,000	96
Electricians	475,000	95
Fire fighting occupations	155,000	90
Health technologists and technicians	808,000	79
Industrial machinery repairers	487,000	96
Insurance sales occupations	200,000	55
Investigators and adjusters, insurance and other	673,000	75
Machine operators and tenders, except precision	3,667,000	96
Machine and precision metalworking	669,000	96
Mail carriers and postal clerks	513,000	89
Managers, properties and real estate	201,000	65
Managers, food service and lodging establishments	469,000	78
Miscellaneous management and administration[*]	2,065	57
Plumbers, pipefitters and steamfitters	287,000	96

Table 2. (continued)

Occupation	Number of Workers	Percent
Police and detectives	353,000	75
Purchasing agents and buyers	260,000	66
Rail transportation occupations	95,000	94
Real estate sales occupations	168,00	54
Registered nurses	656,000	51
Sales occupations, other services	190,000	53
Sales representatives, mining and manufacturing, wholesaling	635,000	56
Science and engineering technicians	287,000	75
Secretaries	2,326,000	90
Stationary engineers (plant and building maintenance) and other plant and system operators	230,000	91
Supervisors, police and fire fighting	92,000	71
Supervisors, mechanics and repairers	181,000	89
Supervisors, construction	419,000	88
Supervisors, production	1,010,000	87
Supervisors, administrative support (clerical, etc.)	519,000	73
Supervisors and proprietors, sales organizations	1,658,000	72
Telephone and telephone line installers and repairers	211,000	95
Truck drivers	2,000,000	96
Welders and cutters	438,000	98
All other occupations	26,021,000	71

* This is a vague U.S. Labor Department category, which includes management and administrative positions at a broad range of nontechnical establishments such as supermarkets, retail stores, gas stations, storage warehouses and so forth.

Even more important, however, is the large number of occupations in which workers without bachelor's degrees can earn $700 or more a week—that is, the same wage and salary scale as workers with bachelor's degrees. Table 2 (on pages 5–6) shows the huge number of opportunities for success *without* a four-year college education. It lists only occupations with at least 50,000 or more workers, in which more than half earn $700 or more a week ($36,400 a year).

In addition to high wages, there are also more than ample job openings right now for eager, motivated workers without four-year college degrees. Indeed, of the 20 fastest growing occupations, according to the Labor Department, only four require a bachelor's degree or higher. Most, as you can see in Table 3 (on page 8) are occupations for which the required training is available in career-education programs at good high schools, two-year community and junior colleges and technical institutes.

Where the New Jobs Will Be

The U.S. Department of Labor estimates that the 20 fastest growing occupations in the United States listed on page 8 will create more than 7.5 million jobs, or more than 40 percent of all the new jobs that will be created between now and the year 2005. Most will be for graduates of vocational and other alternative education programs.

Now those are just the top 20 fastest growing jobs, and they only represent about half the job opportunities that will open up over the next few years. A lot of opportunities will open up in other areas. At this very moment, the machine-tool industry needs 30,000 machinists, and the semiconductor industry has 10,000 openings it needs to fill immediately. In California and Nevada, the utilities industry and Local 1245 of the International Brotherhood of Electrical Workers are eagerly searching the nation for high school graduates—and that's all you need, a high school diploma—to enroll in the lineman apprentice program. In all, American industry will have to fill nearly 17 million new jobs between now and 2005. The retail trades alone will need 2.7 million new workers; there will be 3.8 million new jobs in the business-services sector—computer service and repair, for example. The huge area of health services will need more than 3

Table 3. The 20 fastest growing occupations.

Occupation	New Jobs
Cashiers	562,000
Building maintenance	559,000
Retail salesperson	532,000
Waiters and waitresses	479,000
Registered nurses	473,000
General managers and top executives	466,000
Systems analysts	445,000
Home health aides	428,000
Guards	415,000
Nursing aides, orderlies and attendants	387,000
Teachers, middle and high shcool	386,000
Marketing and sales worker supervisors	380,000
Teacher aides and educational assistants	364,000
Receptionists and information clerks	318,000
Truck drivers	271,000
Secretaries, except legal and medical	267,000
Clerical supervisors and managers	261,000
Child-care workers	248,000
Maintenance repairers, general utility	231,000
Teachers, elementary school	220,000

million more workers, while the field of educational services will need more than 2 million new employees—not just teachers, but teacher aides, construction workers, building maintenance workers and many other men and women with skills they can acquire through alternative education.

Indeed, nearly two-thirds of the 17 million new jobs that will be created over the next few years will be in occupations that do *not* require a bachelor's degree or more education. Despite all the talk about "high-tech" jobs in the United States, only about 21 percent of all workers now have a bachelor's degree or more. Fewer than 21 percent of American workers have four-year college degrees or more. More than 60 percent of American workers learn their skills on the job. Table 4 below shows just how many jobs there are today that require only alternative, as opposed to formal, university education, and the expectations for the year 2005.

Table 4. Number of and percentage of jobs by level of education and training, 1994–2005.

Education and training	1994 (in '000)	Percent	2005 (in '000)	Percent
Total	127,014	100.0	144,708	100.0
Professional degree	1,702	1.3	2,076	1.4
Doctoral degree	976	.8	1,156	.8
Master's degree	1,500	1.2	1,927	1.3
Work experience, plus bachelor's or higher degree	8,191	6.5	9,494	6.6
Bachelor's degree	14,007	11.0	17,771	12.3
Associate degree	3,956	3.1	4,919	3.4
Post-high school vocational training	7,102	5.6	7,845	5.4
Work experience only	9,994	7.9	11,325	7.8
On-the-job training	79,586	62.7	88,192	60.9

Even more important for those just starting out or thinking about switching to a new career, of the more than 49.6 million job openings that will be created by company expansion or net replacements between now and 2005, only slightly more than 13.5 million, or fewer than 23 percent, will be reserved for applicants with at least a bachelor's or higher degree from a four-year college or university. In other words, more than three-quarters of all new jobs opening up between now and the year 2005 will *not* require a four-year college education, but will only require alternative career education or on-the-job training.

Appendix D at the back of the book shows just how many more jobs each industry will have available between now and the year 2000. It also shows which industries will shrink. And Appendix E, which follows, shows the projected changes in the number of jobs in each occupation, along with the kind of training—bachelor's degree, associate degree, on-the-job, etc.—that is needed for each job. In other words, those two appendixes can serve as your personal career planning guide, by showing you which industries are shrinking or expanding, which jobs in each industry will require more or fewer workers, and the training needed to get each of those jobs.

The fact is there are only two good reasons for going to a four-year college or university: a deep desire to study traditional academic subjects (literature, history, philosophy, languages, science, and so on) or a deep commitment to career goals that can only be reached with a university education (law, medicine, engineering, and similar professions).

So if you're one of the millions of Americans who really don't want to or need to go to a university, and your talents and career goals are in areas not requiring a university degree, by all means consider alternative career education. Alternative education can open thousands of career opportunities in the arts, crafts, science and health care, sports, skilled trades, manufacturing, construction, travel, banking and finance and even in your own business—and there's no need to spend thousands of dollars and four precious years at a university if you don't really need to or want to.

What Is Alternative Education?

In simplest terms, alternative education is practical training that will convert your basic skills, talents and interests into a good job and a lasting, rewarding career. Alternative education will help you become a master craftsperson—an expert everyone wants and needs to hire.

Like traditional academics, alternative education is available through courses at almost every level of schooling—high school, community college, technical institutes and four-year colleges and universities. But it's also available in apprenticeship programs and on-the-job training programs provided by many companies and labor unions. In many cases, alternative education involves no formal classroom study. There are many career opportunities where alternative education simply involves getting an entry-level job in which you earn while you learn—and the more you learn, the more you earn. More than 60 percent of all factory workers, tradeworkers, craftspeople and office and clerical workers learn their skills on the job.

How much alternative education you'll need in an area will largely depend on the demands of your work and your employer—and your own interests. In some areas, you may want to continue learning new skills and improving old ones all your life. Some industries require skills that can be learned entirely in high school. Others require skills taught only at technical schools or community colleges, because high schools either don't teach them or don't teach advanced levels. Still other courses are available at four-year colleges and universities, where alternative education students may take them on a full-time or part-time basis during the day or evening, with or without studying for a degree. And that's what this book is about: to show you exactly what type of alternative career education is available, where to get it and how much you'll need to get your first job in a wide variety of careers. The rest of this section will tell you all about alternative education—how to evaluate it and how to pick the right career track for you. Remember: Career education is worthless if it can't help you get a job. Part II lists hundreds of career and talent areas that do not require four-year college or university degrees for entry-level jobs and a clear track to success. Each career listing includes the education or training needed to get started, the pay range and some companies and organizations that need those skills. Part III will show you how to get started in your new career area, with some easy-to-use tips for applying for, and getting, your first job: writing a good resume, completing a successful job application and using the job interview to sell yourself and your talents.

One important thing to keep in mind as you read ahead is that there are almost no limits to the personal *and* financial rewards available from the opportunities described in this book. Even jobs that only pay minimum wage to start can lead to opportunities in management and ownership after you've learned enough about your new craft or trade. Almost all owners and managers started out as ordinary workers in their trades and businesses. Many restaurant owners were once waiters, many store owners started as stock clerks and salespeople and many successful building contractors started as laborers or apprentices. The same is true for managers and owners in almost all of the trades and businesses in Part II, and they got to the top without spending four years at college. You can too. Let's find out how—and good luck!

Getting Started

One exciting thing about alternative education is that it is basically open to all. There are no age limits, for example, and almost no background requirements. To sign up—and to succeed—all you really need is an interest in and a desire to learn a craft or trade. You can start at 16 or 60, whenever *you* are ready. Adults of any age, regardless of educational background, may enroll in virtually every type of program, whether it's on the job, at a two- or four-year college or at a local public high school or technical school. Indeed, more than one-third of all community college and junior college students are more than 30 years old. Most programs are available on weekends and at night as well as during the day, so as not to interfere with any job you may have. More than 80 percent of community college students are enrolled part-time.

Alternative education programs are also available to college students who want to switch from traditional academics or who wish to combine traditional academics with alternative education. High school students often have the same choices: They can switch from traditional academic programs to vocational education or combine the two. So, no matter how old you are or what your circumstances—whether you're in school or not—alternative education programs are open to you. It's only a question of finding the right one.

Even if you've already left high school without getting a diploma, or left so long ago you can't remember what you learned there, you can still take advantage of alternative education. Many alternative education programs don't require a high school diploma for admission. What you may want to consider, however, is enrolling in an equivalency diploma program to brush up on and master basic reading, writing and calculating skills while you take alternative education. Combining the two will give you a marketable skill *and* a high school diploma—a combination guaranteed to open the door to endless opportunities that await all bright, talented, hard-working men and women. Chapter 2 shows you how to get your equivalency diploma, and how to evaluate *yourself*, especially if you're convinced you have no skills. Everyone has skills and talents, and you do too! The problem is that not everyone knows how to determine what his or her talents are. One way is to identify your interests first. Whatever they are—sports, music or science—there are endless jobs to match those interests, even if you're not an athlete, musician or scientist. There are hundreds of vital jobs in every field, and, with alternative education, it's easy to learn how to do them. So keep reading!

Combining Career Education and College

Although none of the career opportunities in this book requires a four-year college degree, if you want to go to college or to a university, by all means do so. College can provide you with a useful and rewarding education, and it may, if you're not sure yet, help you determine how you want to spend the rest of your life. Most colleges are like enormous cafeterias of knowledge, offering endless choices of courses in traditional academics as well as preprofessional and alternative education. Many people, for one reason or another, often fail to recognize the value of traditional academics—the liberal arts. Often it's because they may have had some poor or boring teachers in high school, and they assume they won't enjoy or get anything out of further study in the liberal arts. But the liberal arts are designed to help students develop intellectual and creative abilities that will prove valuable in almost every occupation.

So, you can combine the best of many educational worlds at college and "taste" different areas of knowledge before you make any career decisions. What's more, about 1,000 two- and four-year colleges across the United States now participate with local industries in the growing cooperative education movement to provide a mixture of liberal arts and practical arts education that will assure graduates of immediate jobs at cooperating companies. The exciting career opportunities available through cooperative education are described in the second half of this chapter.

Remember, too, that no matter what career you eventually choose, a degree from a two-year or four-year college will always be a big plus on your resume.

But don't enroll in a full-time, four-year or even two-year college simply because others want or expect you to. For many, college can be the happiest years and worth every penny of tuition invested in it. For others, college can mean years of misery and a waste of a family's life savings. Remember, nearly one-fourth of U.S. college students drop out without getting a degree.

Only you can decide whether you will benefit more from college, alternative education or a combination of both. I hope this book will help you make that decision. One decision to avoid at all costs, however, is to pursue *no* education, either academic or vocational—in other words, to quit school. Fifty years ago, a decision to quit school and go to work at age 16 or 18 was perfectly sound for many people, because there were many jobs for unskilled workers. Elevators in almost every department store and office and apartment building had to be operated by hand. Streets were swept, roads were built and crops were harvested—all by hand. In offices and stores everywhere, all books were kept by hand. Most of this is no longer true. Elevators run automatically; machines sweep streets, pave roads and harvest crops. And scanners register sales at most supermarket and department store checkout counters—and automatically feed all data into computers that keep the books, do the accounting, control inventories and reorder out-of-stock merchandise. Stores won't—and many already do not—need as many bookkeepers, accountants, stocktakers and other behind-the-scenes workers. Self-service long ago eliminated many sales clerks, and scanning equipment is eliminating many cashiers and checkout personnel.

The same is true in almost every industry. ATM equipment is putting bank tellers out of work; e-mail is putting mail handlers out of work; voice mail is eliminating jobs for telephone operators; computers are eliminating the need for file clerks; automatic copying equipment is putting duplicating machine operators out of work. Even computer operators, who set controls and load tapes, disks and paper into big mainframe computers, are losing their jobs as computers themselves become more sophisticated and do more things automatically. In fact, one Japanese robot manufacturing plant is using robots to make robots—to "reproduce themselves," in a sense. The list is endless. Table 5 shows the types of jobs that automation—computers, robots, etc.—will eliminate during the next 10 years.

As you can see, the job opportunities for unskilled and even semiskilled workers are disappearing, because there are almost no more unskilled jobs. Indeed, the unemployment rate among the unskilled—those who dropped out of high school without getting their diplomas—is more than 20 percent, compared to just under 15 percent for high school graduates, less than 8 percent for people with some college but with no degree, 5.4 percent for those with an associate degree

Table 5. Occupations with the largest expected decline in available jobs by the year 2005.

Bookkeeping, accounting and auditing clerks	278,000
Farmers	272,000
Typists and word processors	212,000
Bank tellers	152,000
Sewing machine operators, garment workers	140,000
Household workers	108,000
Computer operators	98,000
Billing, posting and calculating machine operators	64,000
Duplicating, mail, and other office machine operators	56,000
Textile machine operators	47,000
File clerks	42,000
Freight, stock and material movers	41,000
Farm workers	36,000
Machine-tool cutting operators and tenders, metal and plastic	34,000
Central-office telephone operators	34,000
Central-office and PBX installers and repairers	33,000
Electronic and electronic assemblers	30,000
Telephone installers and repairers	26,000
Personnel clerks	26,000
Data-entry keyers	25,000

from a two-year college and 5.2 percent for those with bachelor's degrees or higher from four-year colleges and universities.

In other words, no one can afford to consider quitting school anymore. The only decisions for intelligent people today is what kind of school or training program to attend, what kind of education to get—academic, vocational or a combination of both—and how much education to get. Appendix E at the back of the book lists the kinds of training you'll need for hundreds of different occupations—including the ones you may be considering. Check *now* to see whether you qualify.

Keep in mind that the decision you make is not irreversible. It will naturally be less costly in time and money if you can decide what you'll do the rest of your life before you graduate from high school. But most people don't, and that's a fact. To prove it, just ask your parents or teachers whether they are now doing exactly what they planned to do when they were 16 or 17 years old. The chances are they're not, and, if you're still in high school, it's unfair to expect you to know what you're going to do 25 years from now.

For most people, the decision that seems right at one particular time is often not right at another time. So, if you make a decision now and find you're unhappy about it later on, there is absolutely no reason to feel badly about changing your mind and starting on a new course. It's important to remain flexible and be prepared to change with time and circumstances.

If you decide that vocational education is right for you at this time in your life and others disapprove of your decision, show them this book so they can see how alternative education can help you develop skills and talents to take advantage of rewarding career opportunities. There are many careers that don't require a college education but do provide millions all over the world with successful, rewarding lives. You must fulfill *your* ambitions, not those of your parents or friends or anyone else.

What Kind of Alternative Education Is Best?

Before exploring specific career opportunities, let's look at the various types of alternative education open to you and see how to evaluate them. Careful evaluation is the key to getting good alternative education. Just because your local high school or community college offers vocational courses does not mean you'll gain any useful knowledge if you take them. According to U.S. government studies, as many as half the students who take high school vocational courses graduate with obsolete, *useless* skills (see Table 6 on page 19). So just because a high school or college counselor says a vocational course or program is good doesn't make it good. And just because a vocational school advertises on television doesn't make it good or even honest. Many private trade schools that advertise on television are operated by con artists—which is why careful evaluation of alternative education programs is so important. Many students have wasted their time and life savings pursuing useless vocational education programs. Many have gone into debt without learning useful job skills. Let's make sure that doesn't happen to you.

Let's look at the various kinds of alternative education available, and then at ways to find out if they're any good. There are 10 basic types of vocational education. Although many are not available in all communities, it's important that you know them by name so you can recognize them. They are:

1. Comprehensive high schools
2. Specialized vocational/technical (vo-tech) high schools
3. Cooperative education programs
   a. High schools
   b. Colleges
4. "Two-plus-two" tech-prep programs
5. Community colleges
6. Technical institutes
7. Private, not-for-profit junior (two-year) colleges
8. Private, for-profit (proprietary) trade schools
9. Four-year colleges and universities
10. Employer/union apprenticeship programs
11. Employer-sponsored training programs

Let's take a closer look at each of them and at their advantages and disadvantages. Then let's try to work out the best possible program for you.

1. Comprehensive high schools. A comprehensive high school is an ordinary high school—the kind kids attend everywhere in the United States. It offers *everything* for *everyone*—academic education, vocational education and general education (see page 40). Fewer than 12 percent of all high school students are in vocational education, however. That's a huge drop from 10 years ago, when nearly 27 percent of all high school students enrolled in such programs. More than one-third of the students in high school vocational education courses are older than 30, and many schools offer evening as well as daytime courses to accommodate working adults.

ADVANTAGES: These programs can offer an early opportunity to learn a little about a trade or occupation without making a long-term commitment. Although fewer than 12 percent of all high school students are enrolled in vocational education *programs*, 97 percent take one or more vocational education courses that give them a taste of what each field is like and allows them to decide whether or not they might want to pursue that type of work. Comprehensive vocational education also has the advantage of allowing a student to switch easily from academic to vocational education without having to change schools and make new friends.

DISADVANTAGES: Unless tied to a high school cooperative education program (see Number 3 on page 20), the overwhelming majority of vocational education programs in comprehensive high schools are, by themselves, inadequate. In fact, they're terrible. Half the vocational training in comprehensive high schools centers about agriculture, home economics and industrial arts—all of them areas in which the number of job opportunities is shrinking. Moreover, most comprehensive high schools usually teach only one or two courses in each occupational area, and that's not enough education to get a good job. Most high school vocational courses lack adequate resources and equipment, and so many teachers lack up-to-date training in the fields they teach that many employers simply won't recognize diplomas in vocational education from comprehensive high schools as valid evidence of a young person's skills. And that's why there has been such a dramatic drop in student enrollment. As one U.S. government report put it, the typical high school vocational education program "neglects academic skill development, trains for occupations not in demand, teaches with outmoded equipment, and offers limited placement assistance." The report found that *less than half* of all students who take high school vocational education are able to use what they learned in full-time jobs following high school. As you can see in Table 6, the course utilization rates are poor in some job areas: Less than one-quarter of the men who study communications and less than one-third of the women who study occupational home economics were able to use what they learned after they graduated.

Unemployment among students who graduated from vocational education programs in comprehensive high schools *averages* more than 14 percent, and the average wage for students who do find work is less than $8.00 an hour. There are, of course, some excellent vocational education

Table 6. Rates of high school vocational course utilization by subject area.

According to the U.S. Department of Education, these are the percentages of high school graduates able to use the vocational courses they studied in high school in the jobs they eventually secured after graduating. Even the most gender-oriented education, such as construction or mechanics and repairs for men, proved of no value for more than half the students. Occupational home economics was of value to fewer than one-third of the women students.

	Course Utilization Rate	
Vocational Subject	**Men**	**Women**
Agriculture	43.6%	26.9%
Business	32.4%	65.4%
Marketing	20.9%	38.3%
Health	7.5%	78.8%
Occupational home economics	14.4%	31.5%
Construction	42.0%	0.0%
Mechanics and repairers	45.5%	35.2%
Precision production	36.0%	17.8%
Transportation	6.2%	0.0%
Technical and communications	22.1%	31.6%
Average course utilization rates	38.0%	53.0%

Source: National Assessment of Vocational Education, U.S. Department of Education.

programs in some comprehensive high schools, and the next chapter will show you how to identify them. For the most part, however, it's not a good idea to count on getting a good job based on what you learn in the vocational education program in most comprehensive high schools.

2. Specialized vocational/technical (vo-tech) high schools. These are two- to four-year high schools where all students major in some form of vocational education, although all receive the same fundamental academic instruction of conventional high schools.

ADVANTAGES: Many are outstanding schools. They offer far more comprehensive, in-depth training by skilled craftspeople in each trade than ordinary high schools, thus making each graduate more skilled and employable. Employers generally respect the credentials of graduates from vo-tech schools, which usually have strong job placement services and close ties with employers. Vo-tech students emerge stronger in academics as well, because students learn English, math, science and other subjects in conjunction with their vocational education and, therefore, find these areas more interesting. In other words, they learn *applied* rather than theoretical mathematics. Student self-esteem is usually higher, because the entire administration and faculty are devoted to vocational education instead of traditional academics. In comprehensive high schools, vocational education is often held in low esteem by school administrators, who tend to assign less able teachers to vocational education students than to students in the academic, college-prep curriculum. Another advantage of specialized vo-tech schools is the time and opportunity allowed to sample many trades and occupations before deciding on a specialty. The best vo-tech schools offer prevocational courses that offer students an in-depth look at "career clusters" such as agriculture, manufacturing, health, public service and other broad categories, and then examine the hundreds of specific jobs within those clusters.

DISADVANTAGES: Usually there are none in terms of educational quality. Unfortunately, there are only about 500 vo-tech schools across the entire United States. Most communities have none. If there's a vo-tech school in or near your community, by all means evaluate its program and look into the possibility of enrolling.

3. Cooperative education programs.   There are two kinds of cooperative education programs: One is at the high school level, the other at the college level. Both offer excellent vocational education.

   a. High school cooperative education programs: These programs allow students to take vocational courses at a comprehensive high school in the morning and immediately apply all new knowledge on the job in the afternoon at local companies that provide supervision and instruction and work closely with vocational education teachers.

ADVANTAGES: Skills taught are up-to-date and immediately applicable in the workplace. Close ties with local industry and employers can be a big help in getting students jobs after graduation. Involvement of local industry also assures schools of the most modern equipment and continuous training for teachers.

DISADVANTAGES: The quality of the academic education offered to vocational education students is often inadequate. That's because administrators of comprehensive high schools often hold vocational education in lower esteem than academic education. So they sometimes reserve their best teachers for college-prep programs and assign less-skilled faculty to students of vocational education. These students, however, need just as many skills in reading and comprehensive, mathematics, analysis and problem solving and science as academic track students. Unfortunately, voc-ed students usually do not get an adequate academic education in comprehensive high schools.

The lack of interest by school administrators in vocational education is evident in the small number of comprehensive high schools that have bothered establishing cooperative education programs. Only about 3 percent of high school students are enrolled in formal "coop" programs. From your own personal point of view, another disadvantage of a high school cooperative education program is the possibility that a decision to specialize in a trade at age 16 or 17 may be premature. You may find that, after graduating and working at your new trade for a year, you dislike it intensely. A change then, however, may be economically impossible or, at best, difficult. It will mean going back to school either to learn another trade or to get an academic degree.

b. **College cooperative education programs.** Without question, these provide the finest vocational education for students who are certain about their career goals. Cooperative education programs are available at about 900 public and private two-year and four-year colleges and universities in 48 states and the District of Columbia. The programs integrate your daily college classroom studies with a part-time paying job at a local company, which works closely with your school and your teachers to mesh everything you learn in the classroom with what you'll be doing at work. About 200,000 students now participate in coop-ed programs at every level, from the associate to the doctoral degree. An estimated 50,000 employers in every industry are employing them, including the federal government, which employs 14,000 coop students in 36 federal departments and agencies at almost 2,000 work sites. Although 85 of the 100 largest American corporations employ coop students, the vast majority of coop employers are small organizations employing one to three coop students. There are two types of programs: alternating and parallel. Students in *alternating programs* rotate periods of full-time classroom studies with terms of full-time employment. Students in parallel programs work part-time and attend school part-time during the same term.

ADVANTAGES: This is just about the best vocational education you can get anywhere in the world! Students who do well are almost guaranteed good jobs on the "fast track" after graduation. And remember: You'll be choosing the type of work *you* really want to do—and that's a sure-fire formula for doing well! About 40 percent of coop-ed students continue working for their coop employer after graduation. Another 40 percent find jobs in fields directly related to their coop education, and another 15 percent decide to continue their education by getting bachelor's degrees. Some go on to graduate school programs in law, medicine, dentistry or other professions. Another tremendous advantage of coop-ed is that it allows high school students to concentrate on academics, knowing that they can enroll in excellent community college vocational studies that will almost guarantee them a good job. And still another tremendous advantage of coop education is that you're getting paid while you learn. Students earned between $2,500 and $14,000 a year in wages last year from their coop employers—and they were still eligible for the conventional financial aid available to all college students: scholarships from the colleges they attend and grants and student loans from state and federal government agencies. Some of America's largest companies are involved in coop education: American Airlines, the American Hockey League, American Stock Exchange, Citibank, General Electric, IBM, John Hancock Insurance, Johnson & Johnson, Gillette, Polaroid, Kidder Peabody, the New York Giants (that's right!), Off-Track Betting, Queens Symphony Orchestra, Sears Roebuck . . . the list is endless—and so are the opportunities in virtually every type of occupation you or I could ever think of. And the list of colleges is equally impressive: Boston University, Fairleigh Dickinson University, George Washington University, Michigan State University, Montclair State University, Northeastern University, Pennsylvania State University, Seton Hall University, Syracuse University,

Temple University, University of Connecticut, University of Massachusetts, University of Michigan, U.S. Merchant Marine Academy. . . . Again, the list seems endless—as are the programs they offer: agriculture, natural resources, applied arts and crafts, business, computer science, health care, home economics, technologies and vocational arts, including construction, food service, repair and maintenance, trade and industry. Write for the comprehensive *Directory of College Cooperative Education Programs*, published by Oryx Press for the American Council on Education, Washington, D.C. This is the most complete guide to cooperative education, listing all colleges offering cooperative education, the courses offered and the companies that participate. Appendix F lists 329 colleges with cooperative education programs that are members of the National Commission for Cooperative Education. If you're interested in learning more about any of the programs, write or call the colleges or send a post card to the Commission at 360 Huntington Avenue, Boston, MA 02115, and they'll send you details of the programs from as many as six colleges.

DISADVANTAGES: There are none, except for the lack of similar programs everywhere. Instead of only 900 colleges, every American college and university should be offering similar programs. If you know what career interests you most and you can find a college cooperative education program near you, by all means enroll. Remember that the 20 fastest growing occupations listed by the U.S. Department of Labor (Table 3) usually require some post-high school training, and most employers in those fields prefer an associate degree.

4. "Two-plus-two" tech-prep programs.   Two-plus-two programs are a form of vocational education that combines the last two years of high school with two years of community college education. In other words, it is a *four-year program* that begins in junior year of high school and continues through community college and leads to an associate degree in a particular vocation.

ADVANTAGES: Four years of comprehensive, in-depth training and a college associate degree give students the highest qualifications for the workplace. Because the entire program is usually organized and supervised by the faculty at the community college, a two-plus-two program assures students of superior education at the high school level. Moreover, because it is a comprehensive four-year program, high school seniors must work seriously instead of goofing off and wasting time. Failure to perform well in 12th grade, the second year of the two-plus-two program, can mean failing the entire program. In addition to extensive vocational education, community college faculty see to it that two-plus-two students receive the same academic training and learn the same skills as students in the academic track—that is, reading speed and comprehension, analytical skills, problem-solving, decision-making, computation, computer literacy, human relations and communications skills. Still another advantage is that if, for one reason or another, a student decides against pursuing a particular trade, he or she can either remain in community college and study a new trade or transfer to a four-year college and work toward a bachelor's degree. Two-plus-two programs normally have extremely active and effective job placement services, and employers eagerly recruit graduates from these programs. More than 90 percent of the graduates find work in the fields in which they trained, and the average starting wage is about $10 an hour.

DISADVANTAGES: There are none in terms of educational quality. Unfortunately, the two-plus-two concept is not available in most communities. If it is available in your area, sign up!

5. **Community colleges.** Community colleges were originally designed as two-year public academic institutions that would serve as a transition between high school and four-year colleges and universities. Most still offer a wide range of academic courses, but almost all have added vocational training programs, many of which are among the best in the United States. As previously mentioned, many offer excellent cooperative education programs that allow you to "earn while you learn." Others integrate vocational education with nearby high school programs (see "two-plus-two" tech-prep programs). Still others offer their own independent vocational education programs. Most community colleges try to specialize in only one or two areas of vocational training such as hotel and restaurant management, health care, the graphic arts or some other career cluster.

ADVANTAGES: The cost is relatively low, because community colleges are part of state or city public-university systems. Average tuition for full-time students at American community colleges is $1,200 a year, although costs vary widely from state to state, from as low as $600 to as high as $3,500. Community colleges also offer an opportunity to combine academic studies with vocational training. So, if you feel you need to brush up on academic skills—in math or English, for example—you can do so and still learn a craft or trade. Unlike high school, you can go to school part time and maintain a job while you're continuing your education. You can take as little or as much time as you need to complete your degree. You can take as many or as few courses as you want. You can just study one course to learn a trade without signing up for a degree program. Teachers at community colleges are usually part-time professionals. That's good, because they're up to date and knowledgeable about what's happening in their fields, and they're usually in close touch with job markets. Another point about community colleges: They are usually exceptionally caring institutions that provide far more individual attention than most four-year colleges. Their name, "community," says it all and defines their role: to serve the needs of the community and its students. Most try sincerely to do just that.

DISADVANTAGES: Not all community colleges offer worthwhile vocational education. Indeed, a U.S. Department of Education study found that only about 60 percent of community college students are able to use the college vocational training to get and keep a job. The low "course-utilization rate," however, could reflect a number of things. On the one hand, it might very well reflect poor educational quality. On the other hand, it might also reflect the failure of a lot of students to take enough courses. Students who only take 12 credits—about one-quarter the number needed for an associate degree—have almost three times the unemployment rate of students who take the full complement of credits and graduate from community college with an associate degree. Fewer than 6 percent of students who graduate remain unemployed after a year—almost as low an unemployment rate as those who graduate with a bachelor's degree from four-year colleges.

So, the more courses you take in a particular vocation, the more likely you will be to get a good job and use your training. But it's essential for you to evaluate community college (and all other) vocational programs before enrolling. I'll show you how to do that in the next chapter. Assuming you find a good community college, and many of them are great, it really will be up to you how much you get out of it.

6. Technical institutes.   Like community colleges, these are usually two-year schools, but they are highly specialized and seldom offer extensive academic programs. They expect incoming students to have a firm com-

mand of English, mathematics and basic science. Many offer cooperative education programs of the kind discussed earlier.

ADVANTAGES: Technical institutes usually offer high quality, in-depth training by professionals who are up-to-date on technological advances and in touch with job markets. Technical institutes normally have close working ties with nearby industries and have extensive job-placement facilities for their students.

DISADVANTAGES: Again, there are very few of them across the United States, and most are usually costlier than community colleges and require more intensive study. That makes it difficult for some students to handle the work part time. Indeed, it's best to attend full time.

7.   **Private, not-for-profit junior (two-year) colleges.**   These are the same as community colleges, except that they are privately operated (although not for profit).

ADVANTAGES: On average, they offer much broader academic programs than community colleges and more athletic and other extracurricular activities. Many have boarding facilities for full-time resident students. The main reason for considering private junior colleges is to see whether they offer superior programs or vocational courses and job placement services that may not be available at a local community college. Many offer cooperative education studies as discussed earlier.

DISADVANTAGES: Although usually better than community colleges, they cost more: an average of $7,000 a year, compared to $1,200 for public community colleges.

8.   **Private, for-profit (proprietary) trade schools.**   These are specialized private schools, which usually offer training in one field only, for example, auto mechanics, hair-styling or cosmetology. Most obtain their students by advertising.

ADVANTAGES: Training is quick and concentrated. Students are ready for the job market in as few as two weeks, depending on the trade. In some communities, private trade schools are the only organizations that teach certain trades, such as bartending or barbering. So students may have no choice but to attend a private trade school if they want to learn such trades.

DISADVANTAGES: There are no opportunities for academic work, and all training is limited to one field. Training can be extremely poor, because teachers are paid far less than at community colleges and technical institutes. Unemployment among proprietary school graduates is incredibly high: often above 20 percent. Moreover, wages of proprietary school graduates do not climb substantially with seniority. Most proprietary school training is in single-level occupations such as bartending, barbering or hairstyling. Unless people in these occupations acquire their own businesses (for example, their own tavern or barber shop), their wages will remain relatively constant throughout their careers, affected perhaps only by inflation-impelled increases. Proprietary school graduates are also less likely to get jobs using their vocational training than graduates from community colleges. The biggest disadvantage of proprietary schools, however, is the danger of running into unethical and criminal operators. Some operators advertise their schools on television, accept payment from would-be students then disappear with the money, only to begin again somewhere else. The beautiful school facilities you see on the television commercials may often be cleaned-up garages or beauty parlors whose owners were paid to allow their business places to be videotaped for those commercials. The tragedy of such runaway schools is that they leave many students in debt with loans to repay for education they never received. So, beware of proprietary school advertisements. The promises they make may be lies! There are so many disadvantages to proprietary schools that if there's a good alternative, it's wise to use it. If there's no choice, however—let's say the trade you want to learn is only taught by a proprietary trade school—then be certain the school is *accredited* by the Accrediting Commission of Career Schools and Colleges of Technology, 2101 Wilson Boulevard, Arlington, VA 22201. Chapter 2 will tell you more about the importance of accreditation in evaluating vocational schools. Meanwhile, keep in mind what a U.S. government study of proprietary schools had to say:

> Our study found patterns of misrepresentation to prospective students, lack of attention to . . . standards, low (student) completion rates, and faulty use of federal financial aid programs. Three-quarters of the students admitted without a high school degree and half the students with a high school degree dropped out . . . Certificates from many proprietary schools have little reliability.

9. Four-year colleges and universities. Many state and private four-year colleges and universities offer extensive vocational training programs, including excellent cooperative education programs discussed earlier and listed in the directory of the National Commission for Cooperative Education. Students can enroll full time or part time and take as few or as many courses as they want or need. Like two-year community and junior colleges, you don't have to enroll in a degree-granting program at many colleges or universities. You can just go and study the courses needed to learn a trade.

ADVANTAGES: Training can be more intensive and in greater depth than at two-year colleges, and there are far more opportunities to supplement vocational training with academic courses. You can even transfer from vocational to academic education, or vice versa. Some four-year colleges may offer training in areas not covered by two-year schools. Job placement facilities may also be more extensive. Four-year colleges usually have boarding facilities for resident students and larger recreation facilities.

DISADVANTAGES: Costs are usually much higher than at two-year schools.

10. Employer/union apprenticeship programs. For students with a solid high school education, these programs usually offer the best vocational education in their specialties, especially in fields such as construction, where students earn while they learn. Most programs require about 2,000 hours of supervised, on-the-job training plus related instruction either in classrooms, by correspondence or self-study. There are more than 800 types of apprenticeship programs officially recognized by the U.S. government and the 50 states. As you saw in Table 4, more than 60 percent of all new job opportunities between now and 2005 will be the result of on-the-job training. Appendix A lists the addresses of the U.S. Labor Department's Bureau of Apprenticeship and Training in each state. Check with the office in your state to make certain that any apprenticeship programs you're considering in your area are accredited.

ADVANTAGES: The pay is usually good, and students begin their training with a job already in place. Apprenticeship programs are supervised by master craftspeople and usually represent applied education at its finest.

DISADVANTAGES: There are too few programs, and all are extremely difficult to get into. Less than 2 percent of American high school graduates (usually sons and daughters of union members) get into such programs. Most trades don't even offer apprenticeships. About 300,000 people are enrolled in these programs in the United States today, and fewer than 20 percent are under the age of 23. The programs are mainly meant to train adults in their mid-twenties, and the competition to get in is fierce. That lets employers choose the most skilled and most mature applicants. In other words, it's not the type of training most people can ever count on getting.

11. Employer-sponsored training programs. Unlike apprenticeship programs, these programs are usually not associated with any union. They are taught by master craftspeople and company executives and usually combine on-the-job training with limited classroom training.

ADVANTAGES: As in apprenticeship programs, trainees earn while they learn, and successful completion usually assures them permanent jobs. Instructors are usually the best the company has to offer. Once again, it is "applied" education at its best and, as mentioned earlier, more than 60 percent of all new job opportunities between now and 2005 will result from on-the-job training, either union- or employer-sponsored. Widespread availability makes these programs outstanding opportunities for millions of workers. Here, according to a Rand Corporation study, is the percentage of workers who reported receiving their training from their employers:

DISADVANTAGES: There are two possible disadvantages for applicants to be careful about. The first is that some companies may offer training that is so specific that the trainee never learns to do another job and cannot transfer the skills to another company or occupation. A car assembler who only learns to install door handles won't find many job opportunities if the car plant shuts down. So, it's important that the training program be broad-based and offer *career* training as well as *job* training.

Table 7.   Percentage of workers receiving training from employers.

Job category	Men	Women
Professional and technical workers	61.7%	63.8%
Sales supervisors, representatives and clerks	40.7	29.1
Trade and craftsworkers	38.9	31.1
Office and clerical workers	37.5	33.5
Machine operators and assemblers	26.6	19.5
Transportation workers	16.9	44.9

The other major disadvantage to beware of is an employer's offer to train workers in labor-short markets. Be suspicious whenever you see an advertisement that says, "Carpenters wanted. No experience necessary. Will train. . . ." These ads usually appear when there's a housing boom, often in resort areas that attract young people with few nonrecreational skills. In their eagerness to profit from market conditions, some builders hire workers whose only experience may have been to help their parents complete do-it-yourself projects at home. The jobs offer no real training, only the opportunity to help and observe more experienced workers. The sad results are often shoddy workmanship for the builder's clients and few marketable skills for the young workers. Compared to professionals who trained as apprentices, such trainees are slow and incompetent—even those who have worked many years. Their work may be a quick means of earning money without alternative education, but it is only temporary, because every construction boom eventually ends and workers are left without jobs or real skills. Few professional construction firms in stable labor markets hire workers who have not gone through accredited apprenticeship programs. So it's as important to evaluate employer-sponsored training programs as it is to evaluate all other forms of alternative education.

2

How to Pick the Right Career— And the Right School to Train You for It

As you saw in Chapter 1, there are many types of vocational education, each with its own advantages and disadvantages. With so many choices, how can you decide which is the right program for you?

Well first of all, where you live may limit the number of your choices, because only a few large cities such as New York or Chicago offer all programs listed in Chapter 1. Most areas only offer two or three, and isolated rural areas may only offer one program at the local high school.

No matter how many or how few programs are available, however, it's important for you to evaluate each of them carefully so that you can choose the one that is indeed *the best for you* in your area—and there is almost always one that is better than all others. That's why evaluation is so important—to make certain you pick a program that will get you started properly in a successful and happy career. Remember: *The basic purpose of vocational education is to get a job.* If a school or training program can't teach you the skills you need to get and keep a job, it's a poor school or program, and you shouldn't waste your time with either.

Looking at it from another point of view, vocational education is an investment. You're going to invest a lot of time and perhaps a lot of money. So, as with any investment, it's important to find out *in advance* what the return on your investment will be.

CHECKLIST FOR EVALUATING VOCATIONAL EDUCATION

I. EDUCATIONAL QUALITY

1. Accreditation by appropriate organization in Appendix A   _____

2. Program depth (at least four courses in your field, two at advanced levels)*   _____

3. Link to local vo-tech or community college program*   _____

4. Links to on-the-job training programs in local industry (cooperative education)   _____

5. Up-to-date classroom equipment   _____

6. Strong, required academic program (minimum two years English, math and science)*   _____

7. One-semester course on "World of Work" (resume preparation, interviews, and so on)*   _____

8. Skilled faculty   _____

9. Active job-placement office

10. Readily available performance data

II. EDUCATIONAL RESULTS

1. Program completion rate (at least 75%)   _____

2. Test scores and/or state certification rates (at least 75% passing grades)   _____

3. Training-related job placement rate (at least 80%)   _____

4. Average starting wage (at least twice the minimum wage)   _____

5. Duration of employment (at least two years) and unemployment rate among graduates (no more than 15%)   _____

* Not appropriate for private trade schools.

There are two things to determine in evaluating any vocational education or training program: educational quality and educational results. The above checklist for evaluating vocational education outlines ten factors that make up educational quality and five that measure educational results.

Use this checklist for evaluating a vocational education program. Most of the data should be available from the school's course catalog, the rest from school administrators. Here is how to use it:

I. EDUCATIONAL QUALITY

1. **Accreditation.** *Do not consider* a school or program that is not accredited by an appropriate independent accreditation agency. Accreditation assures you that a program or school has met minimum educational standards set by impartial authorities in the particular field. It also means, first and foremost, that the school clearly has stated educational goals and the methods for achieving those goals. In the case of any vocational high school or college, the goals should be to teach each student a skill and to make sure the student obtains a job practicing that skill. Without such clearly stated goals and effective methods for achieving them, no school can obtain accreditation. Every good high school and college seeks accreditation by one of the six regional accreditation associations for schools and colleges listed in Appendix A on page 138. Lack of school accreditation almost always means substandard education. Don't even bother to continue your evaluation if a school is not accredited. Carefully check that any private trade school you're considering is accredited by the Accrediting Commission of Career Schools and Colleges of Technology, 2101 Wilson Boulevard, Arlington, Va. 22201 and that its owners are approved by the Better Business Bureau and Chamber of Commerce. Check also that the school has been in business for at least 20 years in the same general location. In some areas, some proprietary schools may be set up by con artists, eager to steal student funds. All legitimate trade schools should be accredited. Appendix A lists the names, addresses and telephone numbers of the various school accreditation agencies and associations. Part II on career opportunities gives the names of professional associations that also accredit specific occupational training programs. There is one possible exception to the accreditation rule: Some small companies that train their workers may not have formally accredited training programs. Nevertheless, it's important to evaluate the training they offer as best as you can. Check on the company's reputation in the community by calling the Better Business Bureau and the Chamber of Commerce and by asking employees what they think of the training they received. If you're looking at vocational schools, be certain they are accredited by one of the agencies listed in Appendix A.

2. **Program depth.** With some exceptions such as bartending, which is taught in a single two-week course, a program that offers fewer than four

courses in most occupational areas is probably only providing superficial training, which won't teach you how to be a master craftsperson. Check on the number of advanced *second-level* and *third-level* courses, which offer specific *job* and *career* training as well as *skill* training. A course in basic welding, for example, probably isn't enough to get you a job as a welder even though it teaches you a basic skill. For a welding program to have any market value, it must have courses that show you how to weld parts and materials for *specific jobs*. Vehicle-repair companies usually don't hire "welders;" they hire welders who know how to work on vehicles. So, make sure the program has advanced "occupationally-specific" courses—and that usually means at least four courses (20 credit hours) in each area.

In terms of the "return on your investment," the more courses you take in your major, the better chance you'll have of getting a job with higher wages. Indeed, every additional 30 credit hours in your major will increase your wages 12.2 percent, which is a better return on your investment than you usually can get on Wall Street. Don't consider any school that can't offer you enough credits to get a good job with good pay—or a school that has not been in business for 10 to 20 years at the same location.

3.   Ties to other vocational education institutions (for high schools only). If you're looking at a program at a comprehensive high school, be certain it has ties to a nearby vo-tech high school or community college program in the same field (see cooperative education and "two-plus-two" programs in Chapter 1) so that you can get enough credits to get a good, high paying job.

4.   Integration of theoretical and applied aspects of vocational instruction.   Top-quality high school and college programs link what they teach in classrooms to on-the-job training and application. It's not enough for a school to have a small "shop." It must tie its vocational instruction to a cooperative education program (see Chapter 1) with local employers in the same field and thus link formal school training with work experience.

5.   Up-to-date equipment.   Although few schools or colleges can afford to replace equipment annually, good programs offer students the opportunity to work with "state of the art" equipment that they will encounter on the job. There's no point learning auto mechanics on a Model-T Ford!

6.   Integration of academic skills with vocational skills (does not apply to proprietary trade schools).   Every job today requires a firm knowledge

of oral and written language communication skills as well as skills in computation and problem solving and a knowledge of basic principles of science and
technology.* A top-quality vocational school teaches these and other academic
skills along with vocational skills, because there is a direct connection between
academic disciplines such as science and laboratory experiments, economics,
computer science, mathematics and communication and real-life work such
as accounting, agriculture, clerical and secretarial work, construction, electrical
service, food service, graphic arts, health services, marketing, mechanics, metal
fabrication, transportation and other occupations. Good vocational education
programs have the same academic skill requirements as college prep programs.
One irony of the American job market is that despite increasing shortage of
technically trained workers, too many U.S. schools are graduating uneducated,
unskilled young people who are unable to cope with the expanding technology
of the workplace. Every job in modern society will require that you are able to
read and write well, that you are computer "literate," and that you can make
logical decisions and act on the basis of complex data. That's why it's so
important for you to evaluate carefully any vocational education program
you're considering. As the U.S. Department of Labor explains in its *Occupational Outlook Handbook*, "The connection between high unemployment rates
and low levels of education shows the importance of education in a job market
that increasingly requires more training." An astounding 23 million Americans
can't read, write or calculate adequately to hold a permanent job, and that
number is increasing by about 5 million every 10 years. Make certain you do
not join them.

7. **The World of Work.** Good schools now teach both academic and
vocational students two courses called "The World of Work." One is a
standard prevocational education course that explores a dozen or more "job
clusters"—agriculture, manufacturing, health care, and so on—then explains the function of individual jobs within each cluster. The second course
in "The World of Work" curriculum shows you how to look for jobs, write
resumes, fill out job applications, have job interviews and handle all other

---

* Leading educators agree that a basic course in Principles of Technology should explain the
concepts of force, work, rate, resistance, energy, power, force transformers, momentum, energy converters, optical systems, transducers, time constants, vibrations and radiation.
In evaluating any vocational education program, be certain that a Principles of Technology
course is included and that it covers those topics.

details of looking for, finding and keeping a job. It also teaches basic job skills such as promptness, proper behavior and relationships on the job with coworkers, employers and clients. More employees are fired because they can't get along with others than for *any* other reason. A school that doesn't have courses on "The World of Work" is not doing a good job for its students.

8. Faculty quality.   Teachers in vocational education should have worked in the trade they teach and should continually update their skills. You have a right as a consumer to ask the principal of any school or the director of vocational education whether that is indeed the case. A good school gladly will give you a list of its faculty and their credentials. If not, look for another school or program.

9. Job placement office.   A hallmark of quality in all vocational education programs is an *active* job placement office with skilled *job counselors*. They're not the same as guidance counselors. Job counselors have in-depth knowledge of and *ties to* the job market. They'll study your qualifications, help you write a good resume, then personally *contact* prospective employers for you.

10. Performance information.   Top-quality schools and colleges meas- ure how well their students and graduates are doing, and they are proud to share this data with prospective students. Availability and display of per- formance results are thus two other educational quality hallmarks of any vocational school. Any hedging about such performance results—any failure *to be specific*—is a clear signal that the school is *inferior*. So walk away! The type of data every good vocational school proudly displays—comple- tion rates, job placements, earnings of graduates, and so on—are discussed under "Educational Results." Any vocational school or college that says it doesn't have this data or that the information is confidential is either not truthful or incompetent. In either case, you'll be wasting your time and money by attending.

II. EDUCATIONAL RESULTS

1. Completion rate.   In evaluating any vocational education program, it's important to know how many students complete the program. A high drop-out rate (more than 25 percent) may reflect a poor program, which is unable to sustain student interest.

2. Test scores and certification rates. A key measure of program quality is the percentage of graduates that successfully earns state certification or licensing in a field of study. If the certification rate is less than 75 percent, the program may either be teaching obsolete skills or may be poorly taught. Where no state certification is required, many states nevertheless require schools to administer tests of knowledge and skills in the field studied. Unfortunately, most high schools don't know how their graduates do after graduating, and that indifference is a sign of a poor-quality school. A good school knows and will gladly tell you how its students have performed on certification tests or on tests that measure competency or employability.

3. Job placements *and* the degree to which those placements are *training related*. The quality of job placement assistance is the third important element in evaluating performance results of a vocational education program. After all, if you can't get a job with the training you get, what good is it? Any school or college whose placement service can't find jobs for at least 80 percent of its students either has a poor placement service or is offering inferior training. Nor is it doing a good job if it places its graduates in jobs *unrelated* to their training. There's no point in learning auto mechanics at a school that can only get you a job as a dishwasher after you graduate. Again, these schools don't know how or what their graduates are doing. Good schools do.

4. Average starting wage for graduates and average wage at regular intervals thereafter. A school that does not follow up on the effectiveness of the training it gives its students may be inferior. So, if the program director doesn't know or won't reveal these figures, try to find a better program. The *average* starting wage for graduates of a good vocational or technical school should be at least twice the minimum hourly wage.

5. Duration of employment and unemployment among graduates of the program. Why bother to enroll in a program whose students end up on unemployment lines? You have a right to know whether the program you sign up for is an effective one. If it isn't, don't sign up! There are many other routes to success.

Regardless of what school catalogs and school officials may say about the effectiveness of their program, it's important to protect your interests by double-checking their claims independently. Be especially careful to double-check the educational quality, educational results and accreditation of proprietary schools, that is, the private trade schools that frequently advertise in the media. The best way is to call or meet a few former students and local employers and ask them what they think of the vocational education program at the school you're considering. In the case of graduates, ask them how they're doing. Did the school get them their jobs? Has the training proved useful? Could they have succeeded without the training at school? In other words, did they get their money's worth from the school? In the case of employers, ask how well graduates from the program are doing, how far they've advanced at the company, what they're earning after one, two, five or ten years, and how long they usually last at the company. Don't put 100 percent faith in what the school tells you. Check out some of the school's claims yourself! If a school won't give you a list of graduates or employers, walk out. Cross them off your list. If local companies say they don't know anything about the program or if they're reluctant to discuss it or are unenthusiastic about it, there's probably something wrong. People seldom hesitate to compliment good programs, but they do hesitate to criticize bad ones for fear of lawsuits. If you run into this kind of reluctance after two calls to local companies, pick out a third one—one you'd really like to work for—and ask for an interview with a personnel representative. At the interview, simply ask what qualifications you'd need to get the job you want. Then ask where they think you could get the best training. If they fail to mention the vocational education program you were considering, you know it can't be very good and won't help you get a job at that particular company.

Preliminary Evaluations

Before going to the trouble of making an in-depth evaluation of a school or its program, you can probably save yourself a lot of time and effort by simply getting a course catalog and doing a preliminary evaluation that will allow you to eliminate the poorest schools and programs. Most school course catalogs will give you enough information to fill most of the checklist and thus help you decide if the school is good enough to warrant an in-depth evaluation. If it is, arrange to visit the school and interview the program administrators and a few teachers who can give you the answers to all the questions on the checklist. Then, if you still feel the program is a good one, double-check by contacting some local employers as suggested earlier.

Cross off your list any school without a course catalog and complete descriptions for each course—and, except for one-course trades like bartending, cross off any program that doesn't offer at least four courses in your chosen vocational area, with at least two advanced level courses or two courses that tie into advanced education at a nearby community college (tech-prep).

Selecting the "Right" Program— for You

In general, the "right" program for you is the one that will get you a good job after graduating and put you on the road to a happy and successful career. Employers simply don't hire and keep poorly trained employees. So, after deciding what type of career interests you most, go to the people you'll eventually work for and ask them about the type of education and training they either require or prefer. Then find out if it's available locally. It's also a good idea to contact trade associations and professional organizations in the fields that interest you. Where available, their names and addresses are listed with each occupation in Part II on career opportunities.

As pointed out earlier, many communities in the U.S. simply don't have outstanding vocational education facilities such as area vocational schools, two-plus-two programs, technical institutes or employee/union apprenticeship programs. That leaves most available opportunities for vocational education limited to comprehensive high schools, most of which have inadequate vocational training programs that will only give you a taste of knowledge without any of the in-depth training you'll need to get a good job in the field you want to enter. Indeed, signing up for vocational studies (or even worse, general studies) in many high schools could actually hurt your chances of getting a job in the field you like when you graduate. That's because most comprehensive high schools spend more money on academics than on vocational education, and, as mentioned earlier, they assign their best, highest paid teachers to students studying for academic diplomas in "the academic track." That means students studying for vocational diplomas or general diplomas might get the educational leftovers. That's tragic but true, and it's something you may have to face and respond to appropriately if you plan to succeed in your chosen field. By choosing the vocational track in many high schools, you may get poor vocational and academic training—and that's an educational combination almost guaranteed to lead to unemployment after you graduate.

The General Education Track

Even worse than the vocational track in most U.S. high schools is the so-called "general education" track, which provides the worst academic program available in school and useless pseudo-vocational courses such as home economics, arts and crafts, human relations and personal improvement and equally useless academic courses and personal/hobby courses, which are usually called general science, general social studies, general math and remedial English.

"The high school general-education program," according to Dale Parnell, long-time president of the American Association of Community and Junior Colleges and one of the most respected educators in the United States, "is the academic and vocational desert of American education. [It] relates to nothing, leads to nothing and prepares for nothing." Parnell strongly believes that good education must prepare young men and women for coping with real life as "citizens, wage earners, family members, producers, consumers and life-long learners." The general education programs of U.S. high schools fail utterly in this task. Indeed, most are nothing more than custodial services for non-achievers. Surely, you do not fit that description. Otherwise you would not be reading this book.

There is no way to overemphasize the importance of staying out of the general education program in your school if you're still in high school. *Avoid this program at all costs.* Any guidance counselor, teacher, school administrator or fellow student who urges you to take general education courses in high school is insulting your intelligence—and probably condemning you to a life of unemployment and poverty. General education is a dumping ground for students whom teachers don't want to bother teaching. General education is the worst disaster U.S. high schools have ever experienced. Some 45 percent (about 5.4 million) of American high school students are now enrolled in general education programs—and 63.5 percent *(almost two-thirds)* drop out of school. What happens to them? Well, more than half (54.1 percent) are unemployed, and those who do find work earn an average of less than $6,000 a year—about $112 a week. Any friend who tries to convince you that general studies are fun or easy is no friend; and any guidance counselor, teacher or school administrator who says you'll be "better off" in general studies is lying. You'll be worse off. The U.S. Department of Education and dozens of other organizations have facts and figures to prove it. *Do not enroll in general studies* if you want to assure yourself a successful, secure future after graduating from high school. Stick to academic (college prep) or vocational programs.

"But," you may be asking yourself, "why bother working so hard in the high school academic or vocational track if I can take it easy and have fun in the general education track and still go to college?"

It's true that almost all community colleges and most state colleges and universities admit students on a first-come, first-served "open enrollment" basis. Almost anyone can get into a community or state college or technical institute regardless of the courses they took in high school or their high school grades. But getting *into* college won't get you a good job. You'll have to get *out* of college to do that. You'll have to *graduate* from community or state college, and there simply is no way you'll succeed if you took the easy way out in high school with general studies courses and less than your best effort. That's why more than 50 percent of all college students never finish. They can't. They didn't get a quality high school education to do so—probably because they thought too much about college *entrance* requirements and too little about college *exit* requirements and the type of high school preparation needed to fulfill those requirements.

Most high school students have unrealistic expectations about college, largely because guidance counselors only tell them about entrance requirements and seldom discuss exit requirements. A few years ago, Pennsylvania State University surveyed 18,000 incoming freshmen and found few that had any realistic idea about the requirements for completing their college programs. About 98 percent expected to earn B averages or better at college and 61 percent thought they'd only have to study about 20 hours a week or less. In reality, only about 10 percent of students at colleges such as Penn State earn B averages or better, and most students have to study at least 30 hours or more each week.

Community colleges are seldom as academically demanding as schools such as Penn State, but the expectations of high school students headed for community colleges are no less unrealistic than the Penn State students surveyed about their expectations. The point is not to let the ease of entry into college convince you not to take demanding courses at high school. You'll need that firm academic grounding to fulfill the college's *exit* or graduation requirements. So again, don't let a friend or guidance counselor talk you into taking a general studies program simply because it meets all the college entrance requirements. Over the long term, it will prove useless and the preceding statistics prove that.

Be just as careful about enrolling in vocational studies in any comprehensive high school. No matter how good the school administrators, guidance counselors and teachers say the vocational program is, make certain *you* carefully evaluate the program and the courses offered. *Most vocational education in comprehensive high schools is substandard.* Remember: The statistics in Table 6 (Chapter 1) show how few students actually were able to use the vocational training they received in high school in their workplace after high school. I can't emphasize enough the importance of relying on your own evaluation and not that of a guidance counselor, teacher or school administrator. Let's be realistic: It's unlikely that any counselor, teacher or school administrator will tell you, "Our vocational courses are not adequate, our program is quite poor, and I don't think you'll learn enough to get a good job when you graduate." So, use the rules previously listed and the easy-to-use checklist on page 32 to do your own evaluation; talk to graduates of the program; and get the opinions of local employers. Trust nothing else.

What If There Isn't Any Good Vocational Education?

Let's say your evaluation of the high school vocational education program shows it to be mediocre or poor. What course can you take to achieve your career goals? The best answer may be to postpone your vocational education plans and take advantage of what your high school can offer—namely, a firm grounding in academics in the college prep program.

Most businesses and industries now are demanding that the men and women they hire *for all jobs* be skilled in written and verbal communication, that is, English and perhaps a foreign language such as Spanish. Employers also insist that applicants have a firm command of mathematics and basic principles of science, a good knowledge of history and social studies and a command of basic computer operations. That means that vocational education students must have just about the same high school academic background that students headed for four-year universities have. The importance of academics is that they teach students how to learn, and employers rank the *ability to learn as the most important skill* they seek in employees, regardless of the jobs they perform.

Language, math, science and computers, all academic track courses, are the tools of understanding. With a broad knowledge of academics, you can read complex instructions and understand the mathematical and scientific principles of almost any trade. You can learn almost anything, and that's the type of person American industry needs today, because rapid technological advances are making many jobs obsolete. *Careers* aren't becoming obsolete but the *jobs* are. Let's say you trained to be a secretary by learning shorthand and typing. Most of that training could prove worthless in a company that replaced most of its typewriters with word processors, computers and other high-tech equipment. Word processors and computers won't eliminate secretarial *careers*, but they will eliminate *jobs* as typists and stenographers. Today's secretaries must be administrative assistants with sophisticated skills in communications and business technology. They must be able to write and speak well. The telephone is still the major link between businesses and their clients. Secretaries must have the organizational and mathematical skills needed to maintain records, provide financial data and produce and read spreadsheets, graphs and other reports. And, again, they must be technologically versatile enough to adapt to and use computers and any other new electronic equipment which is developed.

It's the same story in almost every occupation today. What used to be a relatively simple (although back-breaking) job as a building maintenance engineer (once called janitors or superintendents) now requires a keen knowledge of mathematics and electronics. That's because so many functions in new buildings—climate controls, waste disposal and so on—are electronically controlled from computer consoles. Today's maintenance engineer may have to operate the controls for a 100-story skyscraper or a complex of 1,000 or more apartments. That takes a sound education in English, math, basic science and technology.

That's why business and industry are demanding more generalists these days—men and women who have learned how to learn and how to solve problems. Someone with a firm command of written and oral communication skills, mathematics, basic science, computer technology and keyboarding can easily convert his or her job skills from stenography or typing to computer operations or word processing. But if that person's education was limited to shorthand and typing, he or she faces an enormous period of retraining to keep up with fast-changing technology. Similarly, someone who only knows how to shovel coal into a furnace is ill-equipped to move into maintenance engineering and regulate electronic controls in a modern building complex.

So, if you're still in high school and you have no access to good vocational education in a cooperative education program, a two-plus-two tech-prep program or a regional vo-tech school, postpone your plans. Second-rate vocational courses and all general diploma courses will lead only to low-wage jobs, at best, and more likely to unemployment, no matter what your guidance counselor tells you. Stay out of the vocational and general tracks, and select the academic track at your high school; then plan on getting your vocational education in the best available post-high school program you can find at a community college, a technical institute, a four-year college or an apprenticeship or company training program. Almost every employer today prefers employees and craftspeople with strong academic backgrounds, whether the work is in construction, business, health care or building maintenance. Almost every area of work has gone high-tech, and workers without strong academic backgrounds will find it difficult and, in some cases, impossible to adapt.

In addition to knowing how to learn, employees list the following as some essential employability skills: reading, writing, mathematics, computer literacy, communications, inter-personal relations, problem-solving and reasoning, business economics, personal economics and manual and perceptual skills. In cooperation with employers, community leaders and educators, the Colorado Department of Education put together a master list of "Essential Employability Skills" (Appendix B), which gives a more complete picture of what most employers seek in "the perfect employee." Use it only as a guide, and don't worry if you don't fulfill all or even most of the expectations; it's only meant to give you a more realistic picture.

Just because your high school's only outstanding courses are in the academic track doesn't mean you shouldn't take any vocational courses, even if they're mediocre. As you can see in Figure 1 on page 46, even in states with the strictest graduation requirements, you'll have more than 25 percent of your class time available for electives. That means you can take at least 8 elective courses, and in states with even fewer academic requirements for graduation, you can take as many as 12. That will give you ample opportunity to sample vocational courses and at least get a taste of what work is like in those fields. But don't count on any *one* course to teach you enough to get you a job after high school unless it's part of a broader vo-tech, two-plus-two, tech-prep or cooperative education program.

What If I Don't Know What I Want to Do?

Most young people and many older ones don't know what they want to do. Millions make one or more false career starts, and that's all right. There are five easy ways, however, to pick the right career and keep those false starts to a minimum. The first is to broaden your perspective by examining the thousands of different job opportunities waiting for you after you've obtained the right kind of education and training. Take a look at the job listings in Appendix C to get an idea of how many jobs exist. The huge number is not meant to confuse you; it's only meant to prove that there has to be one or more jobs out there that are right for you. Part II of this book will give you some details of occupations, each of which employs at least a half million or more. To get even more complete details of those jobs and others, consult the 500-page *Occupational Outlook Handbook*, which is published every two years by the U.S. Labor Department Bureau of Labor Statistics. It is available in major public libraries and school guidance offices; or you may buy a copy from the Bureau of Labor Statistics, Publication Sales Center, P.O. Box 2145, 9th Floor, Chicago, IL 60690. Telephone: (312) 353-1880. Additional information on occupational categories and individual jobs within those categories is available from the various professional and trade associations listed under specific career opportunities in Part II and in Appendix A.

Figure 1. A typical four-year academic curriculum in comprehensive high schools leaves a mininmum of 8 elective courses that students can select from vocational education offerings. Unless a high school offers at least four courses in a specific area or ties its courses to a cooperative education program with local companies, vo-tech school or community college vocational education program, it's unlikely that such courses will teach you enough to get a job in the trade you studied after you graduate. But even a mediocre vocational education program can give you an opportunity to sample a number of different occupational areas and help you decide whether to pursue vocational education at more advanced levels.

Subject	1st Year	2nd Year	3rd Year	4th Year
English	Grammar and Composition Literary Analysis	Grammar and Composition English Literature	Composition Literary Analysis English/Amer. Literature	Advanced Composition World Literature
Social Studies	Anthropology Ancient History	History: Ancient/Medieval or Modern European	American History and American Govt. The Constitution	Electives
Mathematics	Three Years Required From Among the Following Courses: Algebra I, Plane & Solid Geometry, Algebra II & Trigonometry, Statistics & Probability *(1 sem.)*, Precalculus *(1 sem.)*, and Calculus			Electives
Science	Three Years Required From Among the Following Courses: Astronomy/Geology, Biology, Chemistry and Physics or Principles of Technology			Electives
Foreign Language	Three Years Required in a Single Language From Among Offerings Determined by Local Jurisdictions			Electives
Physical Education/ Health	Physical Education/ Health 9	Physical Eudcation/ Health 10	Electives	Electives
Fine Arts	Art History or Music History	Art History or Music History	Electives	Electives

A second way to help yourself discover your own occupational interests is to use as many high school electives as possible to "taste" vocational courses in several different areas, even if your school's vocational program is a poor one. You'll at least get an idea of what type of work you'd be doing in a variety of careers. Some guidance counselors may try to discourage you from using occupationally oriented programs as a career exploration activity, but don't let that deter you. It's your life, not theirs, and you have a right to use your electives any way you wish.

If you have the opportunity, take the prevocational course called "The World of Work," described earlier in this chapter. That's the course that examines career clusters (agriculture, health care, and so on) and the variety of jobs within each. If you decide to go to a vo-tech school or postpone your vocational education until community college, take a few beginning courses in various trades to see which ones you enjoy, and then take advanced courses in those that appeal to you most.

A third way of exploring careers is to visit businesses and factories in your area when on vacation. Many companies gladly talk to visitors and prospective job applicants about their firms and their industries. Some conduct tours on a regular basis. Even if such tours don't produce any career ambitions, you'll find them interesting and often exciting. To see tons of molten steel (or chocolate) pouring from huge vats and transformed into a thousand different shapes is a thrill for most people, regardless of whether or not they plan a career in that field.

A fourth effective way to pin down career ambitions is to start from a completely different direction and list your personal interests and hobbies instead of job preferences. Forget about jobs for a moment and think about the activities and interests you enjoy most: sports, music, television, science, medicine, stamp collecting—whatever they are and no matter how far they may seem from the world of work. Make a comprehensive list of those *interests*. Only then should you begin to look at the huge number of jobs from Part II that are available and see which ones would allow you to participate in the areas that interest you most. Let's look at a few examples.

Take the sports and recreation industry. You don't have to be an athlete to have an important job in the sports world. As in any other industry, it's the behind-the-scenes office administrators and personnel who keep the sports world functioning smoothly: in team offices, stadium and arena management firms, public relations and advertising firms, catering firms and personal agents' offices. For every athlete on the field or in the arena, there are dozens of administrative and clerical workers in team offices handling promotion, travel arrangements, contracts, endorsements, guest appearances and many other behind-the-scenes activities that are as important to the sports world as the games and players themselves. And that's true for every sport. In addition, every sport needs huge staffs to operate stadiums and arenas and run the concessions; and they need aides in the locker rooms and training camps. They need tradespeople—carpenters, electricians, painters, plumbers, millwrights, groundskeepers—to prepare the stadiums and arenas for the different events.

The same holds true in every area of show business, whether it's the opera and classical concert stage, rock-and-roll music or a Broadway theater. An army of administrative and clerical personnel must prepare all the appearance and travel schedules and arrangements, and just as many carpenters, electricians and other craftspeople are needed to build and tear down sets, set up the complex electrical connections for cameras, microphones and loudspeakers and prepare arenas and stages for performers. Few are performers or have any musical or acting talent, but they're as much a part of show business and participate in it as actively as any performing star.

Every industry needs most of the skills listed under career opportunities in Part II, and the best way to assure yourself a happy and successful career is to apply your skills and training in an area you enjoy most. You don't have to limit yourself to traditional areas. Just because you're good at carpentry or electrical installations doesn't mean you have to work in construction or home renovations unless you want to. You can sell your skills anywhere—at the Metropolitan Opera House, on the Broadway stage, at NBC-TV, or in Hollywood, or you can travel with your favorite rock-and-roll band.

And just as every TV station, theater, concert hall and sports arena needs carpenters, electricians, secretaries and other behind-the-scenes professionals, so does every hospital and newspaper and every other organization you can think of, including Congress and the White House. Every doctor, lawyer, architect, governor, senator, vice president and president needs a secretary, often more than one, and clerical staffs. So when considering what you want to do, don't limit yourself to traditional jobs if they don't interest you. Define your interests first, then match your skills to those interests. For example, just because you're a clerical worker doesn't mean you have to work for an insurance company if insurance doesn't interest you. Filling out job applications at a Hollywood studio or New York City publishing company is no different from filling them out elsewhere. So pick the businesses you enjoy the most. In every area of work, there are more "stars" behind-the-scenes than there are on stage.

The same principle holds true in less visible fields. Let's say you love science or medicine but don't want to go through years of study needed to be a scientist or doctor. Again, there are thousands of administrative support opportunities in hospitals, laboratories, pharmaceutical firms and government agencies involved in science and medicine. If law interests you but you don't want to spend seven years studying to become a lawyer, the huge court systems at city, state and federal levels all need clerks, secretaries, paralegals, carpenters, plumbers, electricians, maintenance personnel, security guards and a host of other support personnel. Most of the people that keep the court house doors open are not judges and lawyers.

Remember that if you work in a field you love, you'll do a better job and be more successful at it. Don't forget that your hobbies also can provide job opportunities. There are many jobs in stores that sell stamps to stamp collectors, coins to coin collectors, books to book lovers and diamonds to diamond lovers.

Finally, a fifth way of helping you choose the right career is to pick the type of people you'd most like to be with perhaps as much as eight hours a day, five days a week, 50 weeks a year. You'd better be with people you like; otherwise you'll wind up miserable, no matter how interesting the job. Let's say you like children. Well, again, that same army of administrative support personnel and craftspeople is needed in schools, pediatric hospitals and children's institutions. If you prefer a more scholarly world, universities and colleges offer many jobs for secretaries, clerks, laboratory technicians, maintenance staffs, craftspeople, security personnel and others. So here again, the principle of picking the right career is to choose the world in which you want to work and adapt your skills to that world. Pick your own world—even if it's in the circus—rather than letting the world pick you.

What If I Have No Skills?

That's what vocational education is all about—to teach you skills. First, get that command of academics discussed earlier. Next, pin down your interests. Then, look at the types of jobs available under each area of interest. Finally, visit a company involved in that area of interest for a first-hand look at available jobs. You'll almost certainly find one and probably more that you'd like to do and could be good at. Then, it's simply a question of learning the particular craft, either at the appropriate vocational school or perhaps at the job itself in a company training program.

What If I Dropped Out of School?

If you dropped out of school, it's easy to catch up. Every state offers a High School Equivalency Testing Program for adults who have not completed a formal high school program. Usually called GED tests (for General Educational Development), they are given over a two-day period. There are five tests, each two-hours long. Test 1 measures spelling, punctuation and grammar skills and the ability to organize ideas in clear, correct sentences. Test 2 measures understanding of social studies, and asks for the interpretation of a series of passages dealing with social, political, economic and cultural problems. Test 3 on the natural sciences offers a series of passages about high school science and asks questions that test your ability to understand and interpret each passage. Test 4 deals with the understanding of literature and asks for an interpretation of a selection of poetry and prose. Test 5 tests abilities in mathematics and covers ratios, percents, decimals, fractions, measurement, graphs, plane geometry and algebra.

To pass and receive a high school diploma, you must get a minimum passing score of 35 (out of 100) on each test but earn a total score of 225 for all five, or an average score of 45 per test.

The most difficult tests for people who have been out of school for a while are tests 1 and 5, but it's easy to prepare for those and the other three in adult education classes which are offered (usually free) in many public schools and community colleges to prepare students for the GEDs. Call the principal of the local public high school for information about the courses in your area. Also helpful are some of the various GED home study books available in major bookstores or directly from the publishers:

1. *How to Prepare for the GED,* Barron's Educational Series, Inc., Hauppauge, NY 11788. Tel.: 1-800-645-3476.
2. *High School Equivalency Diploma Examination,* National Learning Center, Syosset, NY. Tel.: 1-800-645-6337.
3. *High School Equivalency Diploma Workbook,* National Learning Center, Syosset, NY. Tel.: 1-800-645-6337.

After you've completed studying, contact the education department of your state for dates and locations of the tests, and, once you've passed them, you can go to almost any college to study a trade, brush up on academics and even learn how to own and operate your own business. The only disadvantage to a GED is that it does not qualify you for a military career. The U.S. Armed Services require an actual high school diploma obtained by attending four years of high school. So, if you dropped out of high school without graduating and you're interested in the military, contact the principal of your local high school and get information about reenrollment.

Part II Career Opportunities— And How to Find Them

3

Help Wanted: 17 Million Needed

This chapter gives brief descriptions of the many occupations open to serious, motivated men and women who don't want to go to a four-year college or university. Each listing includes the vocational education and training required. Some jobs don't even require a high school diploma; others demand an associate degree from community or junior college or a technical institute. Most jobs fall somewhere in between. If formal training is required, you'll find the appropriate agencies to contact to make sure you attend an accredited school or program for that occupation. Where no specialized accreditation agency is listed, use the accreditation organizations for schools and colleges and for trade schools (see Appendix A). Contacting the appropriate organizations is simple: either call or send a postcard. You can send the same message to each organization. Just say, "Please send me all available information on careers and training in (fill in the career or careers that interest you)." Then legibly write your name and address. There's no need to make it complicated or write formal letters.

Under each occupation, you'll find the pay range for beginning and experienced workers, but they represent national averages. Pay scales may vary widely from region to region as you can see from Table 8 (on the following pages), which lists average annual salaries by state in 1996, according to the U.S. Department of Labor. Although actual salary averages may have changed slightly since then, their relationships to each other and to the national average have not. Use the factor for your state to estimate earnings in your area in the occupations that interest you most. Simply multiply the salary figures for each occupation by the factor for your state to get an approximate idea of what you'd be paid for that work in your state. For example, you'll find in Appendix C that average earnings for agricultural jobs are $285 a week across the U.S. If, however, you live in Alabama, where salaries are below the national average,

Table 8. Average annual salaries in the United States and each state in 1996, according to the U.S. Department of Labor Bureau of Labor Statistics. Next to each salary figure is a comparison with the national average. Use that figure as a factor with which to multiply the national average salary for the occupations that interest you most in Part II to obtain the probable average income for the work in your state. Even if actual average salaries have risen or fallen since 1996, the relationship of state averages to the national average has probably remained relatively unchanged.

State	Average Annual Pay (1996)	Relation to National Average
UNITED STATES	$28,945	—
Alabama	25,180	.87
Alaska	32,461	1.12
Arizona	26,387	.91
Arkansas	22,294	.77
California	31,773	1.10
Colorado	28,520	.99
Connecticut	36,579	1.26
Delaware	30,711	1.06
District of Columbia	44,458	1.54
Florida	25,640	.89
Georgia	27,480	.95
Hawaii	27,353	.95
Idaho	23,353	.81
Illinois	31,285	1.08
Indiana	26,477	.91
Iowa	23,679	.82
Kansas	24,609	.85
Kentucky	24,462	.85
Louisiana	24,528	.82
Maine	23,850	
Maryland	30,293	1.05
Massachusetts	33,940	1.17
Michigan	31.522	1.09
Minnesota	28,869	1.00
Mississippi	21,822	.75

Table 8. (continued)

State	Average Annual Pay (1996)	Relation to National Average
Missouri	26,608	.92
Montana	21,146	.73
Nebraska	23,291	.80
Nevada	27,788	.96
New Hampshire	27,691	.96
New Jersey	35,928	1.24
New Mexico	23,716	.82
New York	36,831	1.27
North Carolina	25,408	.88
North Dakota	21,242	.73
Ohio	27,775	.96
Oklahoma	23,329	.81
Oregon	27,027	.93
Pennsylvania	28,973	1.00
Rhode Island	27,194	.94
South Carolina	24,039	.83
South Dakota	20,729	.72
Tennessee	25,963	.90
Texas	28,129	.97
Utah	24,572	.85
Vermont	24,480	.85
Virginia	28,001	.97
Washington	28,881	1.00
West Virginia	24,075	.83
Wisconsin	26,021	.90
Wyoming	22,870	.79

you'd have to multiply those figures by the factor for Alabama in Table 8—namely .87. That means that agricultural workers in Alabama can probably only count on earning $247.95 a week (.87 × $285). In addition to the jobs and average salaries listed, Appendix C lists the median weekly salaries of full-time workers by job and gender.

Remember, too, that the salaries mentioned do not necessarily translate into cash. In addition to deductions for income taxes and Social Security, there are set-asides for your pension costs and health insurance and other benefits. On average, the average hourly wage paid in private industry in 1995, was $17.10, of which only $12.25, or 71.6 percent, represented actual cash wages *before* taxes. About $4.85, or more than 28 percent, of the hourly wage represented benefits. Although government jobs paid slightly higher wages on average—$17.31 per hour—benefits reduced the cash pay by a whopping $7.65, or more than 44 percent, leaving the actual cash wage a mere $9.75 an hour—*before* taxes.

As you explore each occupation, remember that most listed occupations also offer management and ownership opportunities once you've acquired enough experience. So don't interpret *salary ranges* as limits on potential *earnings* for each job. Beginning workers in animal care facilities may earn only minimum wage, but owners often earn $50,000 to $100,000 a year. A security guard may start at minimum wage but can earn many thousands of dollars more as an owner of a security agency guarding scores of homes and businesses.

Don't, however, consider becoming an owner or even a partner before you've acquired a thorough knowledge of the business. That usually means at least 10 years' experience. Remember, *nine out of ten new businesses end up in bankruptcy!* Your odds for success as an individual entrepreneur, in other words, are not very high. Now that does not mean there is no potential for outstanding success as an individual business owner in every field discussed in this chapter. There is, but you have to know what you're doing; you have to know every aspect of every minute operation in the business you consider—and that, as any successful business owner will tell you, requires at least 10 years' experience.

It is not enough, for example, to be a good cook and be able to prepare tasty dishes to run a successful restaurant. To operate a restaurant—or any other business—successfully, you need complex business-management skills similar to those acquired in MBA programs—programs of study leading to a master's degree in business administration. You must know how to keep costs of materials at a minimum, without lowering quality of meals; how to control personnel costs without reducing quality of service; how to eliminate waste—either because of spoilage or excess give-aways to clients. You must be able to pay for and control costs of a thousand things—food ingredients, beverages, furnishings, maintenance, personnel, and a host of other items—and still manage to make a net profit that will be enough to give you and perhaps your family a decent living. Few restaurant owners can do it. Net profits usually amount to less than 1 percent—as they do in a host of other small, independent businesses, including most retail stores, and most owners work 70, 80 or more hours a week to collect their meager rewards. For most people, it's best to work for someone else. The hours are limited, and, if you're good, you'll make far more than you will trying to start your own business.

So, put the idea of starting your own business out of your mind until you've learned all about the business on the job—working for someone else.

The job descriptions below are brief and are only meant to give you an idea of what you'd be doing if you decide to follow a career in that particular line of work. Occupation listings are limited to those employing at least 500,000 people. Remember, though, not all industries listed are expanding, and, in planning your alternative education, you must be aware of which occupations and industries are shrinking in terms of job opportunities and take these statistics into account. Go back to Table 5 in Chapter 1 for a list of occupations with the largest expected decline in available jobs by the year 2005. Appendix D lists the anticipated job growth or shrinkage by industry between now and the year 2005 and Appendix E lists the anticipated job growth or shrinkage by specific occupation within each industry. Together, these two lists will give you a clear picture of the opportunities—or lack of opportunities—in every industry and every job within each industry—including the ones you may be considering. As you'll see, farm jobs listed in the section on agriculture will experience a net loss of 273,000 jobs over the next few years—hardly a hotbed of opportunity for someone starting out in life. For more complete details of work in these and other jobs, get the *Occupational Outlook Handbook* from the U.S. Department of Labor Bureau of Labor Statistics, Publication Sales Center, P.O. Box 2145, Chicago, IL 60690 (Tel.: 312 353-1880). You can also get more details about each occupation by writing to the trade and professional associations listed under many of the career areas and to leading corporations in each field.

Career Opportunities

AGRICULTURE

If you love the outdoors, agriculture offers a wide variety of jobs in animal care, farming, forestry, conservation, groundskeeping, nursery work and fishing and hunting.

Animal Care

Feed, water, groom, exercise and train animals of all kinds in a variety of settings—ranches, farms, wildlife refuges and fisheries operated by the U.S. Fish & Wildlife Service (Department of Interior), zoos, circuses, amusement and theme parks, pounds, laboratories, animal hospitals, aquariums, kennels, stables and so on. Clean and repair animal quarters, cages, pens and tanks. Work may include careful record keeping, transporting animals and treating sick animals. All training is on-the-job, although some experience with animals (4-H Clubs, for example) preferred. Must demonstrate love for and ability to get along with animals. Salaries range from $9,500 to about $28,000 after five years. Management jobs paying more than $20,000 require a high school diploma with a solid background in math, biology and other sciences plus a community college associate degree or bachelor of science degree from a four-year college or university in animal sciences such as animal hospital technology, animal husbandry or veterinary medicine.

Farm Work

Planting, cultivating, harvesting and storing crops, operating and maintaining farm machinery, tending livestock and poultry, and hauling produce, livestock or poultry to market. No schooling is required. All training is on-the-job. Pay is minimum wage permitted by state and federal laws. Work is seasonal, but workers may be laid off or hired on a day-to-day basis. There is no job security or benefits, but farm work has value as training for eventual ownership of your own farm.

Farm Management

Supervise planting, harvesting maintenance and other farm operations. A highly technical profession requiring extensive skills and at least a community college associate degree (preferably a four-year college bachelor's degree) in horticulture, crop and fruit science, soil science, dairy science, animal science, farm personnel management or agricultural economics, business and finance. Farm management is as complex as managing any company in any other industry and requires a strong background in high school mathematics and science. Pay at large private or corporation farms and ranches averages about $17,000 a year, with starting salaries dipping below $10,000 and the highest paid managers earning more than $30,000. For more career information contact your local county Agricultural Extension Service. For information about certification as an accredited farm manager, contact the American Society of Farm Managers and Rural Appraisers, 950 South Cherry Street, Denver, CO 80222. For information on agricultural education, contact your state university, which has a "land grant college" that usually provides the best agricultural education in the state at the lowest cost.

Forestry Management and Conservation

Planning, development, maintenance and protection of forests and woodlands, planting and raising seedlings, pest and disease control and soil conservation (control of soil erosion and leaching) for lumber companies, pulp and paper companies and the U.S. National Forest Service (Department of Agriculture) and National Park Service (Department of Interior). Although a bachelor's degree from a four-year college or university is usually required, some companies will hire applicants with a community college associate degree in forestry, agronomy or soil sciences. Pay ranges from $12,000 to $16,000 to start and can reach $30,000 after 10 years.

Timber Cutting and Logging

There are almost two-dozen specialized tasks in timber cutting and logging, including site clearing and cutting, trimming, grading, and hauling trees for major lumber companies, pulp and paper companies and logging contractors who hire out to big corporations to fill seasonal demands. Work is seasonal. All training on the job is given by more experienced workers. No experience needed to start, but strength and physical fitness are essential along with maturity and the ability to work with others as a team in an extremely hazardous occupation. There are between 100,000 and 125,000 jobs in the forestry and logging industry, with fewer than 25,000 employed as forest and conservation workers and the rest employed in logging camps by logging contractors. One in four logging workers is self-employed—one of the highest proportions of self-employment in American industry. Average pay is about $19,000 a year, with newcomers starting at less than $10,000 a year and skilled workers with seniority earning as much as $40,000. For more career information contact the school of forestry at your state land grant college or write to the Northeastern Loggers Association, P.O. Box 69, Old Forge, NY 13420; the Timber Producers Association of Michigan and Wisconsin, P.O. Box 39, Tomahawk, WI 54487; and the U.S. Forest Service, Department of Agriculture, 14th Street and Independence Avenue SW, Washington, DC 20013.

Groundskeeping and Gardening, Caretaking

Maintenance of public or private property with hand and power tools. Mowing, trimming, planting, watering, fertilizing, digging, raking, sweeping, landscaping, building maintenance, pool maintenance, animal care and snow removal. Both full-time and part-time jobs are available, but they are seasonal, except in warm weather climates. Pay averages $7 per hour. Supervisory jobs at public parks and gardens, major resorts and amusement parks and some large private estates usually require some high school or community college courses in horticulture and landscape architecture. Pay at the supervisory level is about $27,000 a year. Ownership of landscape maintenance firms can produce an annual net income of up to $40,000 or more.

Nursery Workers

Planting, cultivating, harvesting and transplanting trees, shrubs and plants; landscaping client properties. Seasonal, except in warm climates. Pay is minimum wage. Supervisors, with some background in horticulture, plant and insect science and landscape architecture, can earn from $11,500 to about $20,000, and nursery owners can earn far more.

Fishing and "Outfitting"

Catching fish with nets, seines and lines on board ocean-going fishing vessels; cleaning and repairing equipment. Most companies are small, privately owned firms alongside the wharfs at fishing ports. Outfitters, mostly based in western and New England cities, lead tourists on camping expeditions into the wilderness to fish, hunt or simply hike and camp. Work is seasonal. Pay is usually minimum wage, although earnings for fishers may depend on sharing profits from the catch, while outfitters depend heavily on tips. Ownership of a fishing boat or of an outfitting company can increase earnings substantially, although the seasonal nature of the work and economic conditions make this an insecure occupational area.

ARTS AND CRAFTS

Design

If you're creative, imaginative, have an eye for form and color and are a gifted artist, the opportunities in design are endless. Advancement is only limited by your talent, training, imagination and interest. About 40 percent of designers are self-employed. Most designers specialize in one of seven areas: industrial design, package design, textile design, apparel design, set and display design, interior design and floral design. Except for floral design, which you can learn on-the-job or by taking a one-semester course at a community college or trade school, almost all jobs in design require a minimum of two years' study at a technical institute or community college. Almost all designers now use computers to allow for easy changes at the touch of a few keys and to produce three-dimensional images of their designs. So, in addition to formal design training, computer literacy has become essential in all types and phases of design. The median annual earnings of full-time, salaried designers in all fields is almost $32,000, with the range extending from about $17,500 to just under $60,000, and the vast majority earning between $20,000 and $45,000. Self-employed "stars" in every field but floral design earn somewhere in the range of six figures, and the best Hollywood and Broadway set designers can earn more than $1 million. Write to the National Association of Schools of Art and Design, 11250 Roger Bacon Drive, Reston, VA 22090 for a list of the more than 140 accredited colleges and institutes in the art and design field. Don't consider a school that is not on their list. About one-third of all designers are self-employed. The career opportunities available in design follow.

> **Industrial designers.** Create and draw designs for every conceivable manufactured product, except apparel, textiles, packaging

products, stage sets and buildings. Design cars, home appliances, computers, toys, machinery, medical instruments, office supplies, furniture, sporting goods and other products that must first be in blueprint form before they can be manufactured. Virtually every manufacturer needs industrial designers. It's simply a question of picking the product area that interests you most. Industrial design requires a high school diploma with a strong background in drafting and art and at least a certificate or associate degree in the field from a technical institute, art institute or community college. Many companies and industrial design firms require a four-year college degree. Some require a mechanical engineering degree as well, because industrial designers must have a knowledge of mechanical drawing and computerized design in order to produce all the manufacturing specifications for the products they create. They're not just artists; they often are drafters and engineers and many have graduate degrees. According to the Industrial Designers Society of America, the average base salary of entry-level designers is nearly $26,000, while senior designers with eight years' experience earned an average of nearly $43,000. Industry "superstars," with their own design firms, can earn more than $100,000 a year. Write to Industrial Designers Society of America, 1142 E. Walker Road, Great Falls, VA 22066 for information on careers and educational programs in industrial design.

Package designers.   Design boxes, cans, bottles, and plastic packages and their labels and wrappings. Must have in-depth knowledge of every type of paper, paperboard, metal, plastic and composite material and the structural strength of each, whether it can or should be extruded or molded and which shape is most appropriate for the product it must contain. Just look at the enormous variety of packaging in a drug store or supermarket to get an idea of how complex package design is and why many package designers are graduates of four-year colleges and engineering schools. As in industrial design, however, two years at an art or technical institute is sometimes enough to get started; but a knowledge of mechanical drawing and computer-aided design (CAD) is essential. Average income is about $30,000 a year—about $20,000 to start and

$35,000 for experienced designers. Again, there's almost no limit to the earnings of design "superstars" and owners of their own design firms.

Textile designers.   Design fabrics for garments, upholstery, rugs, draperies and every other type of textile product. Must have thorough knowledge of textiles, fabric construction and fashion trends. Textile manufacturers are the major employers, and pay is about the same as for package designers. Although a bachelor of fine arts degree is a definite plus, there are ample opportunities for designers with an impressive portfolio and a two-year associate degree or certificate in textile or fashion design from a community college or technical institute. For more career information and a list of accredited schools and colleges, write to American Apparel Manufacturers Association, 2500 Wilson Boulevard., Arlington, VA 22201.

Fashion designers.   Design coats, suits, dresses, hats, handbags, shoes, gloves, jewelry, underwear and other apparel for manufacturers and department and specialty stores. Strong portfolio of original designs required plus high school diploma (solid background in art and fashion design) and at least a certificate or associate degree in fashion design from a two-year technical institute or community college. Many fashion designers have four-year university degrees and even graduate degrees in art, although some are so gifted they were able to go right to work after high school with no college training at all. It's important to have studied garment construction, however, along with fashion design and sketching. Knowledge of computer-aided design (CAD) is essential. Salaries range from $15,000 to $35,000, although there's almost no limit to earnings of top high-fashion designers who work for the most exclusive couturiers or for their own clientele. Other high earners in the field are the costume designers who work for theater, opera, television and movie production companies. For information on careers and education, write to the American Apparel Manufacturers Association, 2500 Wilson Boulevard., Arlington, VA 22201.

Interior designers.   Plan and furnish the interiors of private homes, buildings and commercial establishments such as offices, restaurants, hotels and theaters. Draw designs for use of interior space; coordinate colors; select furniture, floor coverings and draperies; design lighting and architectural accents. Must have knowledge of architectural drawing. Although many interior designers work on salary ($15,000 to $30,000) for furniture, home furnishings and department stores, builders, hotel chains and major resorts, the majority are self-employed and have their own clientele, which regularly redecorates their current homes as well as newly acquired residences. Earnings for independent interior designers are limited only by the number and wealth of clients and a willingness to work hard and to find and get along with new clients. Although training varies, the minimum acceptable is a certificate or associate degree in interior design from a technical institute or community college. For career information, write to the American Society for Interior Designers, 608 Massachusetts Avenue NE, Washington, DC 20002.

Set and display designers.   Design stage sets for movies, television and theater, store displays in windows and on selling floors and advertising sets. In addition to artistic skills, set and display design requires a thorough knowledge of architecture and structural materials and the ability to draw rooms, buildings or street scenes in a manner that would *appear* to be realistic from the spectator's point of view at a play, in a movie theater, through a television screen or from the sidewalk looking into store windows. Many TV and movie sets that appear true to life are actually miniatures only inches wide. The camera makes them look life-size, and the set designer must know how to create such special effects. That means taking courses in set design at art school. Opportunities in set design range from small theaters and local television stations to Broadway theaters, major networks, Hollywood film studios, independent film and TV producers and advertising agencies. Starting pay for design assistants is seldom more than $15,000, but there's no limit to the income of an experienced set designer, whose name is featured among the credits for major theater, film and TV productions. Display designers earn between $20,000 and $40,000 depending on the size of the department store or advertising agency and whether it is in a small town or major city. Minimum educational requirements are an associate degree or certificate in set or display design from a technical institute or community college. Most theaters and studios, however, prefer a four-year bachelor of arts degree in theater production and set design.

Floral designers. Arrange flowers in retail flower shops or at hotels, restaurants, banquet halls and other institutional consumers. No high school diploma required, and most florists will train workers on the job. A certificate in floral design from a trade or technical school is a plus, and a degree in floriculture and floristry from a community college is preferred for entry into management or ownership where knowledge of flower marketing and shop management is needed. Salaries range from about $12,000 to start to $16,000 for experienced designers. Managers' salaries average $20,000, while self-employed floral designers and shop owners average more than $30,000. The Society of American Florists (1601 Duke Street, Alexandria, VA 22314) has more career information.

Photography and Camera Work

Here are two exciting areas—with vast, expanding, high-paying job opportunities that don't require a high school diploma or college degree. Both, however, require a deep interest, a lot of imagination, creativity, sense of timing and in-depth technical knowledge acquired either in school or on your own. About 1,000 colleges and vo-tech schools offer courses in photography and camera work, but both are areas where on-the-job training is the primary source of education. The two areas are quite separate, each has its own specialties, and each is a highly competitive field, with far more potential workers than job openings.

Photography involves still shots in portrait, fashion, advertising, industrial, special events, scientific, news or fine arts photography. Photographers may be salaried or work on their own as freelancers; some subcontract their laboratory work, others do their own. Advertising and industrial photographers take pictures of every imaginable person, place or thing—buildings, landscapes, animals, manufactured products, machinery, company executives and personnel for posters, catalogs, shareholders' annual reports, newspapers, magazines, educational presentations and advertising. Job opportunities exist with private photo studios, major corporations, advertising and public relations firms, book publishers, educational institutions and government at every level. Scientific photographers work for educational institutions, corporations in the scientific products and pharmaceutical fields and federal government agencies dealing with scientific research and health. News photographers work for newspapers, magazines, public relations and advertising firms, major corporations and government agencies. Most photographers spend two to three years in on-the-job training as photographers' assistants learning laboratory work, electrical work and camera and lighting set-ups. Starting pay is usually between $15,000 and $20,000 a year, but quickly moves into the $25,000-to-$35,000 range as you begin taking over routine photographic work yourself. After five to ten years, top-notch photographers can earn upwards of $50,000 a year. Self-employed photographers can earn much more. Some portrait photographers for Hollywood stars and other famous people earn more than $200,000 a year. For more information write to Professional Photographers of America, 57 Forsythe Street, Atlanta, GA 30303, and the American Society of Media Photographers, Washington Road, Princeton Junction, NJ 08550.

Camera operators need no formal schooling, but, as in photography, they must show a deep interest and acquired knowledge on their own. Training is on the job as a first and second assistant to a camera operator setting up equipment and electrical gear. Salaries are similar to those of photographers. Skilled camera operators, either freelance or salaried, earn more than $50,000 a year and are in constant demand. Remember: They are the "eyes" of every film producer and the only way producers and directors can convey what they see to the public. (Don't confuse camera operators with projectionists, who set up and operate projection and sound equipment in movie theaters and are only paid by the hour, usually not more than $8. Like theater lighting projectionists, however, pay varies according to geographic area and whether or not the trade is unionized in that area.)

Art Photography

This is a highly specialized field with few opportunities for any but the most artistically talented. Most art photographers are graduates of fine arts colleges or universities and have simply chosen photography as their medium instead of canvas and paints or stone and chisel. Most art photographers rely on some other form of photography for a living.

Fine Arts

The fine arts include drawing, painting, sculpture, ceramics and a wide variety of crafts ranging from weaving to model making and from wood carving to glass blowing. Although no diplomas or college degrees are required, anyone considering the fine arts must demonstrate talent and have a portfolio to prove it. Most fine artists study art at four-year art schools or liberal arts colleges and universities, and many have graduate degrees. Job opportunities are limitless, although most are in commercial or graphic art as illustrators for magazines, books, newspapers, greeting cards, album covers, posters and films. Advertising agencies and the entertainment industry need artists to draw story boards, which tell a story in a series of pictures before the scenes are acted out. Other opportunities exist in the cartoon and comic strip fields as well as in film animation. Salaries range from $15,000 to $50,000, although earnings reach far higher for self-employed "superstars" in the trade. Graphic designers of publications earn between $20,000 and $25,000. The Graphic Artists Guild (11 West 20th Street, New York, NY 10011) has more information about the graphic arts. If you're interested in being an illustrator, write to The Society of Illustrators, 128 East 63rd Street, New York, NY 10021. Outside the commercial and graphic arts fields, fine artists may create original works for sale to the public through galleries and other retail outlets. Other opportunities exist in the decorative arts field in major cities and in the souvenir art field in major resort areas where many tourists prefer paintings of the sights they've seen to ordinary snapshots. In the decorative arts, there are many decorative arts houses in major cities that hire artists to create or reproduce paintings to size, that is, to fit a particular client's wall space in various areas of an apartment or house.

There are fewer opportunities for sculptors than painters. Most opportunities for three-dimensional art are in architecture, the production of public monuments, religious sculptures and mortuary art and existing statuary restoration. Artists' earnings are unpredictable and vary widely, from "starvation" wages to millions.

BUSINESS ADMINISTRATION—ADMINISTRATIVE SUPPORT OCCUPATIONS

This broad category of clerical operations critical to virtually every business and organization includes adjusters (customer complaints), account and bill collectors, advertising clerks (taking orders), bank tellers, billing clerks, bookkeepers, brokerage clerks (Wall Street firms), cashiers, computer operators, court clerks (see Government Service), credit checkers and loan authorizers, customer service representatives (telephone companies, other utilities and businesses), data entry clerks, company dispatchers (scheduling, dispatching workers), emergency dispatchers (police, fire, ambulance—see Government Service), file clerks, general office clerks, hotel desk clerks and cashiers (see Hospitality), insurance claims and policy processing clerks, mail clerks, messengers, meter readers, order clerks, payroll clerks, production planning clerks, real estate clerks, reception and information clerks, reservation and travel clerks, statistical clerks, traffic clerks (shipping, receiving and inventory), travel ticket agents, secretarial positions, stenographers, telephone operators, typists and word processor operators and many others.

Clerical support is essential to every organization in this country—every school, every corporation and business and every government agency—even the White House. Clerks in every organization are responsible for handling the data that makes that organization function. They receive, classify, store (in computers or file cabinets), distribute and retrieve all essential information and paperwork flowing through the organization. The paper they handle may be cash in the case of bank tellers, insurance claims in that industry, purchase orders, invoices and incoming and outgoing checks in every organization and airline tickets and reservation confirmations in the travel business. In addition to handling data, clerks are often "the front line" in an organization's dealings with clients and the public, greeting them over the telephone or in the reception area and either handling client needs themselves or referring clients to the right people or departments. Clerks are the heart of almost every organization, and no organization can function without their skills.

Technological advances, however, have muddied the waters of business administration, and many jobs have been eliminated by new machines and electronic devices. The copier alone has put thousands of typists out of work. The personal computer has eliminated and will continue to eliminate thousands of other clerical jobs; and automatic, computerized telephone answering devices are putting operators out of work. But the elimination of a job does not necessarily mean the elimination of a career, especially in business administration. That is why those entering this career must now get a broader education than many high schools offer. That is why it's essential to evaluate business education courses very carefully. It's essential to check with local employers and graduates of any business education program to determine its value. At most high schools, it will prove far more worthwhile to take good academic courses in English composition and writing skills than to learn obsolete vocational skills that no employer can use. Remember the U.S. government study of vocational education in Chapter 1 (see Table 2), showing that more than half the students who take vocational courses in high school are unable to use what they learn on the job. That's because so many high schools are behind the times and teach skills that became obsolete years ago.

Unless your high school has a strong program in business administration, the best way to a successful career in this field is to take a strong academic program in high school and a strong business administration program at a community college. Anyone planning a career in business administration needs a broad background in technology, and that means high school math, science and English and the study of computers and electronic office equipment either in high school or community college or both. An associate degree in business administration from a community college will help you get a better job and prepare you for a career in which you can shift easily from one job function to another as technology eliminates some jobs but creates others. Here are the salary ranges for a sampling of administrative support occupations:

Adjusters, investigators, and collectors	$29,000–35,000
Bank tellers	10,000–25,000
Clerical supervisors and managers	16,000–50,000
Computer and peripheral equipment operators	13,000–40,000
General office clerks	11,000–35,000
Information clerks (receptionists, new account clerks, reservation and ticket agents, hotel and motel desk clerks, etc.)	11,000–35,000

Mail clerks and messengers	13,000–27,000
Postal clerks and mail carriers	25,000–35,000
Record clerks (bookkeeping, order, billing, filing, personnel, etc.)	16,700–25,000
Stenographers, court recorders, medical transcriptionists	12,000–41,000
Teacher aides	8.29/hour–8.77/hour
Telephone operators	10,300–32,000
Typists, word processors, data entry keyers	15,000–23,000

The U.S. government starts office clerks at about $16,500 a year if they are high school graduates and have had six months' experience. General office clerks and secretaries earn an average of about $25,000 a year. Secretarial salaries in private industry are higher—usually about $27,000 a year on average, and ranging above $40,000, depending on responsibilities. Clerical supervisors earn up to $45,000 a year. For career information in most areas of clerical work, contact Professional Secretaries International, P. O. Box 20404, Kansas City, MO 64195, and the National Association of Legal Secretaries, 2250 East 73rd Street, Tulsa, OK 74136.

CONSTRUCTION TRADES

As in most categories in this section, construction offers endless opportunities to work for oneself, for small or large contractors, for major corporations and organizations, and for municipal, county, state or federal government agencies. Even the White House needs carpenters and plumbers. The construction trades offer opportunities in the city or country building, renovating, repairing and maintaining small structures and large ones, including the world's tallest skyscrapers. Crafts include bricklaying, carpentry, carpet installation, drywall installation and finishing, electric installation, glazing (glass installation), insulation installation, painting and wallpaper hanging, plastering, plumbing and pipefitting, roofing, stone, cement and concrete masonry, structural and reinforcing metal work (erecting steel frameworks of bridges and buildings), tilesetting, paving, heavy equipment operations, road and bridge building, and excavation and loading machine operations. In all areas, a high school diploma is not required, but it is certainly a plus. Today's technology requires a solid background in reading, writing, mathematics and science. The ability to solve problems quickly also is essential. Training can be on the job, but the best training is in apprenticeship programs that last anywhere from two to five years depending on the trade, and include both on-the-job and classroom instruction in subjects such as blueprint reading, layout work, sketching, mathematics, tool and materials technology and safety. Weekly earnings can be quite high, but there's no guarantee of year-round work. Here, nevertheless, are the median weekly earnings of salaried workers in a variety of construction trades—when there's work:

Bricklayers	$486
Carpenters	424
Carpet installers	412
Concrete masons and terrazzo workers	407
Construction and building inspectors	621
Cost estimators	365
Drywall workers and lathers	419
Electricians	574
Excavation and loading machine operators (graders, dozers, etc.)	459
Glaziers	420
Insulation workers	485
Painters and paperhangers	381
Plasterers	385
Plumbers and pipefitters	530
Roofers	371
Sheetmetal workers	444
Structural and reinforcing ironworkers	611
Surveyors	590
Tilesetters	450

For general information about apprenticeship programs in the construction trades write to any of the following:

Associated General Contractors of America, 1957 E Street NW, Washington, DC 20006.

Home Builders Institute, Educational Division of National Association of Home Builders, 1201 15th Street NW, Washington, DC 20005.

For information on apprenticeship programs and careers in specific trades, write to any of the organizations that follow, but also look in Appendix A for the office of the U.S. Department of Labor Bureau of Apprenticeship and Training in your state to check that any local apprenticeship program in your area has been approved by the government and industry.

Bricklaying and stone masonry. National Concrete Masonry Association, 2302 Horse Pen Road, Herndon, VA 22071; Brick Institute of America, 11490 Commerce Park Drive, Reston, VA 22091.

Carpentry, ceiling tile installation, and accoustical carpentry. United Brotherhood of Carpenters and Joiners, 101 Constitution Avenue NW, Washington, DC 20001.

Carpet installation. Floor Covering Installation Contractors Association, P.O. Box 2048, Dalton, GA 30722.

Concrete mason and terrazzo workers. (see also *Bricklaying and stone masonry*). National Terrazzo and Mosaic Association, 3166 Des Plaines Avenue, Des Plaines, IL 60018.

Construction and building inspectors. International Conference of Building Officials, 5630 South Workman Mill Road, Whittier, CA 90601; Building Officials and Code Administrators International, Inc., 4051 West Flossmoor Road, Country Club Hills, IL 60478; American Society of Home Inspectors, 85 West Algonquin Road, Arlington Heights, IL 60005.

Cost estimators. Professional Construction Estimators Association of America, P.O. Box 11626, Charlotte, NC 28220.

Drywall workers and lathers. United Brotherhood of Carpenters (see *Carpentry*); International Brotherhood of Painters and Allied Trades, 1750 New York Avenue NW, Washington, DC 20006.

Electricians. National Electrical Contractors Association, 3 Metro Center, Suite 1100, Bethesda, MD 20814.

Excavation and loading machine operators (graders, dozers, scrapers, pavers, pipelayers, and so on). International Union of Operation Engineers, 1125 17th Street NW, Washington, DC 20036; Industrial Truck Association, 1750 K Street NW, Washington, DC 20006.

Glaziers. International Brotherhood of Painters and Allied Trades, 1750 New York Avenue NW, Washington, DC 20006; National Glass

Association, Education and Training Department, 8200 Greensboro Drive, McLean, VA 22102.

Insulation workers. National Insulation and Abatement Contractors Association, 99 Canal Center Plaza, Alexandria, VA 22314.

Painters and paperhangers. International Brotherhood of Painters and Allied Trades, 1750 New York Avenue NW, Washington, DC 20006.

Plasterers. International Union of Bricklayers and Allied Craftsmen, 815 15th Street NW, Washington, DC 20005; Operative Plasterers' and Cement Masons' International Association of the United States and Canada, 1125 17th Street NW, Washington, DC 20036.

Plumbers and pipefitters. National Association of Plumbing-Heating-Cooling Contractors, P.O. Box 6806, Falls Church, VA 22046; National Fire Sprinkler Association, P.O. Box 1000, Patterson, NY 12563; Mechanical Contractors Association of America, 1384 Piccard Drive, Rockville, MD 20850.

Roofers. National Roofing Contractors Association, 10255 W. Higgins Road, Rosemont, IL 60018; United Union of Roofers, Waterproofers and Allied Workers, 1125 17th Street NW, Washington, DC 20036.

Sheet-metal workers. The Sheet Metal National Training Fund, 601 N. Fairfax Street, Alexandria, VA 22314.

Structural and reinforcing metal workers. International Association of Bridge, Structural and Ornamental Iron Workers, 1750 New York Avenue NW, Washington, DC 20006; National Erectors Association, 1501 Lee Highway, Arlington, VA 22209; National Association of Reinforcing Steel Contractors, 10382 Main Street, Fairfax, VA 22030.

Surveyors. American Congress on Surveying and Mapping, 5410 Grosvenor Lane, Bethesda, MD 20814.

Tilesetters. International Union of Bricklayers and Allied Craftsmen, International Masonry Institute Apprenticeship and Training, 815 15th Street NW, Washington, DC 20005.

GOVERNMENT SERVICE

Village, city, township, county, state and federal government agencies offer secure job opportunities in virtually every category listed in this chapter. Clerical work (see Business Administration) offers the most opportunities, many in especially interesting and unusual areas. Court clerks, for example, must prepare court case dockets, do research and retrieve information for judges and contact witnesses, lawyers and litigants. There are thousands of other job opportunities in government for postal clerks, mail carriers, school crossing guards, emergency dispatchers, firefighters, highway maintenance workers, police officers, correction officers and other positions. Almost all government jobs require a high school diploma, six months' experience and a passing score on the appropriate civil service examination. Salaries range from minimum wage to over $50,000 a year depending on the job and its responsibilities, the level of government and the region of the country. In general, civil service jobs do not pay as much as private industry, and promotions tend to be slower. But there are far more benefits (health insurance, guaranteed retirement pensions and so on), far greater job security, and pay increases are usually automatic and tied to the cost of living and length of time on the job. For more information, contact the Civil Service Commission or state employment office of your state, county or city and the personnel department of the particular branch of government that interests you most. For federal jobs, contact the personnel department of the individual branch or the local U.S. Office of Personnel Management Job Information Center. The Office of Personnel Management (OPM) is what the federal government calls its civil service. OPM has branch offices and testing centers in most major cities. You can get the location and telephone number of the branch nearest you by calling the toll-free number at the Office of Personnel Management in Washington, DC: 1-800-424-9858. They'll also give you all information about job vacancies, salaries and application procedures. For careers in the U.S. Postal Service, contact your local U.S. Post Office. For careers in protective services, contact your local government authorities and any organizations that follow:

Corrections.   For careers on the local level: The American Jail Association, 2053 Day Road, Hagerstown, MD 21740. For careers at the federal level: Federal Bureau of Prisons, National Recruitment Office, 320 First Street NW, Washington, DC 20534; International Association of Correction Officers, 1333 S. Wabash, Chicago, IL 60605.

Firefighting and fire protection.   International Association of Fire Chiefs, 4025 Fair Ridge Drive, Fairfax, VA 22033; International Association of Firefighters, 1750 New York Avenue NW, Washington, DC 20006; Fire Administration, 16825 South Seaton Avenue, Emittsburg, MD 21727.

For information about professional qualifications and a list of two- and four-year college degree programs: National Fire Protection Association, Batterymarch Park, Quincy, MA 02269.

Security officers, guards. Most states have licensing requirements; contact local detective and guard firms, state employment office, state police or state licensing commission.

Police, detectives, special agents. Contact appropriate federal, state and local law-enforcement agencies for career opportunities in all but the following federal agencies: FBI, contact nearest state FBI office; U.S. Marshals Service, Field Staffing Branch, 600 Army Navy Drive, Arlington, VA 22202; Drug Enforcement Administration, Special Agent Staffing Unit, Washington, DC 20537; U.S. Secret Service, Personnel, 1800 G Street NW, Washington, DC 20223.

Private detectives and investigators. Contact state police headquarters.

Police officers, detectives, special agents. Contact your local state or city authorities. OPM handles all federal jobs in this field except those at the FBI, which are handled by state FBI offices.

HEALTH CARE

A high school diploma—and an interest in science and helping people—are all you need to take advantage of some exciting and almost unlimited opportunities in the expanding field of health care. An associate degree from an accredited community college or technical institute opens up many more opportunities, of course, but you can get started in the field with a diploma and move on at your own pace by taking the necessary college courses part time. In addition to the specialized accreditation organizations that follow, make certain that any health care program at a community or junior college or technical institute is also *accredited* by one of these two organizations:

Division of Allied Health Education and Accreditation (CAHEA) of the American Medical Association, 515 N. State Street, Chicago, IL 60610.

Accrediting Bureau of Health Education Schools (ABHES), 2700 South Quincy Street, Arlington, VA 22206.

Write to them both when exploring educational opportunities in the health care field. Otherwise you may waste your time and money and find yourself unqualified for state licensing—and a job.

Here are the opportunities in this rapidly expanding field grouped according to minimum educational requirements:

Health Care Careers Requiring Only a High School Diploma

Dispensing opticians. Most dispensing opticians learn their trade on the job. All that's required to enter the field is a pleasing personality to deal with patients and a high school diploma with a heavy concentration in math and science. High school physics, algebra, geometry and mechanical drawing are important, because training will include the study of optical mathematics, optical physics and use of precision measuring instruments for fitting patients with glasses. Apprenticeships lasting two to five years are required in 22 states to earn a license to practice. Formal training programs lasting from several weeks to two years are available at community colleges, technical institutes, trade schools and lens manufacturers. There are only 40 such programs in the United States and only 15 accredited by the Commission on Opticianry Accreditation, 10111 Martin Luther King Jr. Highway, Bowie, MD 20720. Earnings for salaried dispensing opticians average about $27,000 a year and range from $20,000 to $30,000. Many experienced dispensing opticians go into business for themselves and earn far more—as much as $100,000 a year in some areas. For more information, write to the Opticians Association of America, 10341 Democracy Lane, Fairfax, VA 22030.

Emergency medical technicians (paramedics). The job requires a high school diploma plus a nine-month training program that includes the following three courses: a 110-hour Emergency Medical Technician's (EMT) course designed by the U.S. government and available in all 50 states and the District of Columbia at police, fire and health departments, hospitals and, as a nondegree course, at medical schools, colleges and universities; a two-day course on removing trapped victims; and a five-day course on driving emergency vehicles. Students must also take a 10-hour internship in the emergency room. For the EMT certificate, graduates of accredited EMT training programs must pass a written and practical exam administered by the National Registry of Emergency Medical

Technicians. Earnings range from about $25,000 to start to an average of about $32,000 a year for experienced paramedics. For further information write to your state's Emergency Medical Service Director at the state capital and to these two organizations: National Registry of Emergency Medical Technicians, P.O. Box 29223, Columbus, OH 43229 and National Association of Emergency Medical Technicians, 102 W. Leake Street, Clinton, MS 39056.

Licensed practical nurses.   Rapid advances in medical technology may soon require a two-year associate degree from a community college. For now, however, most states only require a high school diploma and an LPN license available upon completion of a state-approved program given in high schools, community and junior colleges, hospitals and health agencies. Earnings range from $20,000 to $30,000 a year, depending on the area and the type of employer, and average about $21,500. The list of 1,250 approved training programs is available from the National League for Nursing, 350 Hudson Street, New York, NY 10014 and the National Association for Practical Nurse Education and Service, 1400 Spring Street, Silver Spring, MD 20910. Don't enroll in a program that's not on their lists. For more information on a career as an LPN, write to the American Health Care Association, 1201 L Street NW, Washington, DC 20005.

Health Care Careers Requiring an Associate Degree from Community or Junior College or Technical Institute

Cardiovascular technicians.   The job requires a high school diploma with a strong background in health, biology and typing and word processing. Training is on the job and usually lasts eight to sixteen weeks. Licensing by the National Board of Cardiovascular Testing is voluntary but extremely valuable in getting better jobs in this field. Salaries range from about $18,500 a year as a hospital trainee to $25,000 for experienced technicians. Lists of training programs are available from the American Society for Cardiovascular Professionals, 10500 Wakefield Drive, Fredericksburg, VA 22407.

Dental hygienists.   This is an exciting career that yields an average pay of more than $21 an hour, *part time*. That works out to more than $35,000 a year for a 32-hour work week. There is a wide range of opportunities—private dental practice, school systems, hospitals and public health agencies. Hygienists must be licensed by the state. That requires a two-year associate degree from one of the nearly 200 schools of dental hygiene accredited by the Commission on Dental Accreditation of the American Dental Association (ADA) *and* passing a written and clinical examination administered by the ADA Joint Commission on National Dental Examinations. For a list of accredited programs write to the Commission on Dental Accreditation, American Dental Association, 211 E. Chicago Avenue, Suite 1804, Chicago, IL 60611. For information on careers in dental hygiene, write to the Division of Professional Development, American Dental Hygienists' Association, 444 N. Michigan Avenue, Suite 3400, Chicago, IL 60611.

Medical laboratory technicians.   These technicians perform a wide range of routine tests and laboratory procedures in hospitals, clinics, and medical and research laboratories. Training can be on the job, but most lab technicians have at least a two-year associate degree from a community college. Earnings range from $20,000 to $30,000 a year depending on the area of the country and the type of institution. Write to the Accrediting Bureau of Health Education Schools, 2700 South Quincy Street, Arlington, VA 22206, for a list of accredited training programs. No one will hire a lab technician who does not graduate from an *accredited* program. Certification is voluntary, but it's a valuable credential that is often required as an indication of professional competence. Write to the National Certification Agency for Medical Laboratory Personnel, 7910 Woodmont Avenue, Bethesda, MD 20814.

Medical record technicians.   A key figure in hospital care, the medical record technician is in charge of patient medical histories and charts essential for proper treatment and care. Training is available in about 100 two-year associate degree programs accredited by DAHEA. Training includes courses in biological sciences, medical terminology, medical record science, business management, legal aspects of medical and hospital practices and computer data processing. After graduation, medical record technicians obtain professional credentials by passing a written exam of the American Health Information Management Association. Earnings range from more than $13,000 to more than $25,000 a year. Contact the American Health Information Management Association, 7910 Woodmont Avenue, Bethesda, MD 20814.

Radiologic (X-ray) technicians. Technicians in physicians' offices who only take routine X rays are usually trained on the job and need only a high school diploma. The more complex work in hospitals and medical centers requires one to two years of formal training in radiography, radiation therapy technology and diagnostic medical sonography (ultrasound). There are more than 750 programs—mostly two-year associate degree programs at community colleges and technical institutes—accredited by CA-HEA. New technology such as magnetic resonance imaging is making this one of the fastest growing sectors of health care with starting salaries averaging more than $21,000 a year and earnings of experienced radiologic technologists *averaging* about $30,000. The top of the range reaches as high as $50,000. Contact the following organizations: American Society of Radiologic Technologists, 15000 Central Avenue SE, Albuquerque, NM 87123; Society of Diagnostic Medical Sonographers, 12770 Coit Road, Dallas, TX 75251.

Registered nurses. With more patient care responsibilities being handed over to registered nurses, there is growing pressure to make all R.N.s obtain a four-year bachelor's degree. For now, however, there are two other training programs available—a two-year associate degree from community and junior colleges and a three-year diploma program given in hospitals. Both of them, along with four-year R.N. programs at colleges and universities, qualify graduates for entry-level positions as hospital staff nurses. Earnings range from $28,500 to $45,000 and are likely to climb as the demand for nurses grows. Head nurses can earn between $50,000 and $75,000 a year. Nursing homes pay an average of $32,000 a year, compared with $35,000 in hospitals. Nurses also earn extra pay for working evening and night shifts. Don't confuse a *registered nurse* with a practical nurse (LPN) or any other kind of nurse. To become a registered nurse requires attending an accredited program leading to a degree as an R.N. from one of the more than 1,400 accredited programs and a *license*, which is only available after passing a national examination administered by each state. For more information, write to the American Association of Colleges of Nursing, 1 Dupont Circle, Washington, DC 20036; the American Nurses' Association, 600 Maryland Avenue SW, Washington, DC 20024; the American Health Care Association, 1201 L Street NW, Washington, DC 20005.

Surgical technicians.   Although there are fewer than 150 training programs, only about 100 are approved by DAHEA. A high school diploma is required for admission to these programs, which last at least nine to ten months when taken on the job in hospitals but extend to two years at community and junior colleges awarding associate degrees. The shorter, in-hospital programs are generally limited to licensed practical or registered nurses with experience in patient care. The work involves preparing patients for surgery, setting up the operating room and passing instruments and other materials to surgeons and surgeons' assistants during an operation. Starting salaries average about $19,000 a year and, depending on education, experienced technologists can earn about $28,000 a year. Write to the Association of Surgical Technologists, 7108-C S. Alton Way, Englewood, CO 80112.

HOSPITALITY

Food and Beverage Preparation

Chefs, cooks and other kitchen workers need no formal education to start. They can learn all their skills on the job. But that's the hard way. An easier and better way is to get a high school diploma, a strong background in business mathematics and business administration courses and formal training in either an apprenticeship program or a two-year or four-year college. Apprenticeship programs last up to three years and are offered by professional culinary institutes, industry trade associations and trade unions. Two-year community colleges offer associate degrees and a few four-year colleges and universities offer a bachelor degree. Some high schools offer courses in food preparation, but these seldom have any value for obtaining any but the least-skilled jobs in the lowest-paying sectors of the industry, such as fast-food restaurants. Formal training at an accredited culinary institute or other advanced educational institution is the surest way to a good job. For a directory of two-year and four-year colleges with courses in the food service field, write to the Educational Foundation of the National Restaurant Association, 250 South Wacker Drive, Suite 1400, Chicago, IL 60606. Also write for a directory of colleges and schools from the Council on Hotel, Restaurant and Institutional Education, 1200 17th Street NW, Washington, DC 20036-3097. There's some duplication in the two catalogs, but it's worth having them both. And finally, write to the American Culinary Federation, P.O. Box 3466, St. Augustine, FL 32084, which offers apprenticeship programs and certifies chefs at the levels of cook, chef, pastry chef, executive chef and master chef. Earnings in the food preparation field vary widely, from minimum wage for inexperienced beginners to $100,000 a year for world-renowned master chefs at elegant French restaurants in cities such as New York or San Francisco. On average, however, food preparation personnel earn between $9,000 and $20,000 a year depending on years of experience, position in the kitchen hierarchy and type of restaurant. Fast-food restaurants pay the least—usually minimum wage, regardless of experience. Elegant "white-tablecloth" restaurants usually pay the most but demand the most experience. In many areas, especially in big cities, hotel and restaurant workers must join unions.

Food and Beverage Service Workers

This category includes dining room attendants (busboys and busgirls), bartender assistants, serving persons, hosts and hostesses and bartenders. Most bartenders go to private trade schools for a standard two-week course, but most other food and beverage service work is learned on the job. Most employers prefer applicants with high school diplomas, a solid grounding in mathematics (for accurate handling of meal charges) and pleasing personalities. Pay ranges from minimum wage to $25,000 a year for an experienced host or hostess who has been on the job for many years at an elegant "white tablecloth" restaurant in a major city. Average earnings, however, are about $14,000 a year; but tips, which run between 10 percent and 20 percent of guest checks for waiters and waitresses, can double the totals. Bartenders earn similar salaries and can also double their incomes with tips. More information on hospitality careers is available from the Council on Hotel, Restaurant, and Institutional Education, 1200 17th Street NW, Washington, DC 20036-3097; the Educational Foundation of the National Restaurant Association, 250 South Wacker Drive, Chicago, IL 60606; and the Accrediting Commission of Career Schools and Colleges of Technology, 2101 Wilson Boulevard, Arlington, VA 22201.

Other Career Opportunities in Hospitality:

- Amusement and recreation park attendants, fee collectors, carnival and amusement park ride and concession stand operators, facility preparers at indoor game parlors (billiards, pinball machines, video machines and so on), servers at sports clubs and spas.
- Hotel baggage porters and bellhops.
- Business administration: hotels, amusement and theme parks, restaurants, stadiums and sports arenas. Clerical functions (office clerks, secretaries, reservations clerks, desk clerks and cashiers) are as essential to the hospitality industry as they are to every other industry. Basic training for these jobs, along with cash and materials management, desk clerks, operators, cashiers and receptionists is discussed in the section on Business Administration. Additional training to adapt business administration skills to the hospitality industry should take place on-the-job, although some might want to consider courses in hotel and restaurant administration at a community or technical college. Some institutions, such as Hocking Technical College in Nelsonville, Ohio, operate their own motel, restaurant, travel agency and support systems as part of their Hospitality Program.
- Housekeeping. See "Janitors and cleaners" under Service Occupations.
- Sports and activities supervision. See Sports and Recreation.
- Maintenance. See "Grounds maintenance" under Agriculture or "Janitors and cleaners" under Service Occupations.
- Theater ushers, lobby attendants, ticket takers, cashiers.

MARKETING AND SALES

Retailing

Retailing offers many job opportunities as cashiers, wrappers, floor and counter sales clerks and stock clerks in all types of consumer outlets, specialty stores, supermarkets, department stores, theaters, laundries, dry cleaners, video rental stores and car rental agencies to name a few. All training is on-the-job and applicants don't need high school diplomas, although employers prefer a strong background in mathematics for handling cash accurately and a pleasing personality for dealing diplomatically with customers. To advance into management ranks or to go into business for yourself, however, a high school diploma and at least a community college associate degree in business administration are essential. Some high schools call their vocational programs for retailing "Distributive Education." Don't let the fancy name confuse you.

Here are the median weekly earnings in eight different types of retail sales for 1994:

Motor vehicles and boats	$534
Furniture and home furnishings	427
Radio, television, stereos, appliances	401
Parts	378
Hardware and building supplies	333
Street and door-to-door sales workers	323
Shoes	280
Apparel	265

For more general information on retail sales, write to the National Retail Federation, 325 Seventh Street NW, Washington, DC 20004. If you're interested in training for a career in car sales, write to the National Automobile Dealership Association, 8400 Westpark Drive, McLean, VA 22102.

Real Estate Agents

Although real estate agents must be licensed in every state and be high school graduates, most states do not require a college degree. All that's necessary is to pass a 60-to-90-hour course that is offered by many large real estate firms and by more than 1,000 universities, colleges, and junior and community colleges. At some colleges, students can earn an associate degree or bachelor degree in real estate. Average earnings were almost $30,000 a year in 1994, and ranged from $10,000 to more than $100,000. Earnings are almost all from commission and depend on general market conditions and property values. For career information and a list of colleges offering courses in real estate, contact the National Association of Realtors, 430 North Michigan Avenue, Chicago, IL 60611.

Wholesale Sales

Wholesalers, who buy goods from manufacturers and resell them to retailers, have armies of salespeople who sell in two ways: "Inside" salespeople solicit sales by telephone, while "outside" salespeople sell by personal solicitation with visits to retail store owners and managers. The variety of products sold by wholesalers is as wide as the variety of products in any department or discount store. Wholesale trade salespeople usually need associate degrees from community colleges and are then trained on-the-job—first as stock clerks to become familiar with the merchandise the wholesaler may carry and the complex pricing of such goods. Initial training generally leads to "inside" sales jobs, first as an order taker on incoming reorders from steady customers, then eventually as a troubleshooter soliciting telephone orders from customers who have not reordered. After two years on the inside, top salespeople acquire outside sales routes. College courses in wholesale distribution, marketing and business administration can speed advancement into management. Wholesale trade salespeople earn as little as $15,000 a year as trainees but quickly rise into the $20,000 to $40,000 range when they become outside salespeople. Top salespeople earn upwards of $70,000 a year. Other career opportunities in wholesaling include the range of business administration functions (see Business Administration) and inventory controls and handling stock as it moves on and off company shelves. Stock work is usually a minimum wage job, but salaries improve with increased responsibilities. Write to the Manufacturers' Agents National Association, P.O. Box 3467, Laguna Hills, CA 92654.

MECHANICAL TRADES

The mechanical trades—mechanics, installers and repairers—offer some of the widest opportunities for personal and financial success of any professional area. Mechanics keep America's machinery running. They are the men and women who make it safe for us to fly in airplanes and ride in cars, trucks, transit systems and building elevators; they make it safe to use home appliances and keep our heating and cooling equipment operating; they keep us in touch with the world by maintaining and repairing communications equipment such as telephones, radios, televisions and computers. American industry could not produce the goods and services we all need without mechanics to keep production machinery humming. Indeed, without mechanics, our nation would be unable to function.

Here are just a few of the opportunities in this enormously important field of installation, maintenance and repair: aircraft and aircraft engines; diesel engines; cars and trucks; car bodies; office equipment and cash registers; computers; commercial and industrial electronic equipment (everything from radar and missile installations to medical diagnostic equipment); telephones and communications equipment; television and stereos; elevators; farm equipment; heating; air-conditioning; refrigeration equipment; home appliances and power tools; industrial machinery; heavy equipment; vending machines; musical instruments; boats and motorcycles and small engines. Any piece of equipment you can think of needs an expert who knows how it works to keep it running smoothly and fix it when it breaks down. That person is a mechanic.

Years ago, it used to be easy for anyone with "good hands" to go into the mechanical trades, even without a high school diploma. But like the field of business administration, the mechanical trades have become an area of constant change due to rapid technological advances. As in business administration, automation and other devices are eliminating jobs. They're not eliminating careers—just jobs. The auto repair business, for example, still offers wonderful career opportunities, but the job of hand-tuning engines on most cars has disappeared. The same is true in all areas of the mechanical trades, and that's why today's mechanics must be so well-educated.

A high school diploma is virtually a must in every area of mechanical trades along with a solid understanding of mathematics and basic scientific principles (especially physics), and the ability to read and understand complex materials relating to the functioning and repairing of complex machinery and equipment.

In addition to academic requirements, entry into most mechanical trades requires two to four years of solid vocational education either in high school, an accredited trade school, community college or a formal company training program. And finally, at least two to four years on-the-job are needed to reach the status of master craftsperson. The rewards for this investment in time and study can be great. There are mechanics in almost every specialty previously mentioned earning as much as $50,000 a year. Computer service technicians, for example, average more than $30,000 within five years and can earn $40,000 to $50,000 when they reach the top of their trade. Diesel engine mechanics in the transportation industry average $30,000 a year or more; automotive mechanics, $23,000; farm-equipment mechanics, $20,000; telephone installers, about $35,000; and office machine repairers, $24,000. The salary range for mechanics is quite wide; demand is great, and so are the rewards.

As in every other professional area, it's important to get the proper training. What follows are organizations which will send you career information, certification requirements (if any) and lists of accredited schools and colleges for each mechanical trade:

Aircraft
Aviation Maintenance Foundation, P.O. Box 2826, Redmond, WA
   98073 (career information).
Professional Aviation Maintenance Association, 500 Northwest Plaza,
   St. Ann, MO 63074 (career information).

Automotive
Automotive Service Association, Inc., 1901 Airport Freeway, Bedford,
   TX 76021.
Automotive Service Industry Association, 25 Northwest Point, Elk
   Grove Village, IL 60007.
Chrysler Dealer Apprenticeship Program, 26001 Lawrence Avenue,
   Center Line, MI 48015.
Ford Motor Company, Training Department, Parts and Service
   Division, 3000 Schaefer Road, Dearborn, MI 48121.
General Motors Automotive Service Educational Program, General
   Motors Service Technology Group, 30501 Van Dyke Avenue,
   Warren, MI 48090.

National Automotive Technical Education Foundation, 13505 Dulles
   Technology Drive, Herndon, VA 22071-3415 (list of certified automotive training programs).

Commercial and Industrial Electronic Equipment
Electronic Technicians Association, 604 North Jackson, Greencastle,
   IN 46135 (career, certification and placement information).

Communications Equipment Line Installers and Splicers
Communications Workers of America, 501 3rd Street NW, Washington,
   DC 20006 (employment opportunities).
United States Telephone Association, 1401 H Street NW, Washington,
   DC 20005 (career information).

Your local telephone or long distance company (career opportunities).

Diesel Mechanics
ASE, 13505 Dulles Technology Drive, Herndon, VA 22071-3415
   (training information).
American Trucking Association, 2200 Mill Road, Alexander, VA
   22314 (career information).
Automotive Service Industry Association, 25 Northwest Point,
   Elk Grove Village, IL 60007.
National Automotive Technical Education Foundation, 13505 Dulles
   Technology Drive, Herndon, VA 22071 (list of certified programs).

Electronic and Home Entertainment Equipment
Electronic Industries Association, 2001 I Street NW, Washington,
   DC 20006 (career information).
National Electronic Sales and Service Dealers Association and the
   International Society of Certified Electronics Technicians, 2708
   West Berry Street, Fort Worth, TX 76109 (career and certification
   information).
Electronics Technicians Association, 604 North Jackson, Greencastle,
   IN 46135 (career information).

Farm Equipment

North American Equipment Dealers Association, 19877 Watson
  Road, St. Louis, MO 63127.
Deere and Co., John Deere Road, Moline, IL 61265.

Heating, Air-Conditioning and Refrigeration

Associated Builders & Contractors, 1300 North 17th Street, Rosslyn,
  VA 22209 (career information).
Air-Conditioning and Refrigeration Institute, 4301 North Fairfax
  Drive, Arlington, VA 22203 (career information).

Heavy Equipment (Bulldozers, and so on)

Motor and Equipment Manufacturers Association, Technical Training
  Council, P.O. Box 13966, Research Triangle Park, Raleigh, NC
  27709 (career information).

Industrial Machinery

The Association for Manufacturing Technology, 7901 Westpark
  Drive, McLean, VA 22102.
Associated General Contractors of America, 1957 E Street NW,
  Washington, DC 20006.

Millwrights

(Note: Millwrights install and dismantle the machinery and heavy equipment used in virtually every factory in America. They're the mechanics who
unpack, inspect and set into place all new production machinery with
cranes or whatever other equipment is needed. Earnings can reach above
$40,000 a year, depending on the area of the country.)

Associated General Contractors of America, 1957 E Street NW,
  Washington, DC 20006 (career information).

Small Engines (Motorcycles, Boats, and so on)

Motorcycle Mechanics Institute/Marine Mechanics Institute, 2844 W.
  Deer Valley Road, Phoenix, AZ 85027.

Musical Instruments (Repair and Tuning)

National Association of Professional Band Instrument Repair Technicians, P.O. Box 51, Normal, IL 61761 (career information).

Vending Machines

National Automatic Merchandising Association, 20 N. Wacker Drive, Chicago, IL 60606 (list of accredited schools).

Other Career Opportunities (On-the-job or Private Trade School Training Only)

Bicycle repairs, medical equipment repairs, instrument and tool repairs, rail car repairs, rigging, tire repairs, watch repairs.

Additional Information

Accrediting Commission of Career Schools and Colleges of Technology, 2101 Wilson Boulevard, Arlington, VA 22201.

Your state labor department (in the state capital) for lists of apprenticeship programs in various trades.

Your state employment service (job opportunities).

PERFORMING ARTS

Unlike other professions, there is no sure way to success in the performing arts. Many talented actors, singers and dancers have spent their lifetime waiting tables in restaurants only steps away from Broadway theaters—waiting for the "big break" that never came. And many performers with questionable talents have made millions because they did get a "big break," or perhaps they had the right "connections." In either case, there are factors beyond one's control that can affect careers in the performing arts far more than in many other professions where study and hard work are usually the surest means of success.

Unlike many other professions, too, the performing arts offer opportunities for men and women with widely varying levels of formal education. Many have university degrees; others dropped out of high school and never spent another minute studying their crafts. Obviously, careers in classical music, ballet or theater require years of formal study. That's not necessarily the case for careers in popular music, dance or theater. What most successful artists have in common, however, is talent, and most have spent years practicing what they do—whether it's acting, singing, dancing, playing a musical instrument or announcing on radio and television. Those who stayed in school have worked on school and college productions of all kinds or in local theater groups and informal musical groups.

Formal training can be a big help, because it often puts students in touch with professionals and job opportunities. Formal study in most of the performing arts is available at all levels: high schools, community colleges, four-year colleges and universities and private trade schools. For high school students, the finest education in the performing arts is at so-called "magnet" schools such as LaGuardia High School (once known as the High School of Performing Arts in New York City, the school portrayed in the TV show "Fame"). There are similar magnet schools in other major cities, all part of the public school system of their states. But admission is competitive by audition and restricted to the most-talented applicants.

In some states such as North Carolina, magnet schools have boarding facilities for applicants who live too far away to commute. Many community colleges and four-year universities have outstanding departments in one or more of the performing arts. Check with the state superintendent of schools to see if there are any magnet high schools for the performing arts in your state. Use the various guides to two-year and four-year colleges to identify those with outstanding music, theater or dance departments. Peterson's directory of two-year colleges even has a form you can send in with your special areas of interest, and the publisher's computer will pick all the appropriate schools for you to contact. Barron's Educational Series (250 Wireless Boulevard, Hauppauge, NY 11788) has helpful guides for four-year-colleges, universities and graduate schools.

The performing arts also includes behind-the-scenes opportunities discussed elsewhere. These include broadcast technicians (see Technical Trades), administrative and clerical work (see Business Administration), camera crews (see Arts and Crafts, Photography and Camera Work), instrument tuning and maintenance (see Mechanical Trades), set design (see Arts and Crafts, Design) and carpentry and electrical work (see Construction Trades).

PRODUCTION TRADES

Production workers make every product produced by American industry—apparel, fabrics and textiles, toys, furniture, home furnishings, shoes and leather goods, books and publications, tools and machinery, eyeglass rims, dental bridges, jewelry, cars, ladders and every other product you can think of. It's an endless list. Everything you see around you has to be made by hand or machine. The products that are mass-produced by machine are made by production workers who earn between $10,000 and $60,000 a year depending on the area of the country, the specific industry and the skills and training involved. Tool and die makers, who need four to five years of apprenticeship training, are in great demand. They earn about $20,000 to start and average nearly $35,000 after several years. The top 10 percent of their craft earn more than $60,000 a year. Most production workers earn between $12,000 and $15,000 to start. In 1988, earnings for production work averaged $28,000 a year for all industries and ranged from $20,000 to $35,000 a year for workers with five to 10 years' experience. Skilled workers able to deal effectively with people can work their way up to supervisory positions as inspectors, graders, testers and, of course, production line and plant floor supervisors. Those jobs usually pay between $25,000 and $60,000 a year. Almost all training for production work is on-the-job, either in a formal apprenticeship program or as an assistant to a skilled worker who serves as a mentor. Not all industries require workers to have high school diplomas, but in today's world of advanced technology, most manufacturers prefer applicants with high school diplomas and strong backgrounds in math, science (especially physics) and English (for reading complex instructions). Many high schools, vocational schools, community colleges, technical institutes and private trade schools offer formal training in specific production areas. Here is a sampling of the types of production trades and the organizations to contact for more information about career opportunities and training programs.

Apparel Workers

American Apparel Manufacturers Association, 2500 Wilson Boulevard, Arlington, VA 22201.

Check college directories for specialized textile colleges.

Bakers, Butchers, Meat-Poultry-Fish Cutters, Cooking Machine Operators, Dairy Processors

United Food & Commercial Workers International Union, 1775 K Street NW, Washington, DC 20006.

Bindery Workers (Production of Books, Magazines, Catalogs, Folders, Directories)

Education Council of the Graphic Arts Industry, 1899 Preston White Drive, Reston, VA 22091.

Compositors and Typesetters, Lithographers and Photoengravers, Printing Press Operators, Screen Printing Setters

Education Council of the Graphic Arts Industry, 1899 Preston White Drive, Reston, VA 22091.

Graphic Communications International Union, 1900 L Street NW, Washington, DC 20036.

Dental Laboratory Technicians (Production and Repair of Dental Fittings and Appliances)

American Dental Association Commission on Dental Accreditation, Division of Educational Measurement, 211 E. Chicago Avenue, Chicago, IL 60611.

National Association of Dental Laboratories, 3801 Mt. Vernon Avenue, Alexandria, VA 22305.

Electric Power Generating Plant Operators, Power Distributors and Dispatchers

Edison Electric Institute, P.O. Box 2800, Kearneysville, WV 25430.

International Brotherhood of Electrical Workers, 1125 15th Street NW, Washington, DC 20005.

Utility Workers Union of America, 815 16th Street NW, Washington, DC 20006.

Jewelers

Jewelers of America, Time-Life Bldg, 1185 Avenue of the Americas, New York, NY 10036.

Machinists and Metalworkers, Numerical-control Machine Tool Operators, Plastics Fabrication Machine Operators, Tool and Die Makers, Metal Fabricators, Sheet-metal Workers,

Metal Pourers and Casters, Extruding and Forming Machine Operators

The Association for Manufacturing Technology, 7901 Westport Drive, McLean, VA 22102.

The National Tooling & Machining Association, 9300 Livingston Road, Fort Washington, MD 20744.

National Screw Machine Products Association, 6700 W. Snowville Road, Brecksville, OH 44141.

The Tooling and Manufacturing Association, Education Department, 1177 South Dee Road, Park Ridge, IL 60068.

Precision Metalforming Association, 27027 Chardon Road, Richmond Heights, OH 44143.

Ophthalmic Laboratory Technicians (Production of Optical Goods and Eyeglasses)

Commission on Opticianry Accreditation, 10111 Martin Luther King Jr. Highway, Bowie, MD 20715.

Painting and Coating Machine Operators

Automotive Service Industry Association, 25 Northwest Point, Elk Grove Village, IL 60007.

Automotive Service Association, P.O. Box 929, Bedford, TX 76021.

National Institute for Automotive Service Excellence, 13505 Dulles Technology Drive, Herndon, VA 22071-3415.

Photographic Process Workers

Photo Marketing Association International, 3000 Picture Place, Jackson, MI 49201.

Shoe and Leather Workers

Shoe Service Institute of America, 5024-R Campbell Boulevard, Baltimore, MD 21236.

Stationary (Operating) Engineers (Operation and Maintenance Repair of Power Generating Equipment)

International Union of Operating Engineers, 1125 17th Street NW, Washington, DC 20036.

National Association of Power Engineers, 1 Springfield Street, Chicopee, MA 01013.

Textile Machinery Operators

American Textile Manufacturers Institute, 1801 K Street NW, Washington, DC 20006.

Institute of Textile Technology, P.O. Box 391, Charlottesville, VA 22901.

Water and Waste Water Treatment Plant Operators

American Waterworks Association, 6666 West Quincy Avenue, Denver, CO 80235.

Water Environment Federation, 601 Wythe Street, Alexandria, VA 22314.

Welders, Solderers, Brazers, Cutters and Welding Machine Operators

American Welding Society, 550 NW LeJeune Road, Miami, FL 33126.

National Association of Trade and Technical Schools, P.O. Box 10429, Rockville, MD 10850.

Woodworking

American Furniture Manufacturers Association, Manufacturing Services Division, P.O. Box HP-7, High Point, NC 27261.

Institute for Woodworking Education, 1012 Tenth Street, Manhattan Beach, CA 90266.

International Woodworkers of America, U.S. Research and Education Department, 25 Cornell Avenue, Gladstone, OR 97027.

Other Career Opportunities in Production Trades (On-the-job and Trade School Training Only)

Boiler operators; cannery workers; chemical equipment controllers and operators; chemical plant and system operators; coil winders and tapers; crushing and mixing machine operators; cutting and slicing machine operators; electrical and electronic assemblers; electronic semiconductor processors; furnace, kiln and kettle operators; gas and petroleum plant and systems operations; hand grinders and polishers; laundry and dry-cleaning machine operators; machine assemblers; machine feeders and offbearers; miners; packagers; quarry workers; roustabouts (oil field workers); tunneling machine operators; packaging and filling machine operators; separating and still machine operators; shipfitters and tirebuilding machine operators.

SERVICE OCCUPATIONS

Barbers

No high school diploma is required, but all states require barbers to be licensed. That means attending a state-approved barber school (9 to 12 months), then taking an examination for an apprentice license, working as an apprentice for one to two years and, finally, taking another examination for a license as a registered barber. Barbers seldom earn salaries. Instead, they earn 60 percent to 70 percent of the money they take in—and they get to keep all tips. Earnings averaged about $15,000 a year in 1996, but ranged up to $30,000 for experienced hairstylists—plus tips. Many barbers own their shops and earn more. A list of accredited barber schools is available from the Accrediting Commission of Career Schools and Colleges of Technology, 2101 Wilson Boulevard, Arlington, VA 22201.

Childcare Workers

Although no experience or formal training is required, most day care centers and other employers expect workers to have at least a high school education and to have studied some psychology, sociology, home economics, nutrition, art, music, drama and physical education. Moreover, a growing number of employers now require formal training and certification in childcare at the community college level. Many high schools and community colleges offer a one-year training program leading to a Child Development Associate (CDA) certificate. The program is open to anyone at least 18 years old with some childcare experience or related classroom training. For details, write to the Council for Early Childhood Professional Recognition, 1341 G Street NW, Washington, DC 20005. For career information write to the Association for Childhood Education International, 11501 Georgia Avenue, Wheaton, MD 20902, and to Head Start Bureau, P.O. Box 1182, Washington, DC 20013. Earnings in childcare are low, starting at minimum wage for beginners and seldom exceeding $15,000 a year.

Cosmetologists (Beauticians and Hairstylists)

State requirements vary, but all states require licensing, and that means being at least 16 years old, passing a physical examination and graduating from a state-licensed school of cosmetology. Some states require a high school diploma; others only require an eighth grade education. Unlike barbering, cosmetology instruction is offered in both public and private schools. Public high schools and vocational schools usually offer free training combined with useful academic education. Private trade schools, which charge fees, only teach the trade. Students in both public and private cosmetology schools must buy their own tools. Day courses usually take six months to a year to complete, while evening courses take longer. After graduation, cosmetologists must take a state licensing examination, part written and part practical demonstration. Earnings vary widely from area to area but usually average about $15,000 and reach $25,000 for experienced professionals. Tips are an important factor, and many cosmetologists in wealthy communities earn between $30,000 and $50,000 a year. Gifted cosmetologists can earn even more working with a private clientele or in the performing arts—television, movies and theater—preparing actors and actresses for performances. For additional information contact the National Accrediting Commission of Cosmetology Arts and Sciences, 901 North Stuart Street, Arlington, VA 22203, and the American Association of Cosmetology Schools, 901 North Washington Street, Alexandria, VA 22314.

Homemaker and Home Health Aides

Although a high school diploma is desirable, most agencies only require an ability to read, write and complete a one- to two-week training program as a homemaker/home health aide, which the agencies usually pay for. Some agencies and states require a nursing aide certificate. Earnings range from $5.00 to $9.00 an hour for a 20 to 36 hour work week. The Foundation for Hospice and Homecare, National Certification Program, (519 C Street NE, Washington, DC 20002) has more details on training and career opportunities.

Building Custodians (Janitors) and Cleaners

Most training is on-the-job, although workers must know simple arithmetic, how to read and write and how to make simple repairs. Shop courses at school can be helpful. No other formal education is required. Earnings average about $15,000 a year and range up to nearly $30,000 a year depending on the area of the country, hours worked and type of employer. About one-third of the more than 2.5 million janitors and cleaners work part time, that is, less than 35 hours a week. The largest employers are schools (including colleges and universities) and private maintenance firms, which clean buildings under contract. These two sectors employ about 20 percent each of the custodial work force. Hospitals and hotels each employ 10 percent, and the rest of the custodial force works in restaurants, apartment buildings, office buildings, manufacturing plants, government buildings and churches and other religious buildings. The field offers outstanding opportunities for experienced custodians willing to study small business management to establish private-home and apartment cleaning services. More information is available from the Building Service Contractors Association, 10201 Lee Highway, Fairfax, VA 22030.

Pest Control

This is usually a minimum wage job, although opportunities for self-employment after learning the trade can raise the annual income to between $30,000 and $50,000.

Private Household Workers

Usually no training or formal education is required, although most employers insist on an ability to clean well and/or cook and/or take care of children—skills generally learned while helping with housework at home. Courses in home economics, cooking, childcare, child development, first aid and nursing can lead to broader opportunities and better-paying jobs. Two-thirds of the one million private household workers work part time. Earnings range from minimum wage to $10 an hour, depending on the area of the country. Live-in workers employed by wealthy families earn more, between $800 and $1,000 a week plus room, board, medical benefits, a car, vacation days and education benefits, but such jobs require special training at schools for butlers, chauffeurs, nannies, governesses and cooks.

SPORTS AND RECREATION

Recreation workers are needed on a full-time or part-time basis at various establishments—commercial recreation areas, hotels, resorts, amusement parks, sports and entertainment centers, wilderness and survival excursion companies, tourist centers, vacation excursion firms, camps, health spas, athletic clubs, apartment and condominium complexes, ocean liners, civic and religious organizations, social service organizations (day care and senior citizens centers), residential care facilities and institutions, industrial plants and city, state and federal parks. To work at most schools and colleges, recreation workers and coaches must have a bachelor's degree in physical education from a four-year college and a teaching certificate. For other areas mentioned, only a high school diploma may be required along with experience in one or more recreational areas (art, music, drama and so on) or sports. Some jobs, such as lifeguards, require special certification. For career-track jobs, most employers now require an associate degree in park and recreation programs (available at about 200 community and junior colleges). Earnings range from $12,000 to $30,000 a year but average only $16,000. Write to the National Recreation and Park Association, 2775 South Quincy Street, Arlington, VA 22206 for career information, a list of approved academic programs and a twice-monthly bulletin of job opportunities. Additional information is available from the National Employee Services and Recreation Association, 2211 York Road, Oakbrook, IL 60521; and the American Camping Association, Bradford Woods, 5000 State Road, 67 N, Martinsville, IN 46151. For careers with the YMCA, write to the YMCA National Office, 101 North Wacker Drive, Chicago, IL 60606.

TECHNICAL TRADES

Broadcast Technicians

An associate degree from a technical institute or community college is required for operating and maintaining the complex electronic equipment, which records and transmits radio and television programs. Also required is a radio-telephone operator license issued by the Federal Communications Commission after successful completion of a series of written exams. Those entering the field must have strong backgrounds in high school algebra, trigonometry, physics, electronics and other sciences. Starting jobs at small stations pay about $15,000. As a profession, technicians average between $20,000 and $25,000 but can earn $50,000 or more at network-owned radio and television stations. Supervisory jobs can pay close to $100,000 at such stations. For information on licensing procedures, write to the Federal Communications Commission, 1270 Fairfield Road, Gettysburg, PA 17325. For career information, write to the National Association of Broadcasters Employment Clearinghouse, 1771 N Street NW, Washington, DC 20036 and to the National Cable Television Association, 1724 Massachusetts Avenue NW, Washington, DC 20036. For a list of accredited schools, write to the Broadcast Education Association, National Association of Broadcasters, 1771 N Street NW, Washington, DC 20036. For information on certification, write to the Society of Broadcast Engineers, 8445 Keystone Crossing, Indianapolis, IN 46240.

Drafters

Drafting—the drawing of exact design dimensions and specifications of every product and part that is manufactured and every structure that is built—is a profession requiring a two-year associate degree from a technical institute, community college or trade school. Training includes courses in mathematics, physics, mechanical drawing and, of course, drafting. Salaries range from $16,000 for beginners and climb to more than $50,000 for senior drafters. The average salary is about $30,000 a year. Use Peterson's *Two-Year Colleges* guide to find appropriate community colleges and technical institutes.

Engineering Technicians

This is an exciting profession for the mechanically gifted with aptitudes in math and science, and it requires only an associate degree from a technical institute or community college. Be extremely cautious about selecting the right education for this field, however. Contact the Junior Engineering Technical Society (JETS), 1420 King Street, Alexandria, VA 22314 for more information. The work of engineering technicians pays between $15,000 and $50,000 a year and involves assisting engineers and scientists in government and industry research and development. Engineering technicians set up experiments, help develop new products and solve customer problems with equipment ranging from production machinery to NASA missiles, space shuttles and satellites.

Legal Assistants (Paralegals)

Although many employers prefer training their own legal assistants, more than 800 formal training programs for paralegals are available to high school graduates at community and junior colleges, four-year colleges, law schools and legal assistant associations. Lists of approved legal assistant training programs, career information and job opportunities are available from these organizations:

Legal Assistant Management Association, P.O. Box 40129, Overland Park, KS 66204.

National Association of Legal Assistants, 1601 South Main Street, Tulsa, OK 74119.

National Federation of Paralegal Associations, 104 Wilmot Road, Deerfield, IL 60015-5195.

National Paralegal Association, P.O. Box 406, Solebury, PA 18963.

Standing Committee on Legal Assistants, American Bar Association, 750 North Lake Shore Drive, Chicago, IL 60611.

Depending on the area of the country and the size of the law firm or employer, legal assistants earn between $15,000 and $40,000 a year.

Library Technicians

Library technical assistants, as they're often called, perform all the support activities of a library. They help librarians prepare, organize and catalog materials; help the public; operate audio-visual equipment; organize exhibits and help clients with microfiche equipment and computers. Library technicians need a two-year community college associate degree in library technology. Salaries vary widely but average $25,000. It's important for you to know, however, that credits earned for an associate degree in library technology *do not* apply toward a degree in library science, which is a four-year professional degree from a college or university in preparation for a job as a librarian. For more information write to the American Library Association, Office for Library Personnel Resources, 50 East Huron Street, Chicago, IL 60611.

Science Technicians

For those with an interest in science, this profession offers the opportunity to work in research and development in the chemical, petroleum and food processing industries as well as in college, university and government research laboratories and the labs of research and development firms. Most junior and community colleges offer two-year associate degrees in science, mathematics and specific technologies such as food technology. Earnings of science technicians range from $14,500 to $47,000 a year. For information about a career as a chemical technician in chemistry-related fields including food, contact the American Chemical Society, Education Division, Career Publications, 1155 16th Street NW, Washington, DC 20036. For information about a career as a biological technician in biology-related fields, contact the American Institute of Biological Sciences, 730 11th Street NW, Washington, DC 20001.

TRANSPORTATION

Air Transport

With the exception of flight crews, most airline and ground service personnel (flight attendants, ground crews, and so on) and airport operations staffs need no college education, although flight attendants on international routes must know appropriate foreign languages. Most training is on-the-job in formal company training programs. Earnings average about $22,000 a year. Most airlines require pilots to have two years of college and many insist on a four-year college degree. Pilots must attend a certified pilot school or pass a Federal Aviation Administration military competency exam if they learn to fly in the military. Pilot salaries average $80,000 and range as high as $165,000 for senior pilots on major airlines. For more information about career opportunities in air transport, write to the airlines themselves, to air transport companies such as United Parcel Service or Federal Express, to Future Aviation Professionals of America, 4959 Massachusetts Boulevard, Atlanta, GA 30032, and to the Air Line Employees Association, Job Opportunity Program, 6520 South Cicero Avenue, Chicago, IL 60638.

Ground Transport

Bus drivers. Must be 18 to 24 years old, preferably high school graduates, and, depending on state regulations, have a commercial driver's license or special schoolbus license. In addition, intercity bus drivers must meet state or U.S. Department of Transportation qualifications. Training is on-the-job in formal company or transit system training programs lasting two to eight weeks. Drivers in local transit systems earn between $21,000 and $40,000 a year. Experienced intercity bus drivers can earn more than $50,000 a year. Information on school-bus driving is available from the National School Transportation Association, P.O. Box 2639, Springfield, VA 22152, and you can get information on local transit bus driving from the American Public Transit Association, 1201 New York Avenue NW, Washington, DC 20005.

Truck drivers. Qualifications vary widely depending on the types of trucks and where goods will be carried. In general, truck drivers need to be in good physical condition and at least 21 years old to engage in interstate commerce. They must have a commercial motor vehicle operator license and take written examinations on the Motor Carrier Safety Regulations of the U.S. Department of Transportation. Many firms won't hire new drivers under 25 years old because of insurance costs. Local drivers are paid by the hour, but wages vary from community to community and whether drivers are unionized. Average income ranges from $8 an hour for driving light trucks to about $15 an hour for driving medium trucks. Long-distance tractor-trailer drivers, many of whom belong to the International Brotherhood of Teamsters (union), earn from $20,000 to more than $50,000 a year. For more information, write to American Trucking Associations, Inc., 2200 Mill Road, Alexandria, VA 22314. For a list of certified tractor-trailer driver training programs, write to the Professional Truck Driver Institute of America, 8788 Elk Grove Boulevard, Elk Grove, CA 95624.

Other Transportation Industry Opportunities

- Shipping. Seamen on ocean-going vessels; mates aboard coastal and inland ships, boats and barges.
- Railroads. Locomotive engineers; brake, signal and switch operators; conductors; yard masters; yard equipment operators.
- Surface transport. Taxi drivers and chauffeurs; limousine drivers; hearse drivers; car delivery drivers for new car dealers; service station attendants; parking lot operators; car wash operators.

ARMED SERVICES (FOR NONMILITARY JOBS, SEE GOVERNMENT SERVICE)

The U.S. Armed Services—the army, navy, marines and coast guard—offer millions of American men and women endless opportunities to learn a trade and serve their country at the same time. All branches require a high school diploma, and applicants must pass written examinations. Applicants must be at least 18 years old (or 17 with parental consent) and must agree contractually to serve at least two and usually three to four years. Together, the four services are the largest employers in the U.S. and offer the most job training and benefits. They offer training and work experience in nearly 2000 occupations, most of which are valuable in civilian life. Here are the jobs, in 12 broad categories, which are open to enlisted personnel (nonofficers) with no college education or previous experience. All training is on-the-job at full pay and at government expense.

1. Human services: recreation.
2. Media and public affairs: musicians, photographers, camera operators, graphic designers and illustrators and foreign language interpreters and translators.
3. Health care: medical laboratory technologists and technicians, radiologic technologists, emergency medical technicians, dental assistants, pharmaceutical assistants, sanitation specialists and veterinary assistants. Military training as a health care specialist automatically entitles a person to civilian certification.
4. Engineering, scientific and technical occupations: mapping technicians, computer programmers, air traffic controllers and radio and radar operators.
5. Administrative, clerical and functional support jobs: accounting clerks, payroll clerks, personnel clerks, computer programmers, computer operators, accounting machine operators, chaplain assistants, counseling aides, typists, word processor operators, stenographers, storekeepers and other clerical jobs.
6. Service occupations: military police, correction specialists, detectives, firefighters, food preparation and service.
7. Vehicle and machinery mechanics: maintenance and repair of aircraft, missiles, conventional and nuclear powered ships, boats and

landing craft, trucks, earth moving equipment, armored vehicles and cars.

8. Electronic and electric repair: repairs of radio, navigation and flight control equipment, telephones and data processing equipment.

9. Construction trades: carpenters, construction and earthmoving equipment operators, metalworkers, machinists, plumbers, electricians, heating and air-conditioning specialists and every other building trades occupation related to construction and maintenance of buildings, roads, bridges and airstrips.

10. Machine operating and precision work: laboratory technicians, opticians, machinists, welders and shipfitters.

11. Transportation and materials handling: truck drivers; aircrews; seamen; warehousing and equipment handling specialists and all jobs associated with the operation of transportation equipment, including trucks, ships, boats, airplanes and helicopters; and maintaining inventories of all spare parts.

12. Infantry, gun crews and seamen specialists: the one area with few applications to civilian life, although some munitions experts find work in law enforcement and demolition, while seamen specialists often find jobs on merchant and passenger vessels.

Enlistment is a contract in which *you* specify the occupational areas that interest you most and in which you want to be trained before you join. You can also apply for Officer Candidate School, and if accepted, become an officer trained in managerial and administrative skills. Service in the military entitles you to scholarship funds to attend college while you're in the military or after discharge. Although the military can be a stepping stone to a rewarding civilian career, it is also a rewarding career in itself and should be considered seriously as such. Aside from pride of service, the military offers the most benefits and job security of any U.S. employer. Enlisted personnel earn an average of more than $25,000 a year in take-home pay and housing and subsistence (food) allowances. Cash income ranges from $800 to $1300 a month along with free room and board (or a housing and subsistence allowance), free medical and dental care, a military clothing allowance, free on-base recreational facilities and 30 days paid vacation a year. Warrant officer earnings average more than $42,000 a year and commissioned officers average nearly $53,000 a year in cash and equivalents. Military personnel are eligible for retirement benefits after only 20 years of service, including a pension worth 40 percent of base (cash) pay. Any veteran with two or more years of service is eligible for free medical care at any veterans administration hospital. For information on military careers, stop in at any military recruiting station or state employment service office. Most high schools, colleges and public libraries have similar materials. You may also write to:

Department of the Army, HQUS Recruiting Command, Fort Sheridan, IL 60037.

USAF Recruiting Service, Randolph Air Force Base, TX 78150.

Commandant of the Marine Corps, Headquarters, Washington, DC 20380.

Navy Recruiting Command, 4015 Wilson Boulevard, Arlington, VA 22203-1991.

Commandant, G-PRJ, U.S. Coast Guard, Washington, DC 20590.

4 Getting Started in Your New Career

Once you've selected the industry and career that interests you most and you've completed your alternative education for that career, you'll have to get a job. If you attended a cooperative education program, it's likely that the employer that helped train you will offer you a permanent job. In that case, you're all set. Good luck in your new job.

If you did not participate in such a program, but carefully evaluated the one you did attend and picked a good one, that program's job placement service will put you in touch with employers looking for your skills. You'll also want to contact employers on your own. With or without help from others, the job of getting a job is simple. It will take time; it may be frustrating; but the techniques are simple. Don't complicate them and don't let others complicate them or discourage you. Many friends and relatives will tell you "you're doing it all wrong" and flood you with endless articles and books about "How to Get a Good Job" and "How to Write a Good Resume." Chances are all those articles and books contain good pointers, but you may find yourself spending more time reading about how to get a job instead of going out and getting one.

The principles in all those books and articles are the same. Identify your skills and positive traits, get them down on paper in summary or *resume* form and get that resume into the hands of the one employer in ten or one hundred or one thousand who is looking for your combination of skills and personality.

Writing Resumes

A resume is not an autobiography. It is a *sales pitch*—a written advertisement of skills and services for sale. It's the reverse of a help wanted ad. A help wanted ad never tells you any negatives about a job, only the positives. Like all ads, it's a teaser, which lures readers into contacting the employer to get more details. Which of these ads would tease you into making a call to get more details?

> *Administrative Assistant:* Top salary, flexible hours, interesting, congenial atmosphere on TV talk show team. Must be able to handle contacts with guest personalities. Call 555-0000.

> *Secretary:* Take dictation (80 words/min), type letters, file documents, answer telephones, carry messages, run errands for busy executive. Hours 9 to 5, five days a week, but must be ready to work evenings and some weekends. Salary: $18,000. Call XYZ Productions. . . .

The two jobs are identical, but the top ad makes it more attractive by keeping details to a minimum and only listing positive aspects of the job. And that's what you've got to do with your resume. Every job has negative characteristics, but the ad that features them will get no takers. The same is true for resumes. We all have our weaknesses, but they don't go in our resumes. Similarly, too many details can destroy the value of an ad by discouraging a response from an applicant who doesn't fit the job perfectly—the otherwise perfect candidate who can only take dictation at 60 words a minute, for example. That candidate might respond to the first ad but not the second, and the company would be the loser by not even getting a chance to interview the perfect candidate.

These same rules apply to resumes. Once again, a resume is not your life history. It is an ad, a sales promotion piece. Keep it short (no more than one page); keep it simple; keep it positive; and, as in all ads, show its readers how your skills and services can so benefit them that they'll invite you for an interview. And that's what your resume is for—to get you an invitation for an interview. Don't misunderstand its purpose: A resume will never get you a job, only a job *interview*.

A resume has two elements: form and content. There are simple rules for both. Break these rules and your prospective employer will assume you cannot follow any rules. Your resume will end up in a special file for rejected applications—the waste basket. The important thing to keep in mind in writing a resume is that it is one of the few aspects in the job application process that is totally under your control. You cannot control job market conditions or the quality of other applicants competing with you. But you can control what goes into your resume.

Here are the rules for resume form:

1. **Brevity.** *No more than one page long.* An inability to reduce a resume to one page shows either a lack of command of the English language, an inability to follow directions or an inflated sense of self-importance—none of which are characteristics that employers admire.

2. **Neatness.** Absolute perfection is the rule. There is no excuse for not being able to produce a perfect resume in the quiet and privacy of one's home away from all pressures. If you can't produce an absolutely neat one-page paper, potential employers will assume you can't do anything neatly.

3. **Factual accuracy.** Potential employers will check the facts in your resume. Be certain they are accurate. If they're not, a potential employer will conclude that you are either dishonest or unable to do accurate work.

4. **Honesty.** Don't exaggerate by calling your summer job as a file clerk an "administrative assistant." And if you cut lawns as a summer job or picked vegetables, say so. Don't call yourself a landscape or agricultural technician.

5. **Writing accuracy.** Your resume must be free of spelling, grammatical and typographical errors. Again, if you can't produce a one-page paper free of errors, employers will conclude you can't do any error-free work.

6. **Personal data.** You should not include a photograph of yourself or personal information such as height, weight, sex, race or religion. It is against state and federal law to mention any characteristics associated with discrimination based on race, religion, gender or age.

7. **Standard presentation.** Don't use off-sized or off-color paper. You are writing for businesspeople. Be businesslike. Use standard 8-in. x 11-in. white paper. Artistic attention-getting devices, which parents and teachers may have thought cute or even imaginative in school, will only be tossed away as unbusinesslike by potential employers.

8. **Well organized.** The resume should be organized into four or five basic categories, that is, each headed by a capitalized or underlined heading. There are three basic methods of organization: chronological (in order of occurrence), functional (in order of importance) and combined chrono-

logical and functional. The last format is usually the most effective and the one used in the following sample. It orders the broad categories by importance for the job you're applying for, but orders the information within each category chronologically, either backwards or forwards, depending on which is more effective.

9. Typography. Resumes should be typed and printed or copied on print-quality dry copying machines or prepared on a letter-quality word processor. Do not use a dot matrix printer, and never send a carbon copy! Word processing is by far the most preferable, because it allows you to use a basic format, which you can adapt slightly or "custom design" for each prospective employer. Someone interested in a secretarial career might want to modify the objective to read "Secretarial work in health care field" for one prospective employer and "Secretarial work, scientific research" for another. In other words, you can show a specific interest in a particular company. That's almost impossible with a printed resume, whose tone must be general enough to send to a wide variety of prospective employers. It says the same thing to every company and shows no particular interest in any.

Here are the rules for content, followed by a sample resume on page 115, which you can use by substituting your own data for the fictitious information:

Name, address and telephone number, centered at the top of the page

Career Objective

Notice that I've used the word *career* rather than occupational or job objective. That's because by stating a broad career goal, you give a potential employer who likes your resume more flexibility than you would by stating the specific job you're seeking. If you list bartending as a job objective, for example, and there are better, more experienced applicants, you'll be rejected. But if you list restaurant and hotel service, the same employer who might reject you for the bartender's job may be eager to give you some other opportunity as a waiter or assistant host if your training warrants it. Similarly, the modest applicant who specifies "entry-level position in public relations" may get no job at all (because there is no entry-level job) or he might win that entry-level job and miss getting a better job for which his resume kept him from being considered. If you specify an entry-level job, that's all you'll probably be considered for. So, again, don't close doors of opportunity on yourself by narrowing your goals or being unnecessarily modest.

Job Qualifications

The next category of data should tell the employer that you know how to do the job he or she has. If you've just graduated from school and learned those skills in a vocational education program, you should put "Education" as the next category in your resume. If, on the other hand, you learned most of the skills you need through previous work experience, then "Work Experience" should be next. Within the category of job qualifications, list each experience chronologically, with the most recent one first. With each experience, indicate *briefly* what skill you learned or used that will be of value to your prospective employer. Also mention any special award or accomplishment associated with each experience. Whether you're submitting your resume to a giant corporation or a local grocery store, prospective employers want to know the same thing: that you can do the job they're trying to fill. You can demonstrate that to them by showing that you either learned how at a good vocational school or that you've actually done it on-the-job.

References

List the names, addresses and telephone numbers of former employers or teachers who had key roles in teaching you the skills needed for the job you're applying for. There's no point listing a 9th-grade teacher who likes you a lot. The only teachers you should consider are those who taught you your trade and, perhaps, the director of the program in which you learned that trade.

Optional Categories

Special skills. If you're fluent in a foreign language or have some other special skill or knowledge not mentioned under "Experience"—it could be a hobby or travel experience—that might prove *useful* to your employer, mention it under this listing. Remember: It must prove useful, not just interesting.

Awards and affiliations. If you've won an award or have some position in a club or organization where you display other talents your employer could use, then add this category to your resume. An example might be, "Treasurer, Smithville Boys Club. Managed membership dues collections, club solicitations, investments and disbursements and maintained accounts ledgers." Such an example shows your familiarity with handling and managing organization funds and with accounting and bookkeeping. It also reflects a community's faith in your honesty and trustworthiness. It displays another positive element of your character in just a few words, without any bragging or exaggeration.

Writing Style

Keep each statement short. Do not use complete sentences such as, "I worked as a salesperson behind the greeting card counter." Instead, the description of such a previous job should read, "Salesperson, greeting cards. Actively managed customer sales, cash flow, inventory controls, reorders of 16 product lines from five vendors." And, if your work was particularly notable, you would add to the description, "Salesperson of the Month Award, December 1997," or "Reorganized inventory controls to reduce perennial shrinkage from 3.24 percent of purchasing costs to 0.14 percent with annual savings of $46,542 to the department."

There are two other important elements in a good resume writing style. One is the use of active, meaningful verbs to describe what you did on the job or learned in the classroom—for example, "reorganized" rather than "changed" or "managed" rather than "responsible for." Be careful not to write a job description, only what you did on the job and only those accomplishments that might be of use to your new employer. Follow each job title with an action verb: "introduced," "inspected," "maintained," "prepared," "organized," "controlled," "planned," "initiated," "executed," "analyzed," "documented," "designed," "monitored," "modified," "systematized," "streamlined," "converted," "promoted" and so on. In describing classroom training experiences, use the phrase "hands-on operation" or "hands-on production" to indicate you actually operated some equipment or produced some product.

The other important element in a good writing style is the avoidance of jargon, which is a wordy, meaningless phrase for which a single word can be substituted. Our daily speech is filled with jargon: "at this point in time" instead of "now"; "at some future point in time" instead of "soon"; "in order to" or "for the purpose of" or "with a view toward" instead of "to"; "with respect to" instead of "about." In other words, keep your sentences short and to the point.

Figure 2 on page 115 is a sample resume in which the job applicant is seeking a career in merchandising, or retailing. He has learned his skills both in college and working at summer jobs. Had he majored in English instead of marketing, his work experience would have been listed first. But the broad nature of his business education warrants its appearance before his work experience, which, after all, was only summer work and probably did not give him the in-depth understanding of retail operations that he studied in college. Had this been a resume of a young man who had graduated two years earlier and then worked for two years in a department store, his work experience would have been listed before his education.

The resume is purposely "average"—no awards, no super achievements—because most of us are average. The trick to resume writing is to display the solidity, dependability and skills that someone with an average background and education can develop. Notice, too, how the resume can be used to match individual employer needs with as little as a single word change. As it stands, it is a valid resume for any department store. But, if he changed his career goal from "Merchandising" to "Fashion Merchandising" or "Merchandising, Menswear," it would be a particularly effective resume for any menswear retailer. By leaving his career objective as it is, however, and by expanding his experience in the student book store, he could send his resume to any store that sells student supplies in or near a college or university.

The Cover Letter

In some cases, you hand-deliver your resume to a prospective employer. Every resume that's sent by mail, however, should have a cover letter regardless of how you made initial contact with a prospective employer. Just as the resume is designed to get you an interview, the cover letter is designed to get the recipient to read your resume. The cover letter, therefore, is not a rehash of your resume. It must be different. Like the resume, it must be a teaser and intrigue its reader to look at the enclosed resume.

Eugene Everett Richards
687 Saybrook Court
Yalesville, CT 10101
Tel: (718) 563-4839

CAREER OBJECTIVE:	Merchandising
EDUCATION:	Rockdale Community College, Associate Degree, Marketing, June 1998. Courses: Accounting, Retail Computer Applications, Marketing, Merchandising, Store Management.
	Rockdale High School. Graduated, June 1996 with honors. Academic Program with marketing and accounting electives.
WORK EXPERIENCE:	September 1997–May 1998. Hands-on management (as part of "Store Management" course), RCC Student Book Store: purchasing, pricing, inventory controls, reorder of books and student supplies, including stationery, toiletries and college souvenir clothing; employee relations.
	Summer 1997. Salesman, men's furnishings (shirts, socks, underwear, handkerchiefs), Binghamton Department Store. Active selling: Guided customer selection with emphasis on sales of latest, high mark-up designer brands and fashionwear; processed all aspects of sales transactions.
	Summer 1996. Stock clerk, men's apparel, Binghamton Department Store. Managed restocking of floor racks and shelves with suits, sport shirts, dress shirts, socks, underwear and other furnishings; processed automatic reorders via computer terminals.
	Binghamton Department Store, summers, 1994, 1995.
SPECIAL SKILLS:	Fluent in conversational and commercial Spanish.
REFERENCES:	Mr. Donald Director
	President
	Binghamton Department Store
	321 Downtown Mall
	Binghamton, NJ 07698
	Dr. Emma Educator
	President
	Rockdale Community College
	876 Wisdom Road
	Rockdale, NY 10893

Figure 2. Sample resume of a graduating community college student.

The principles of resume writing apply to the cover letter. It must be short (one page only), neat, accurate, free of spelling, grammatical and typographical errors and prepared on a typewriter or letter-quality word processor on standard paper or stationery in standard business-letter format, as in the following sample. If you have business-type stationery with your own letterhead, use it. Otherwise, type your letterhead in the upper right hand corner. Do not use small or decoratively printed personal stationery. Again, avoid cuteness such as "Hi!" or a pompous attitude, such as "Here's the letter you've been waiting for!" As in the case of the resume, the cover letter is another aspect of keeping the job application process completely under your control. Produce a letter that will make you a desirable candidate.

You are writing to conservative business people who have one goal—to improve company operations. Your letter must be conservative and businesslike and indicate that you can make a contribution to the company. You can use the sample letter on page 117 by substituting the facts of your own background for those of the fictitious job applicant.

In general, a cover letter should be no longer than three paragraphs, preferably two. You must make three points:

1. Why you are writing.   Although the saying, "It's not what you know, it's who you know" doesn't always apply, contacts often can be important factors in getting a job. If you get the job, of course, you'll have to prove yourself, and contacts won't help you much. But for getting that first chance, the person with contacts and good references will usually win out over the applicant without them, all other things being equal. So, your opening sentence in any cover letter should mention your contact, if you have one, and his or her connection to either the company or to you. The contact may be a friend of the person you're writing; an official in the company; the job placement counselor at your school or college; a teacher or official at your college or school; an employment agent or a parent or relative. Whoever the contact, if you have one, use it—and use it to begin your opening sentence. Don't waste time: play your strong cards immediately.

"Ms. Doris Manning, vice-president of marketing, suggested I write to you . . ." or "My father, Samuel Richards, an attorney at . . ." or "Dr. Frederick Walker, president of Rockdale Community College . . ." or "Mrs. Patricia Lane of the Rockdale Community College Job Placement Office, suggested I write you . . .".

Eugene Everett Richards
687 Saybrook Court
Yalesville, CT 10101

May 1, 1998

Ms. Cherie Lorraine
Director
Executive Training Program
Smith's Department Store
Barclay Square
New York, NY 10036

Dear Ms. Lorraine:

Mr. Donald Director, president of Binghamton Department Store, suggested I write to you to apply to Smith's Executive Training Program. As you can see in my enclosed resume, I will be graduating from Rockdale Community College this June with an Associate Degree in Marketing. As part of my course in store management, I had the opportunity to participate in hands-on management of the Rockdale Community College bookstore. Together with my two summers as a stock clerk and a third summer as a salesperson in men's furnishings at Binghamton Department Store, my work in merchandising—especially with goods designed for younger men and women—has proved the most exciting experience in my life. I want to make it my career, and I would love to work at Smith's.

I would be most grateful for the opportunity of an interview with you to see if you think I might qualify for Smith's Executive Training Program.

With many thanks for your consideration.

Sincerely,

Eugene Everett Richards

If you do not have a contact, explain what motivated the letter: "I saw your advertisement . . ." or, if you contacted the company "cold" by telephone, "I enjoyed talking with you today about the possibility of my working at . . .".

Once you've explained who or what put you in touch with the company, finish the opening by explaining the reason for writing: ". . . about the opening for a salesperson in the Smith's Menswear Department" or "about an opening in the Smith's Executive Training Program" or "about the possibility of a job in merchandising at Smith's."

2. Who you are. Again, keep this short. You're either a graduate of or will soon graduate from a school or college where you studied some courses or trade important in the job you're applying for. In one sentence say why you want to make that trade your career and why you want to work at the company you're writing to. Those two short sentences are probably the most difficult sentences any job applicant ever has to write. They sound simple enough, but they're not. They require considerable soul searching and research—but you must do it. Anyone who eventually hires you will want to know why you want to go into your chosen field and why you want to work for that particular company. So, you might just as well pinpoint the reasons now. And if you can't figure out the reasons, perhaps you're going into the wrong trade or applying for a job at the wrong company. The way to get started is to list all the characteristics you like about the trade you've chosen. Then reword those characteristics to have more meaning for others who may be unfamiliar with that industry. Take the fictitious job applicant in the preceding letter who obviously likes working in stores. Why would anyone want to spend eight to ten hours a day on his feet five or six days a week listening to complaining customers? Well, those who make a career out of and love merchandising don't see those as negative aspects. They see the positiveness—the excitement of facilitating the huge flow of goods from manufacturer to consumer. They enjoy the satisfaction of filling consumer needs, of discovering new products, of setting new fashion trends. They see themselves, to paraphrase a General Electric Co. advertising slogan, bringing good things to their community and its people.

In the interview, which follows, you'll have to explain in detail why you like the trade you've chosen. For the second sentence of your cover letter, however, you must summarize it in one line, as the fictitious applicant has done: ". . . merchandising . . . goods designed for younger men and women has proved the most exciting experience in my life." And in the next line, explain why you want to work for that company. Your reasons may have to do with the company's standing in the community, in the industry or in the nation or your own experience with its products or services. They cannot be trivial or selfish. Just because you can walk to work is not a good primary reason. It's a good secondary reason, which you can bring up in the interview. After all, proximity to your work is valuable to your employer as well as to you, because it reduces employee lateness and absenteeism. But proximity cannot be a reason to put in your cover letter. It's essential to research the reasons for wanting to work for a company. Get an annual report to shareholders; study company brochures about its operations and its products and services; and speak to current and former employees and to customers. You may find you don't want to work for that company. But if you do, tell them why in one short sentence of your cover letter.

3. What you want the reader to do. Obviously, you want the reader of your letter to read your resume and interview you for a job. Say so quickly and politely at the end of your cover letter, as the applicant has done in the sample. You may use any acceptable sign-off: "Sincerely," "Sincerely yours" or "Yours truly."

Do not enclose any other material—only your resume and a cover letter. If you have any supporting materials, such as letters of recommendation or charts or spreadsheets that show the kind and quality of work you did, bring those with you to the interview. Never send them by mail unless you are specifically requested to do so and then include a self-addressed, stamped envelope for their return.

The Personal Interview

As in the case of the resume and cover letter, the personal interview is another aspect of the job application package under your control. It is an opportunity for you to display a depth of knowledge and aspects of your personality that dry facts and statistics on an application or resume cannot exhibit. The interview—sometimes there may be a series of two or three for the job you're seeking—is the final stage of your quest for employment. Do well in it, and you'll probably be hired.

The Interview Guidelines on page 123 lists the range of questions interviewers at one large U.S. corporation asks job applicants. The forms they use show you exactly how they handle the entire interview process. As you can see, the first thing interviewers look for is the applicant's appearance. So do enough advance research to determine the proper dress for the job you're trying to get. If people who hold similar jobs normally wear dresses or ties and jackets, then you must do so also. A company is not like school where the person who stands out in the crowd because of unusual conduct or dress will win some admiration. The interview is the moment to prove you can be part of the company's team and play by the company's rules. In addition to dress, posture and grooming are important elements of everyone's appearance. Slouching in one's seat can cost an applicant a job. Failure to look the interviewer in the eye, nervous habits and any other unusual behavior can all go down as negatives in an application folder.

Here is the full range of questions most good interviewers will ask job applicants. Can you answer the ones appropriate for your background and the type of job you're seeking? If not, start practicing. There are three sections to the interview package. The first section lists a range of questions to ask. The second section tells the interviewer what to listen and look for—especially appearance, manner, self-expression and responsiveness on the part of the applicant. And the third section asks the interviewer to rate the applicant on appearance, work experience, education and present activities and interests—and then recommend for or against hiring. Use this material to help you prepare for your interviews.

INTERVIEW GUIDELINES

Outlined below are the four major areas of the applicant that you should investigate: Work Experience, Education and Training, Goals and Ambitions, and Self-Assessment. The questions within each area are suggested topics for you to explore. Ask these questions in your own words and style, and add any questions you feel necessary within each category. Be sure to cover each area thoroughly. Remember, the following are only sample questions and are, by no means, an exhaustive list.

Work Experience

1. Please describe your present responsibilities and duties.
2. What were some of the things that you particularly enjoyed when you were working for the ABC Corporation?
3. What do you consider to have been your chief accomplishments at the ABC Corporation?
4. Tell me about the personal progress that you made during your association with the ABC Corporation.
5. Looking back at the time spent with the ABC Corporation, what do you feel you have gained from your association?
6. What were your reasons for leaving the ABC Corporation?
7. In the past, for what things have your superiors complimented you? For what have they criticized you?
8. What were some of the problems that you encountered on your job and how did you solve these problems?
9. As you see it, what would be some advantages to you were you to join our company? What disadvantages or drawbacks might there be?
10. Describe a typical day on your last job.

Education

1. How did you select the college or type of school you attended?
2. What did you hope to do with your education?
3. How do you think college or alternative education contributed to your development?
4. How would you describe your academic achievement?
5. Have you had any additional training or education since graduating?
6. Looking back at your education, how do you feel it has prepared you for a position as a _____?
7. How did you select your major course of study?

Goals and Ambitions

1. What are you looking for in a job?
2. Why does this job sound appealing to you?
3. What would you like to be doing in 3 years? 5 years?
4. What would you want in your next job that you are not getting now?
5. What are some of the things in a job that are important to you?
6. In considering joining a company, what are some of the factors that you take into account?
7. What are your present salary expectations?

Self-Assessment

1. In general, how would you describe yourself?
2. What do you regard to be your outstanding qualities?
3. Why have you progressed to where you are?
4. What kinds of situations in circumstances make you feel tense or nervous?
5. In which areas do you feel you would like to develop yourself?
6. What do you feel you have to offer us?
7. We all have our strengths and weaknesses. What do you feel are your greatest strengths, and what are those areas that you would like to improve upon?

Interviewers will note both the manners and language of applicants. The repetitive use of the word *like* and the phrase "ya know," as in "Like . . . ya know . . ." will certainly produce negative reactions from interviewers. So will responses such as "Cool!" and immature speech patterns such as, "Well, ya know, I kinda like computers, ya know, and, uh, like, ya know, electronic equipment and, ya know . . ." Clear, effective communication is important in every job involving other people. Everyone on the team has to be able to understand what other team members say and write. An applicant who has not yet learned how to communicate effectively will find it difficult to get a good job, because most employers seek applicants who have the ability to articulate well.

One-word answers also leave interviewers unimpressed and hurt any chances of getting a job—as it did this applicant, whose interview began this way:

Interviewer: Did you find your way here all right?
Applicant: Yeah.
Interviewer: No trouble at all, eh?
Applicant: Nah.
Interviewer: Well, have a seat.
Applicant sits without replying.
Interviewer: Let's see . . . you're applying for the sales job in meanswear, right?
Applicant: Yeah.

Although such answers may be the result of shyness, they usually appear to others as unfriendly and rude. The ability to engage in conversation is always seen as a sign of good manners and friendliness.

Another error that can earn a job rejection is poor grammar, especially for office jobs. A lot of poor grammar such as "Things are going good" instead of "well" or "Me and my friends went to the movies" instead of "My friends and I . . ." may be the result of bad habits, not lack of knowledge. If that's the case for you, begin changing those habits in your everyday speech now before you begin the round of job interviews. Poor grammar can hurt your chances of getting a good job, and it can affect your entire career.

In addition to proper conduct, dress and speech, it's important to go into an interview knowing as much about a particular company as possible. Almost every interviewer will ask why you want to work for his or her company, and it's important that you know why, specifically, on the basis of your in-depth reading of its annual report, sales brochures, product catalogs and any other printed materials. Most major libraries carry directories of corporations—*Moody's*, for example, or *Standard & Poor's*, or *Value Line*—that contain much data about all major companies. When an interviewer asks what you know about the company, you should know more than "just what I read in the newspapers." Your answer should demonstrate initiative and interest. You should know its history, the products and services it offers and something about its top officials. You should know what makes the company unique and exactly why you want to work for it. An applicant who doesn't know why he or she wants a job at a particular company should not be there in the first place. Even if the real reason is because you need a job and are willing to take anything you can get, don't say so. You'll probably never get work that way. Nor are you likely to get a job by saying that your friends work there, and they say, "It's a nice place."

Remember that most interviewers are probably quite proud of their companies. They see their firms as unique, and they see the job you're applying for as a unique opportunity. Do enough research to find out what makes each firm unique and why the job you're after is indeed a great opportunity for you. If you don't see it as such, perhaps you should consider waiting for a better opportunity.

In addition to knowing as much as possible about the company and the job, it's important to know all about yourself. Remember that the interview represents a common measuring stick for all applicants—no matter what schools or colleges they attended; no matter what contacts they have; no matter what previous jobs they've held and no matter what their social backgrounds. Everybody walks into the interview facing the same test. Whether you're shy or outgoing, the interview is something you'll have to face all your life. It's a chance to sell yourself. Use it to good advantage. If you're not skilled at having interviews, practice with friends or family. Have them ask you questions. The following is a list of typical questions asked by professional job interviewers. Rehearse your entrance into the interviewer's office. Walk into the room with quiet self-confidence, smiling and looking him or her straight in the eye and firmly shaking hands. Rehearse your exit: shaking hands again, saying thanks for the interview, then turning and walking out, again with quiet self-confidence. Rehearse often. Move the furniture around in a room at home to make a stage set of an interviewer's office with a desk or table in the middle, you on one side and a friend or relative on the other.

Interview techniques vary widely from company to company and interviewer to interviewer. Some interviewers may be as new at it—and as nervous—as you. You might even be the first person they have ever interviewed. Most personnel executives, however, are quite skilled. Some will purposely make the situation more stressful for you than others to see how you respond to pressures. Typical stress interviews begin with such questions such as, "What can I do for you?" or "Tell me about yourself"; "What kind of job are you looking for?"; "Why do you think you're the right person for this job?"; "What do you know about the job (or company or 'me,' if the interviewer is your prospective boss)?"; "Where else are you looking?"; "Why did you leave your last job?"; "What did you like least about your last job?"; "Can you work under extreme pressure?" These are all tough questions, and you should be prepared for them in advance by thinking them through carefully and having a specific, direct answer—nothing vague.

Remember that you are there to describe your qualifications for the job. Don't let yourself get side-tracked. Answer the stressful questions, but immediately steer the conversation back to your skills. *Don't* focus on the stresses of the situation but on the reason for being there: to display the elements of your background, character, education, skills and personality that make you uniquely qualified for the job you're applying for.

Most interviewers will begin with a series of random questions to try to put you at ease. They'll find some topic that will get you talking comfortably so that you'll relax enough to talk openly and honestly about yourself. Good interviewers want applicants to do most of the talking during the 30 to 45 minutes of the interview so that they can get an idea of the applicant's personality and the way they think.

Before going into an interview, it's important to make a careful assessment of all those characteristics that qualify you for the job. Write them on a list in order of importance, and learn them so well that you can discuss your life and talents in any order—either in piecemeal answers to many questions or in an interesting discourse in answer to a single, general question such as, "Tell me about yourself." And don't be afraid to take notes with you. It's perfectly acceptable to refer to them during the interview. Try to know them by heart, of course, but don't be afraid to pause and look at them and say, "I just want to make sure I've covered everything." Be sure that you talk about your qualifications for the job. Describe specific, concrete examples of what you've done either in the classroom, school laboratory or on some other job that demonstrate your ability to do the job you're applying for and to fulfill the company's needs.

Take a notepad and pencil. It's important to listen to what your interviewer has to say and to demonstrate that you are a good listener and interested enough to take notes on what you consider essential information.

Notes are also helpful for questioning your interviewer. "Do you have any questions?" is a question almost every interviewer will ask—and you'd better have some or risk a poor score on your interview. One important one is to get an outline of the responsibilities of the job you're seeking. Some other obvious questions are, "What kind of person are you looking for?" "Why did the last person leave this job?" or "Where might this job lead, if I do very well?" Some better ones would be, "How would you like to see the work done on this job? Has it been done that way? How would you like to see it improved? What's a typical day on the job like? What's the best thing about the job? The worst thing? What are some of the problems I'll face on the job?" On a broader level, your reading about the company might produce these questions: "I read in the papers that sales are (slipping) (growing). Does this mean the company might (cut back) (expand) operations? Would this job (be in jeopardy) (have more responsibilities)?"

KEEP QUESTIONS OPEN-ENDED

Introduction

Cover:		Look for:
Greeting		Appearance
Small talk		Manner
Opening question		Self-expression
Lead question		Responsiveness

Work Experience

Cover:	Ask:	Look for:
Earliest jobs, part-time, temporary	Things done best? Done less well?	Relevance of work
Military assignments	Things liked best? Liked less well?	Sufficiency of work
Full-time positions	Major accomplishments?	Skill and competence
	Most difficult problems faced? How handled?	Adaptability
	Ways most effective with people? Ways less effective?	Productivity
	Level of earnings?	Motivation
	Reasons for changing jobs?	Interpersonal relations
	What learned from work experience?	Leadership
	What looking for in job? In career?	Growth and development

Education

Cover:	Ask:	Look for:
Elementary school	Best subjects? Subjects done less well?	Relevance of schooling
High school	Subject liked most? Liked least?	Sufficiency of schooling
College	Reactions to teachers?	Intellectual abilities
Specialized training	Level of grades? Effort required?	Versatility
Recent courses	Reasons for choosing school? Major field?	Breadth and depth of knowledge
	Special achievements? Toughest problems?	Level of accomplishment
	Role in extracurricular activities?	Motivation, interests
		Reaction to authority
		Leadership
		Team work

KEEP QUESTIONS OPEN-ENDED (continued)

How financed education?
Relation of education to
  career?
Considering further
  schooling?

Summary

Cover:	Ask:	Look for:
Strengths	What bring to job?	PLUS (+) AND
Weaknesses	What are assets?	MINUS (−)
	What are best talents?	Talents, skills
	What qualities seen by	Knowledge
	self or others?	Energy
	What makes you good	Motivation
	investment for	Interests
	employer?	Personal qualities
	What are shortcomings?	Social qualities
	What areas need	Character
	improvement?	Situational factors
	What qualities wish to	
	develop further?	
	What constructive	
	criticism from others?	
	How might you be risk for	
	employer?	
	What further training, or	
	experience, might you	
	need?	

Closing remarks

Cover:

Comments regarding
  interview and applicant
Further contacts to be made
Course of action to be taken
Cordial parting   _____

Applicant: _____ Date: _____

Position: _____

Interviewer: _____

Comment on the applicant's background and behavior, taking into conside ration the
elements listed in the right-hand column of each section. Then circle a rating for each
section based on the evidence you have cited. Finally, at the end of this report, make
one overall rating of the candidate.

Initial Impression

Manner
Self-expression

Favorable 1   2   3   4   5   Unfavorable   Responsiveness

Work Experience

Relevance of work
Sufficiency of work
Skill and competence
Adaptability
Productivity
Motivation
Interpersonal relations
Leadership

Favorable 1   2   3   4   5   Unfavorable   Growth and development

Education

Relevance of schooling
Sufficiency of schooling
Intellectual abilities
Versatility
Breadth and depth of knowledge
Level of accomplishment
Motivation, interests
Reaction to authority
Leadership

Favorable 1   2   3   4   5   Unfavorable   Team work

Present Activities and Interests

Maturity and judgment
Intellectual growth
Diversity of interests
Social skills

Favorable 1   2   3   4   5   Unfavorable   Leadership

Summary of Strengths (+)   Summary of Weaknesses (–)

Overall Summary Recommendations (write three paragraphs)

1. In favor of hiring: _____

_____

2. Against hiring: _____

_____

3. Final recommendations: _____

_____

4. Overall Rating:
            Favorable 1   2   3   4   5   Unfavorable

Thank you for your feedback. Please forward to Personnel.

Another type of question to ask, depending on the interviewer's personality, is the interviewer's own experiences and length of service at the company. "How long have you been here, and what do you see as the strengths and weaknesses of the company?" Remember, the word "interview" means "to see one another." Most people think it means one person questioning another, but the original meaning is for two people to see each other. Use the situation to establish a rapport with your interviewer and get a friendly, two-way conversation going. If you think the offices are beautiful, say so; if the building or factory is impressive, say so. Conversation is an art that will certainly help you score well in any interview situation.

Write your questions down in advance, and don't be afraid when the time comes to say, "Yes. I wrote a few down," and then refer to your notes.

One of the "loaded" questions most interviewers will almost certainly ask you is to tell them about your weak points. Nobody's perfect, and your interviewer knows that. You'll appear rather conceited if you say you have none, and you'll show a lack of self-knowledge if you say you don't know what they are. There are two rules for handling the problem. The first is to discuss all weak points that will ultimately surface in a check of your application facts and your references. You're far better off discussing such weaknesses in advance so that they don't come as a surprise later and force the company to reject your application. Often, by explaining some weak point at the interview, you can reduce it's importance and make it seem insignificant.

If no weak points will ever turn up in the company's check into your background and references, the way to prepare for an interviewer's question about them is to list them all before the interview at the same time you list all your strong points. Be honest with yourself. No one will see the list but you. Then cross out the worst of the weak points and save the most common, almost humorous ones that will not or cannot in any way affect your job performance. Then discuss them with a smile and show yourself to be human.

An important rule in interview techniques is never to begin or end an interview on a negative note, and, after any discussion of weak points, be certain to show how you've converted a weakness into a strength. Someone weak in high school math, for example, might well have taken a special summer school course to strengthen mathematical skills.

Another "loaded" question many prospective employers will ask is, "What kind of salary do you expect to get on the job?" If you've done your homework, you should know what the pay range is for the type of job you want, and, if you're just starting out, show the boss that you have done your homework by saying, "Well, I understand the company usually pays beginners _____ dollars (an hour, a week, etc.)."

Another important rule at job interviews is to show that you want the job. If an interviewer doesn't think you want it, you won't get it. As in any relationship, clear communication is vital in interviews. You must tell other people what you need and want or they'll never know. So, at an appropriate point—usually, toward the end of the interview when you're asked if you have any other questions or if "there's anything else you'd like to discuss"—speak up and say something like, "I just want you to know that I'd really like to work for this company, and I'd really like this job. I think I can do a good job and make a contribution to the company." Or, if the interviewer is the person you'll actually be working for: "I'd really like to work for you. I know I can do a good job and make a contribution to your department." Don't be afraid to say things such as, "I promise you won't be sorry if you hire me" or "This job is exactly what I've been looking for—it ties in perfectly with everything I've ever learned and studied about . . ." Be enthusiastic, however, and say you want the job!

Chances are you won't get a job offer on the spot. Usually, the interviewer will tell you that the company will give your application careful consideration and that they will let you know within a few days. Regardless of how friendly or enthusiastic your interviewer may seem, keep looking for other jobs while awaiting the company's decision.

After your interview, write a thank-you letter that reinforces your interest in and qualifications for the job. Below is a sample letter.

Don't be disappointed if you don't get the job. Remember, there is no way for you to know the qualifications of other job applicants. Moreover, many companies make mistakes, and there's nothing you can do about it except to keep applying at other companies until you find the job that's right for you at a company that's eager to have you on its team.

Eugene Everett Richards
687 Saybrook Court
Yalesville, CT 10101

June 1, 1998

Ms. Cherie Lorraine
Director
Executive Training Program
Smith's Department Store
Barclay Square
New York, NY 10036

Dear Ms. Lorraine:

It was kind of you to take so much time to see me yesterday. I enjoyed meeting you and learning so much about Smith's and the Executive Training Program. I'm even more excited now about the prospect of a career in merchandising, and there's no place I'd rather work than at Smith's. Obviously, a chance to join the Smith's Executive Training Program would be the opportunity of a lifetime, and I promise that, given that chance, I would not let you or Smith's down.

All my thanks for your consideration.

Sincerely,

Eugene Everett Richards

Filling in Applications

As in all other written work in the job application process, your application must be filled in neatly with no spelling, grammatical or typographical errors. Unlike resumes and letters, however, you probably won't be able to fill in your job application in the serenity of your home. In all likelihood, a personnel department official will give you the application and a pen or pencil and direct you to a small corner table or desk where you'll have to fill it in on the spur of the moment. So, be prepared. The following is a sample of a typical application. First, practice filling it in carefully and neatly. Make a few copies and see if you can do it error free without having to cross out or erase any entries. Next, use it to make a list of the information and vital statistics *you know* every job application will demand. There is nothing worse than having to tell the personnel office that you don't have or forgot some information about yourself—like your social security number—and that you'll telephone them later with the information. That is inefficiency of the worst kind—and usually unforgiveable, because it demonstrates what you may be like on the job. So make a list of the data required in most job applications and have it with you whenever you visit a prospective employer.

And, once again, good luck!

Figure 3. A standard employment application used by companies across the United States. Make a copy and practice filling it out neatly and *error-free*. Make a list of the data required so you have all the pertinent facts with you when you have to fill applications in actual situations.

APPLICATION
FOR EMPLOYMENT

We consider applicants for all positions without regard to race, color, religion, sex, national origin, age, marital or veteran status, the presence of a non-job-related medical condition or handicap, or any other legally protected status.

(PLEASE PRINT)

Position(s) Applied For	Date of Application

How Did You Learn About Us?

❑ Advertisement   ❑ Friend   ❑ Walk-In

❑ Employment Agency   ❑ Relative   ❑ Other _____

Last Name	First Name	Middle Name

Address	Number	Street	City	State	Zip Code

Telephone Number(s)	Social Security Number

If you are under 18 years of age, can you provide required proof of your eligibility to work?   ❑ Yes   ❑ No

Have you ever filed an application with us before?   ❑ Yes   ❑ No

If Yes, give date _____

Have you ever been employed with us before?   ❑ Yes   ❑ No

If Yes, give date _____

Are you currently employed?   ❏Yes   ❏No

May we contact your present employer?   ❏Yes   ❏No

Are you prevented from lawfully becoming employed in this
country because of Visa or Immigration Status?
Proof of citizenship or immigration status will be required upon employment.   ❏Yes   ❏No

On what date would you be available for work?   _____

Are you available to work: ❏Full Time   ❏Part Time   ❏Shift Work   ❏Temporary

Are you currently on "lay-off" status and subject to recall?   ❏Yes   ❏No

Can you travel if a job requires it?   ❏Yes   ❏No

Have you been convicted of a felony within the last 7 years?
Conviction will not necessarily disqualify an applicant from employment.   ❏Yes   ❏No

If Yes, please explain   _____

_____

_____

_____

_____

_____

_____

_____

_____

WE ARE AN EQUAL OPPORTUNITY EMPLOYER

EDUCATION

	Elementary School	High School	Undergraduate College/University	Graduate/ Professional
School Name and Location				
Years Completed	4 | 5 | 6 | 7 | 8	9 | 10 | 11 | 12	1 | 2 | 3 | 4	1 | 2 | 3 | 4
Diploma/Degree				
Describe Course of Study				

Describe any specialized training, apprenticeship, skills and extra-curricular activities	
State any additional information you feel may be helpful to us in considering your application	

Indicate any foreign languages you can speak, read and/or write

	FLUENT	GOOD	FAIR
SPEAK			
READ			
WRITE			

List professional, trade, business or civic activities and office held.

You may exclude memberships which would reveal sex, race, religion, national origin, age, ancestry, or handicap or other protected status.

References

Give name, address and telephone number of three references who are not related to you and are not previous employers.

1. _____

2. _____

3. _____

Have you ever had any job-related training in the United States military?

❏ Yes   ❏ No

If Yes, please describe _____

Are you physically or otherwise unable to perform the duties of the job for which you are applying?

❏ Yes   ❏ No

EMPLOYMENT EXPERIENCE

Start with your present or last job. Include any job-related military service assignments and volunteer activities. You may exclude organizations which indicate race, color, religion, gender, national origin, handicap or other protected status.

	Employer		Dates Employed		Work Performed
1.			From	To	
	Address				
	Telephone Number(s)		Hourly Rate/Salary		
			Starting	Final	
	Job Title	Supervisor			
	Reason for Leaving				
2.	Employer		Dates Employed		Work Performed
			From	To	
	Address				
	Telephone Number(s)		Hourly Rate/Salary		
			Starting	Final	
	Job Title	Supervisor			
	Reason for Leaving				
3.	Employer		Dates Employed		Work Performed
			From	To	
	Address				
	Telephone Number(s)		Hourly Rate/Salary		
			Starting	Final	
	Job Title	Supervisor			
	Reason for Leaving				
4.	Employer		Dates Employed		Work Performed
			From	To	
	Address				
	Telephone Number(s)		Hourly Rate/Salary		
			Starting	Final	
	Job Title	Supervisor			
	Reason for Leaving				

If you need additonal space, please continue on a separate sheet of paper.

Special Skills and Qualifications

Summarize special job-related skills and qualifications acquired from employment or other experience.

APPLICANT'S STATEMENT

I certify that answers given herin are true and complete to the best of my knowledge.

I authorize investigation of all statements contained in this application for employment as may be necessary in arriving at an employment decision.

This application for employment shall be considered active for a period of time not to exceed 45 days. Any applicant wishing to be considered for employment beyond this time period should inquire as to whether or not applications are being accepted at that time.

I hereby undersand and acknowledge that, unless otherwise defined by applicable law, any employment relationsip with this organization is of an "at will" nature, which means that the Employee may resign at any time and the Employer may discharge Employee at any time with or without cause. It is further understood that this "at will" employment relationship may not be changed by any written document or by conduct unless such change is specifically acknowledged in writing by an authorized executive of this organization.

In the event of employment, I understand that false or misleading information given in my application or interview(s) may result in discharge. I understand, also, that I am required to abide by all rules and regulations of the employer.

_____   _____
Signature of Applicant   Date

FOR PERSONNEL DEPARTMENT USE ONLY

Arrange Interview   ❏ Yes   ❏ No

Remarks _____

_____   _____
                                                          INTERVIEWER   DATE

Employed   ❏ Yes   ❏ No   Date of Employment _____

                                                         Hourly Rate/
Job Title _____   Salary _____   Department _____

                    By _____   _____
                                                  NAME AND TITLE   DATE

NOTES _____

_____

_____

_____

Appendix A

Nationally Recognized Accrediting Associations

The following regional and national accrediting associations are recognized by the U.S. Secretary of Education as reliable authorities on the quality of secondary, postsecondary education or training offered by educational institutions or programs. Contact any of the appropriate associations to check whether the educational institution you're considering is accredited and approved.

REGIONAL INSTITUTIONAL ACCREDITING ASSOCIATIONS AND COMMISSIONS FOR HIGH SCHOOLS, COMMUNITY COLLEGES, JUNIOR COLLEGES, TECHNICAL INSTITUTES AND FOUR-YEAR COLLEGES AND UNIVERSITIES

Middle States Association of Colleges and Schools (Delaware, District of Columbia, Maryland, New Jersey, New York, Pennsylvania, Puerto Rico, Virgin Islands), 3624 Market Street, Philadelphia, PA 19104. Tel. (215) 662-5606.

New England Association of Schools and Colleges (Connecticut, Maine, Massachusetts, New Hampshire, Rhode Island, Vermont), Sanborn House, 15 High Street, Winchester, MA 01890. Tel. (617) 729-6762.

North Central Association of Colleges and Schools (Arizona, Arkansas, Colorado, Illinois, Indiana, Iowa, Kansas, Michigan, Minnesota, Missouri, Nebraska, New Mexico, North Dakota, Ohio, Oklahoma, South Dakota, West Virginia, Wisconsin, Wyoming), 15440 30th Street, Boulder, CO 80306. Tel. (80) 525-9517.

Northwest Association of Schools and Colleges (Alaska, Idaho, Montana, Nevada, Oregon, Utah, Washington), Education Building No. 528, Boise State University, Boise, ID 83725. Tel. (208) 385-1596.

Southern Association of Colleges and Schools (Alabama, Florida, Georgia, Kentucky, Louisiana, Mississippi, North Carolina, South Carolina, Tennessee, Texas, Virginia), 1866 Southern Lane, Decatur, GA 30033-4097. Tel. (404) 329-6500.

Western Association of Schools and Colleges (California, Hawaii), 1606 Rollins Road, Burlingame, CA 94010. Tel. (415) 697-7711.

National Apprenticeship Program

U.S. DEPARTMENT OF LABOR EMPLOYMENT AND
TRAINING ADMINISTRATION

**State Offices, Bureau of Apprenticeship and Training
(To Check On Accreditation of Apprenticeship Programs)**

ALABAMA
USDL-BAT
Medical Forum Building
Room 648
950 22nd Street North
Birmingham,
Alabama 35203
205/731-1308

ALASKA
USDL-BAT
Calais Building
3301 C Street, Suite 201
Anchorage, Alaska 99503
907/271-5035

ARIZONA
USDL-BAT
Suite 302
3221 North 16th Street
Phoenix, Arizona 85016
602/640-2964

ARKANSAS
USDL-BAT
Federal Building
Room 3507
700 West Capitol Street
Little Rock, Arkansas 72201
501/324-5415

CALIFORNIA
USDL-BAT
Suite 1090-N
1301 Clay Street
Oakland, California
94612-5217
510/637-2951

COLORADO
USDL-BAT
U.S. Custom House
721 19th Street, Room 469
Denver, Colorado 80202
303/844-4793

CONNECTICUT
USDL-BAT
Federal Building
135 High Street, Room 367
Hartford, Connecticut
06103
203/240-4311

DELAWARE
USDL-BAT
Lock Box 36
Federal Building
844 King Street
Wilmington,
Delaware 19801
302/573-6113

FLORIDA
USDL-BAT
City Centre Building
Suite 4140
227 North Bronough Street
Tallahassee, Florida 32301
904/942-8336

GEORGIA
USDL-BAT
Room 6T81
Atlanta Federal Center
61 Forsyth Street SW
Atlanta, Georgia 30303
404/562-2323/2321

HAWAII
USDL-BAT
Room 5113
300 Ala Moana Boulevard
Honolulu, Hawaii 96850
808/541-2519

IDAHO
USDL-BAT
Suite 128
3050 North Lakeharbor
    Lane
Boise, Idaho 83703-6217
208/334-1013

ILLINOIS
USDL-BAT
Room 708
230 South Dearborn Street
Chicago, Illinois 60604
312/353-4690

INDIANA
USDL-BAT
Federal Building and
U.S. Courthouse
46 East Ohio Street
Room 414
Indianapolis, Indiana 46204
317/226-7592

IOWA
USDL-BAT
210 Walnut Street
Room 715
Des Moines, Iowa 50309
515/284-4690

KANSAS
USDL-BAT
444 SE Quincy Street
Room 247
Topeka, Kansas 66683-3571
913/295-2624

KENTUCKY
USDL-BAT
Federal Building
Room 187-J
600 Martin Luther
King Place
Louisville, Kentucky 40202
502/582-5223

LOUISIANA
USDL-BAT
Suite 1043
501 Magazine Street
New Orleans, LA 70130
504/589-6103

MAINE
USDL-BAT
Federal Building
68 Sewall Street, Room 401
Augusta, Maine 04330
207/622-8235

MARYLAND
USDL-BAT
300 West Pratt Street
Room 200
Baltimore, Maryland 21201
410/962-2676

MASSACHUSETTS
USDL-BAT
Room E370
JFK Federal Building
Boston, Massachusetts
02203
617/565-2291

MICHIGAN
USDL-BAT
801 S. Waverly
Room 304
Lansing, Michigan 48917
517/377-1746

MINNESOTA
USDL-BAT
316 Robert Street
Room 146
St. Paul, Minnesota 55101
612/290-3951

MISSISSIPPI
USDL-BAT
Federal Building, Suite 410
100 West Capitol Street
Jackson, Mississippi 39269
601/965-4346

MISSOURI
USDL-BAT
1222 Spruce Street
Room 9.102E
Robert A. Young Federal
    Building
St. Louis, Missouri 63103
314/539-2522

MONTANA
USDL-BAT
Federal Office Building
301 South Park Avenue
Room 396, Drawer #10055
Helena, Montana
59626-0055
406/441-1076

NEBRASKA
USDL-BAT
Room 801
106 South 15th Street
Omaha, Nebraska 68102
402/221-3281

NEVADA
USDL-BAT
301 Stewart Avenue
Room 311
Las Vegas, Nevada 89101
702/388-6396

NEW HAMPSHIRE
USDL-BAT
143 North Main Street
Room 205
Concord, New Hampshire
03301
603/225-1444

NEW JERSEY
USDL-BAT
Parkway Towers
Building E, 3rd Floor
485, Route #1, South
  Iselin
New Jersey 08830
908/750-9191

NEW MEXICO
USDL-BAT
505 Marquette, Room 830
Albuquerque, New Mexico
87102
505/766-2398

NEW YORK
USDL-BAT
Leo O'Brien Federal
Building, Room 809
North Pearl &
  Clinton Avenue
Albany, New York 12207
518/431-4008

NORTH CAROLINA
USDL-BAT
Somerset Park, Suite 205
4407 Bland Road
Raleigh, North Carolina
27609
919/790-2801

NORTH DAKOTA
USDL-BAT
New Federal Building
Room 428
657, 2nd Avenue
North Fargo, North Dakota
58102
701/239-5415

OHIO
USDL-BAT
Room 605
200 North High Street
Columbus, Ohio 43215
614/469-7375

OKLAHOMA
USDL-BAT
Suite 202
1500 S. Midwest Blvd.
Midwest City,
Oklahoma 73110
405/732-4338

OREGON
USDL-BAT
Federal Building, Room 629
1220 SW 3rd Avenue
Portland, Oregon 97204
503/326-3157

PENNSYLVANIA
USDL-BAT
Federal Building
228 Walnut Street
Room 773
Harrisburg, Pennsylvania
17108
717/782-3496

RHODE ISLAND
USDL-BAT
Federal Building
100 Hartford Avenue
Providence, Rhode Island
02909
401/528-5198

SOUTH CAROLINA
USDL-BAT
Strom Thurmond Federal
  Building
1835 Assembly Street,
Room 838
Columbia, South Carolina
29201
803/765-5547

SOUTH DAKOTA
USDL-BAT
Oxbow I Building, Room
  204
2400 West 49th Street
Sioux Falls, South Dakota
57105
605/330-4326

TENNESSEE
USDL-BAT
Airport Executive Plaza
1321 Murfreesboro Road
Suite 541
Nashville, Tennessee 37210
615/781-5318

TEXAS
USDL-BAT
VA Building, Room 2102
2320 LaBranch Street
Houston, Texas 77004
713/750-1696

UTAH
USDL-BAT
Suite 101
1600 West 2200 South
Salt Lake City, Utah 84119
801/975-3650

VERMONT
USDL-BAT
Federal Building
11 Elmwood Avenue
Room 629
Burlington, Vermont 05401
802/951-6278

VIRGINIA
USDL-BAT
700 Centre, Suite 546
704 East Franklin Street
Richmond, Virginia 23219
804/771-2488

WASHINGTON
USDL-BAT
Suite 100
1400 Talbot Road South
Renton, Washington 98055
206/277-5214

WEST VIRGINIA
USDL-BAT
Suite 203
1108 3rd Avenue
Huntington, West Virginia
25701
304/528-7540, 7541, 7542

WISCONSIN
USDL-BAT
Federal Center
Room 303
212 East Washington Avenue
Madison, Wisconsin 53703
608/264-5377

WYOMING
USDL-BAT
American National Bank
Building
1912 Capitol Avenue
Room 508
Cheyenne, Wyoming
82001-3661
307/772-2448

Appendix B

Essential Employability Skills

Together with employers, community leaders and educators, the Colorado Department of Education developed the following list of "employability skills" that every good career education program should be teaching its students. If your school's vocational education program is not teaching most of these skills, it is not preparing you for the world of work. If you cannot find a high school career education program that teaches these skills, switch to a strong academic program and postpone plans for vocational education until you graduate from high school and can enroll in a community college, technical institute or some other post-high school career training program.

Identification of Essential Employability Skills

DIRECTIONS: Check those skills that are essential for students to acquire so that they will be well prepared to obtain employment and be successful on the job. In making judgments consider your own job experience. Add to part "M. Other" any skills which you consider essential which are not listed.

Name _____

Date _____

Please refer to the handout entitled "Identification of Employability Skills" for examples of each skill.

A. JOB SEEKING—CAREER DEVELOPMENT SKILLS

❏ 1. Knows sources of information

❏ 2. Knows own abilities, aptitudes, interests

❏ 3. Knows occupational characteristics

❏ 4. Identifies career/occupational goals

❏ 5. Develops a career plan

❏ 6. Identifies and researches potential employers

❏ 7. Knows employment position(s) desired

❏ 8. Accurately completes:

❏   a. Inquiry letter

❏   b. Resume

❏   c. Follow-up letter

❏ 9. Accurately completes job application

❏ 10. Handles interview without errors

❏ 11. Seeks information about future education/training

B. MATH SKILLS

❏ 1. Understands importance of math in jobs

❏ 2. Performs basic calculations $(+, -, \times, \div)$

❏ 3. Performs calculations in:

❏   a. Fractions

❏   b. Percentages

❏   c. Proportions/Ratios

❏ 4. Makes reasonable estimates

❏ 5. Uses values from graphs, maps, tables

❏ 6. Uses English/metric measurement

❏ 7. Compares numerical values

❏ 8. Applies geometric principles

❏ 9. Uses formulas correctly

❏ 10. Constructs diagrams, tables, records

❏ 11. Uses elementary statistics

❏ 12. Uses instruments to solve problems:

❏   a. Gauges, Meters, Scales

❏   b. Calculators

❏   c. Computers

C. COMPUTER SKILLS

❏ 1. Becomes aware of computer functions

❏ 2. Inputs and accesses data from computer

❏ 3. Has experience with computer programs

❏   a. Business applications

❏   b. Data management

❏   c. Simple programming

❏   d. Word processing

❏ 4. Understands issues associated with computer use

D. READING SKILLS

❏ 1. Understands the importance of reading in jobs

❏ 2. Develops vocabulary related to careers and occupations

❏ 3. Reads for details and special information

❏ 4. Interprets pictures, graphs and symbols

❏ 5. Locates information in reference materials

❏ 6. Follows intent of written directions/instructions

❏ 7. Interprets ideas and concepts (comprehension)

❏ 8. Reads accurately at appropriate rate

E. WRITING SKILLS

❏ 1. Understands the importance of writing in jobs

❏ 2. Develops handwriting legibility

❏ 3. Composes formal letters

❏ 4. Fills out forms

❏ 5. Records messages

❏ 6. Writes memorandums

❏ 7. Composes ads/telegrams

❏ 8. Writes instructions and directions

❏ 9. Writes reports

❏ 10. Develops summaries

❏ 11. Takes notes and/or outlines

❏ 12. Corrects written materials

F. COMMUNICATION SKILLS

❏ 1. Reports accurately/concisely

❏ 2. Follows intent of oral directions/instructions

❏ 3. Speaks distinctly

❏ 4. Formulates questions

❏ 5. Answers questions accurately

❏ 6. Explains activities and ideas clearly

❏ 7. Uses appropriate vocabulary/grammar

❏ 8. Gives clear instructions and directions

❏ 9. Stays on topic

❏ 10. Uses nonverbal signs appropriately

❏ 11. Develops oral presentations

❏ 12. Presents information effectively to groups

G. INTERPERSONAL SKILLS

❏ 1. Functions cooperatively with fellow students

❏ 2. Functions cooperatively in team efforts

❏ 3. Functions cooperatively with adults outside school

❏ 4. Exhibits openness and flexibility

❏ 5. Seeks clarification of instructions

❏ 6. Exercises patience and tolerance

❏ 7. Utilizes suggestions about improving skills

❏ 8. Uses initiative in getting work done

❏ 9. Expresses opinions with tact

❏ 10. Demonstrates ability to negotiate differences with others

H. BUSINESS ECONOMIC SKILLS

❏ 1. Understands business organization

❏ 2. Understands business competition

❏ 3. Knows about processes of marketing

❏ 4. Knows about processes of production

❏ 5. Understands business costs

❏ 6. Understands factors affecting profits

I. PERSONAL ECONOMIC SKILLS

❏ 1. Knows how to evaluate products and services

❏ 2. Knows how to access community resources/services

❏ 3. Can compute working hours/wages

❏ 4. Knows how to handle financial affairs

❏ 5. Can handle records of income and expenses

❏ 6. Knows how to make price-quality comparisons

❏ 7. Knows how to prepare state/federal tax forms

❏ 8. Can evaluate insurance programs

❏ 9. Knows how to determine credit costs

❏ 10. Understands legal rights in agreements

❏ 11. Maintains and utilizes various forms of transportation

J. MANUAL PERCEPTUAL SKILLS

❏ 1. Constructs/assembles materials

❏ 2. Uses specific hand tools and instruments

❏ 3. Develops visual presentations

❏ 4. Masters keyboard skills

☐ 5. Operates power equipment

K. WORK ACTIVITY SKILLS

☐ 1. Produces type/amount of work required

☐ 2. Maintains punctuality

☐ 3. Meets attendance requirements

☐ 4. Accepts assignments/responsibilities

☐ 5. Takes responsibility for own actions

☐ 6. Maintains consistent effort

☐ 7. Works independently

☐ 8. Manages time effectively

☐ 9. Respects rights and property of others

☐ 10. Adheres to policies and regulations

☐   a. Health

☐   b. Honesty

☐   c. Safety

☐ 11. Presents a neat appearance

☐ 12. Keeps work area in good/safe condition

☐ 13. Exhibits interest in future career

☐ 14. Suggests or makes workplace improvements

☐ 15. Knows sources of continuing education

☐ 16. Knows about basic employee/student rights

☐ 17. Knows about basic employee/student responsibilities

☐ 18. Knows basic steps in getting a raise or promotion

☐ 19. Knows how to terminate employment

L. PROBLEM SOLVING/ REASONING SKILLS

☐ 1. Recognizes problems that need solution

☐ 2. Identifies procedures

☐ 3. Obtains resources

☐ 4. Prepares or sets up materials/equipment

☐ 5. Collects information

☐ 6. Organizes information

☐ 7. Interprets information

☐ 8. Formulates alternative approaches

☐ 9. Selects efficient approaches

☐ 10. Reviews progress

☐ 11. Evaluates activities

☐ 12. Corrects errors

☐ 13. Makes conclusions

☐ 14. Summarizes and communicates results

☐ 15. Uses results to develop new ideas

M. OTHER

☐ 1. _____

☐ 2. _____

☐ 3. _____

☐ 4. _____

☐ 5. _____

☐ 6. _____

☐ 7. _____

☐ 8. _____

☐ 9. _____

Source: Colorado Department of Education

Appendix C

Here are the median weekly earnings in 1996 of salaried workers in a wide variety of different jobs, ranging from doctors to bartenders and requiring vast differences in training and formal education. As you'll see, there are significant differences in the salaries paid to men and women, with women receiving far less on average. The figures are compiled annually by the U.S. Department of Labor's Bureau of Labor Statistics.

Occupation	1996					
	Both sexes		Men		Women	
	Number of workers	Median weekly earnings	Number of workers	Median weekly earnings	Number of workers	Median weekly earnings
Total, 16 years and over	90,918	$ 490	51,895	$ 557	39,023	$418
Managerial and professional specialty	27,222	718	13,934	852	13,288	616
Executive, administrative, and managerial	13,300	699	7,187	846	6,113	585
Administrators and officials, public administration	593	753	328	847	265	638
Administrators, protective services	54	621	35	(1)	19	(1)
Financial managers	567	782	253	979	314	635
Personnel and labor relations managers	120	781	60	1,150	60	658
Purchasing managers	126	799	67	976	58	659
Managers, marketing, advertising, and public relations	588	912	377	1,043	211	674
Administrators, education and related fields	550	804	258	956	292	657
Managers, medicine and health	607	685	157	988	450	610
Managers, food serving and lodging establishments	908	458	487	516	421	391
Managers, properties and real estate	314	548	141	620	173	481
Management-related occupations	3,622	622	1,519	749	2,103	567
Accountants and auditors	1,269	630	547	771	722	561
Underwriters	97	603	31	(1)	66	588
Other financial officers	614	665	277	845	337	606
Management analysts	159	760	81	940	78	716
Personnel, training, and labor relations specialists	371	622	127	707	245	597
Buyers, wholesale and retail trade, except farm products	155	575	75	639	80	478
Construction inspectors	61	648	57	670	4	(1)
Inspectors and compliance officers, except construction	232	695	152	750	80	606

Occupation	1996					
	Both sexes		Men		Women	
	Number of workers	Median weekly earnings	Number of workers	Median weekly earnings	Number of workers	Median weekly earnings
Professional specialty	13,922	730	6,747	857	7,175	647
Engineers, architects, and surveyors	1,957	938	1,776	954	181	787
Architects	93	760	75	799	18	[1]
Engineers	1,844	949	1,685	963	158	793
Aerospace engineers	73	1,097	70	1,099	3	[1]
Chemical engineers	92	1,012	80	1,084	12	[1]
Civil engineers	217	884	198	899	18	[1]
Electrical and electronic engineers	567	994	521	1,002	46	[1]
Industrial engineers	247	841	216	863	31	[1]
Mechanical engineers	335	956	311	969	24	[1]
Mathematical and computer scientists	1,192	883	826	929	366	790
Computer systems analysts and scientists	968	891	694	931	274	813
Operations and systems researchers and analysts	191	815	112	889	80	737
Natural scientists	462	762	325	822	137	674
Chemists, except biochemists	139	851	96	900	43	[1]
Biological and life scientists	101	698	64	738	37	[1]
Medical scientists	59	659	30	[1]	30	[1]
Health diagnosing occupations	489	1,090	336	1,256	153	763
Physicians	426	1,133	295	1,378	131	802
Health assessment and treating occupations	2,005	703	342	766	1,663	692
Registered nurses	1,410	697	120	729	1,290	695
Pharmacists	131	992	81	1,047	51	931
Dietitians	77	478	7	[1]	69	484
Therapists	337	672	106	658	231	678
Respiratory therapists	76	636	36	[1]	40	[1]
Physical therapists	83	757	35	[1]	48	[1]
Speech therapists	68	689	5	[1]	64	692
Physicians' assistants	51	806	28	[1]	23	[1]
Teachers, college and university	566	870	351	937	215	765
Teachers, except college and university	3,740	641	1,023	723	2,718	613
Teachers, prekindergarten and kindergarten	357	361	7	[1]	350	358
Teachers, elementary school	1,617	662	278	719	1,339	648
Teachers, secondary school	1,101	697	498	760	603	643
Teachers, special education	301	646	48	[1]	252	652
Counselors, educational and vocational	219	689	64	799	155	659
Librarians, archivists, and curators	139	654	28	[1]	111	640
Librarians	123	660	21	[1]	102	649
Social scientists and urban planners	278	673	127	736	152	642
Economists	123	715	53	871	69	654
Psychologists	124	633	53	668	71	589
Social, recreation, and religious workers	1,134	513	545	577	589	485
Social workers	641	524	204	591	437	507
Recreation workers	85	343	23	[1]	62	314
Clergy	314	534	278	540	36	[1]
Lawyers and judges	559	1,150	369	1,258	191	970
Lawyers	530	1,149	343	1,261	187	970
Writers, artists, entertainers, and athletes	1,181	614	635	728	546	529
Technical writers	59	787	35	[1]	23	[1]
Designers	375	592	195	767	180	441
Actors and directors	75	620	44	[1]	31	[1]
Painters, sculptors, craft artists, and artist printmakers	91	517	52	532	39	[1]
Editors and reporters	212	688	106	756	106	608
Public relations specialists	132	660	53	908	79	586
Technical, sales, and administrative support	26,116	441	9,988	567	16,128	394

Occupation	1996					
	Both sexes		Men		Women	
	Number of workers	Median weekly earnings	Number of workers	Median weekly earnings	Number of workers	Median weekly earnings
Technicians and related support	3,215	573	1,662	650	1,553	498
Health technologists and technicians	1,172	482	263	537	909	470
Clinical laboratory technologists and technicians	296	520	87	578	209	508
Radiologic technicians	106	559	37	(1)	70	557
Licensed practical nurses	294	468	14	(1)	280	466
Engineering and related technologists and technicians	834	605	683	621	151	542
Electrical and electronic technicians	341	610	300	622	41	(1)
Drafting occupations	209	601	166	608	43	(1)
Surveying and mapping technicians	58	461	53	459	5	(1)
Science technicians	221	519	140	598	81	443
Biological technicians	66	485	28	(1)	39	(1)
Chemical technicians	79	599	58	648	21	(1)
Technicians, except health, engineering, and science	988	706	576	806	412	611
Airplane pilots and navigators	88	1,138	87	1,143	2	(1)
Computer programmers	518	772	363	797	156	741
Legal assistants	245	549	36	(1)	208	545
Sales occupations	9,041	474	5,114	589	3,927	353
Supervisors and proprietors	2,969	519	1,845	608	1,124	415
Sales representatives, finance and business services	1,583	607	866	727	717	485
Insurance sales	416	606	212	767	205	471
Real estate sales	306	605	149	695	157	510
Securities and financial services sales	273	747	179	977	94	541
Advertising and related sales	131	500	53	607	78	421
Sales occupations, other business services	457	582	273	631	184	486
Sales representatives, commodities, except retail	1,329	694	1,005	735	324	583
Sales workers, retail and personal services	3,136	299	1,390	386	1,746	259
Sales workers, motor vehicles and boats	251	593	230	597	22	(1)
Sales workers, apparel	163	265	39	(1)	123	260
Sales workers, furniture and home furnishings	119	403	77	406	42	(1)
Sales workers, radio, television, hi-fi, and appliances	155	423	123	428	32	(1)
Sales workers, hardware and building supplies	171	372	134	399	36	(1)
Sales workers, parts	139	409	122	427	17	(1)
Sales workers, other commodities	674	298	260	340	414	273
Sales counter clerks	84	303	37	(1)	47	(1)
Cashiers	1,215	247	289	274	926	240
Street and door-to-door sales workers	106	372	46	(1)	60	398
Administrative support, including clerical	13,860	405	3,212	489	10,648	391
Supervisors	634	557	261	624	374	506
General office	356	541	121	638	235	503
Financial records processing	79	604	13	(1)	66	576
Distribution, scheduling, and adjusting clerks	168	541	108	553	61	509
Computer equipment operators	332	430	139	538	194	401
Computer operators	329	433	139	538	191	403
Secretaries, stenographers, and typists	2,907	404	63	389	2,844	404
Secretaries	2,401	406	36	(1)	2,365	406
Stenographers	55	412	6	(1)	49	(1)
Typists	451	395	21	(1)	430	397

| Occupation | 1996 | | | | | |
| | Both sexes | | Men | | Women | |
	Number of workers	Median weekly earnings	Number of workers	Median weekly earnings	Number of workers	Median weekly earnings
Information clerks	1,273	345	145	367	1,127	343
Interviewers	115	356	11	(1)	104	364
Hotel clerks	73	267	20	(1)	52	267
Transportation ticket and reservation agents	209	421	64	458	146	397
Receptionists	633	333	18	(1)	615	333
Records processing, except financial	651	387	152	396	498	383
Order clerks	184	455	51	466	132	451
Personnel clerks, ecxept payroll and timekeeping	58	445	11	(1)	47	(1)
File clerks	203	328	57	334	146	325
Records clerks	149	389	23	(1)	126	383
Financial records processing	1,503	403	166	439	1,338	400
Bookkeepers, accounting, and auditing clerks	1,081	399	110	450	971	396
Payroll and timekeeping clerks	145	444	16	(1)	129	441
Billing clerks	141	397	20	(1)	121	399
Billing, posting, and calculating machine operators	87	395	12	(1)	75	391
Duplicating, mail and other office machine operators	60	362	22	(1)	39	(1)
Communications equipment operators	140	376	17	(1)	123	367
Telephone operators	126	363	13	(1)	112	359
Mail and message distributing	815	599	526	628	289	521
Postal clerks, except mail carriers	283	643	159	673	124	612
Mail carriers, postal service	284	678	207	684	76	646
Mail clerks, except postal service	151	339	80	383	72	314
Messengers	98	360	80	366	17	(1)
Material recording, scheduling, and distributing clerks	1,642	412	953	444	689	379
Dispatchers	218	471	113	518	105	420
Production coordinators	191	517	89	618	101	462
Traffic, shipping, and receiving clerks	550	367	395	382	155	339
Stock and inventory clerks	432	429	245	470	188	366
Meter readers	53	434	43	(1)	10	(1)
Expediters	137	361	43	(1)	94	346
Adjusters and investigators	1,372	438	344	532	1,029	416
Insurance adjusters, examiners, and investigators	377	506	106	649	271	458
Investigators and adjusters, except insurance	763	415	184	486	579	400
Eligibility clerks, social welfare	103	455	14	(1)	88	441
Bill and account collectors	129	407	39	(1)	91	406
Miscellaneous administrative support occupations	2,531	369	426	426	2,105	358
General office clerks	510	372	108	423	402	361
Bank tellers	279	315	26	(1)	253	313
Data-entry keyers	566	366	79	407	488	360
Statistical clerks	83	397	8	(1)	74	392
Teachers' aides	331	273	29	(1)	302	272
Service occupations	9,957	305	4,958	357	5,000	273
Private household	365	212	19	(1)	346	213
Child care workers	136	198	2	(1)	134	198
Cleaners and servants	214	220	16	(1)	198	221
Protective services	1,902	538	1,627	562	275	439
Supervisors	176	742	159	773	18	(1)
Police and detectives	93	793	81	845	12	(1)

Occupation	1996					
	Both sexes		Men		Women	
	Number of workers	Median weekly earnings	Number of workers	Median weekly earnings	Number of workers	Median weekly earnings
Fire fighting and fire prevention	221	653	216	657	5	(^{1})
Firefighting	208	658	204	661	4	(^{1})
Police and detectives	939	606	797	616	141	520
Police and detectives, public service	549	667	481	679	68	617
Sheriffs, bailiffs, and other law enforcement officers	127	513	107	517	20	(^{1})
Correctional institution officers	263	513	210	541	53	449
Guards	566	333	455	343	111	295
Guards and police, except public service	531	336	440	343	91	302
Service occupations, except private household and protective	7,690	285	3,312	304	4,379	272
Food preparation and service occupations	2,839	265	1,496	278	1,343	253
Supervisors	234	312	93	357	141	294
Bartenders	177	310	82	378	96	277
Waiters and waitresses	518	271	155	308	363	253
Cooks, except short order	1,221	264	792	279	430	242
Food counter, fountain, and related occupations	71	217	23	(^{1})	49	(^{1})
Kitchen workers, food preparation	105	264	36	(^{1})	69	265
Waiters' and waitresses' assistants	208	259	124	239	84	278
Miscellaneous food preparation occupations	304	231	192	226	112	239
Health service occupations	1,688	299	231	342	1,457	293
Dental assistants	128	361	2	(^{1})	126	359
Health aides, except nursing	237	314	50	355	187	306
Nursing aides, orderlies, and attendants	1,323	292	179	339	1,144	286
Cleaning and building service occupations	2,140	298	1,325	321	815	266
Supervisors	148	391	102	468	46	(^{1})
Maids and housemen	455	264	96	300	359	253
Janitors and cleaners	1,476	301	1,069	313	407	272
Pest control	55	421	53	421	2	(^{1})
Personal service occupations	1,024	291	260	360	764	276
Hairdressers and cosmetologists	274	292	32	(^{1})	242	288
Attendants, amusement and recreation facilities	103	348	57	364	46	(^{1})
Public transportation attendants	59	417	11	(^{1})	48	(^{1})
Welfare service aides	57	285	10	(^{1})	46	(^{1})
Early childhood teachers' assistants	207	231	5	(^{1})	202	230
Precision production, craft, and repair	11,020	540	10,076	560	944	373
Mechanics and repairers	3,834	568	3,672	571	162	510
Supervisors	212	707	193	712	18	(^{1})
Mechanics and repairers, except supervisors	3,622	559	3,479	563	144	502
Vehicle and mobile equipment mechanics and repairers	1,443	524	1,432	524	11	(^{1})
Automobile mechanics	644	478	638	480	6	(^{1})
Bus, truck, and stationary engine mechanics	300	545	299	545	1	(^{1})
Aircraft engine mechanics	131	720	130	722	1	(^{1})
Automobile body and related repairers	144	463	141	459	3	(^{1})
Heavy equipment mechanics	144	613	144	613	–	–
Industrial machinery repairers	527	569	513	574	14	(^{1})
Electrical and electronic equipment repairers	607	645	533	669	74	542
Electronic repairers, communications and industrial equipment	146	602	139	609	8	(^{1})

Occupation	1996					
	Both sexes		Men		Women	
	Number of workers	Median weekly earnings	Number of workers	Median weekly earnings	Number of workers	Median weekly earnings
Data processing equipment repairers	170	573	134	588	37	(1)
Telephone installers and repairers	163	717	138	746	25	(1)
Miscellaneous electrical and electronic equipment repairers	64	714	64	713	–	–
Heating, air conditioning, and refrigeration mechanics	244	543	240	544	4	(1)
Miscellaneous mechanics and repairers	784	557	745	569	39	(1)
Millwrights	86	669	85	665	1	(1)
Construction trades	3,653	516	3,585	518	68	389
Supervisors	438	662	429	667	10	(1)
Construction trades, except supervisors	3,215	502	3,157	503	58	388
Brickmasons and stonemasons	111	483	111	483	–	–
Carpet installers	51	402	51	402	–	–
Carpenters	804	475	795	476	9	(1)
Drywall installers	122	430	120	436	2	(1)
Electricians	647	611	633	612	14	(1)
Electrical power installers and repairers	125	710	125	710	–	–
Painters, construction and maintenance	270	381	254	392	17	(1)
Plumbers, pipefitters, steamfitters, and apprentices	434	586	427	586	7	(1)
Concrete and terrazzo finishers	66	467	65	461	1	(1)
Insulation workers	53	508	53	508	–	–
Rooters	127	363	127	363	–	–
Structural metalworkers	58	598	57	600	2	(1)
Extractive occupations	128	699	124	700	4	(1)
Precision production occupations	3,405	526	2,695	583	710	356
Supervisors	1,141	619	952	650	189	458
Precision metalworking occupations	865	581	798	595	66	367
Tool and die makers	132	716	129	714	2	(1)
Machinists	481	543	450	555	32	(1)
Sheet-metal workers	118	605	110	612	8	(1)
Precision woodworking occupations	81	395	71	409	10	(1)
Cabinet makers and bench carpenters	55	401	50	407	5	(1)
Precision textile, apparel, and furnishings machine workers	116	346	63	390	52	308
Precision workers, assorted materials	472	368	216	412	256	337
Optical goods workers	53	457	24	(1)	29	(1)
Electrical and electronic equipment assemblers	324	340	118	355	206	334
Precision food production occupations	350	354	240	392	109	310
Butchers and meat cutters	221	366	172	402	48	(1)
Bakers	98	327	60	347	38	(1)
Precision inspectors, testers, and related workers	135	572	113	603	23	(1)
Inspectors, testers, and graders	128	570	108	601	20	(1)
Plant and system operators	246	634	241	638	5	(1)
Water and sewage treatment plant operators	59	551	57	562	2	(1)
Stationary engineers	118	621	117	620	1	(1)
Operators, fabricators, and laborers	15,100	391	11,613	422	3,487	307
Machine operators, assemblers, and inspectors	7,100	380	4,527	437	2,573	307
Machine operators and tenders, except precision	4,605	372	2,918	427	1,686	300
Metalworking and plastic working machine operators	385	436	327	459	58	346

Occupation	1996					
	Both sexes		Men		Women	
	Number of workers	Median weekly earnings	Number of workers	Median weekly earnings	Number of workers	Median weekly earnings
Punching and stamping press machine operators	94	418	76	448	18	(1)
Grinding, abrading, buffing, and polishing machine operators	125	408	106	428	19	(1)
Metal and plastic processing machine operators	157	401	126	416	31	(1)
Molding and casting machine operators	99	396	75	409	24	(1)
Woodworking machine operators	110	373	95	387	15	(1)
Sawing machine operators	73	355	64	368	9	(1)
Printing machine operators	356	473	289	500	67	395
Printing press operators	281	484	250	502	31	(1)
Textile, apparel, and furnishings machine operators	905	268	221	310	684	257
Winding and twisting machine operators	50	357	19	(1)	31	(1)
Textile sewing machine operators	535	254	91	287	444	249
Pressing machine operators	77	244	18	(1)	59	230
Laundering and dry cleaning machine operators	128	254	38	(1)	90	243
Machine operators, assorted materials	2,676	396	1,848	432	828	327
Packaging and filling machine operators	377	313	156	344	222	302
Mixing and blending machine operators	100	383	92	395	8	(1)
Separating, filtering, and clarifying machine operators	56	609	53	608	3	(1)
Painting and paint spraying machine operators	191	422	170	441	20	(1)
Furnace, kiln, and oven operators, exc. food	56	510	52	512	4	(1)
Slicing and cutting machine operators	157	359	112	407	45	(1)
Photographic process machine operators	57	314	24	(1)	32	(1)
Fabricators, assemblers, and hand working occupations	1,783	403	1,247	448	536	320
Welders and cutters	555	478	525	482	30	(1)
Assemblers	1,117	378	648	430	469	322
Production inspectors, testers, samplers, and weighers	712	379	361	471	351	323
Production inspectors, checkers, and examiners	513	407	254	499	259	346
Graders and sorters, except agricultural	144	265	65	279	79	258
Transportation and material moving occupations	4,254	476	3,982	486	272	350
Motor vehicle operators	3,052	473	2,836	484	216	345
Supervisors	73	583	60	634	14	(1)
Truck drivers	2,396	481	2,314	485	82	359
Drivers—sales workers	146	506	139	515	6	(1)
Bus drivers	287	396	184	468	103	329
Taxicab drivers and chauffeurs	119	374	109	381	10	(1)
Transportation occupations, except motor vehicles	181	691	178	696	3	(1)
Rail transportation	116	740	114	742	2	(1)
Water transportation	65	586	64	592	1	(1)
Material moving equipment operators	1,021	461	968	469	53	374
Operating engineers	226	516	219	518	7	(1)
Crane and tower operators	76	552	74	558	2	(1)
Excavating and loading machine operators	66	487	66	487	–	–

Occupation	1996					
	Both sexes		Men		Women	
	Number of workers	Median weekly earnings	Number of workers	Median weekly earnings	Number of workers	Median weekly earnings
Industrial truck and tractor equipment operators	505	417	472	420	33	(¹)
Handlers, equipment cleaners, helpers, and laborers	3,747	330	3,105	343	642	295
Helpers, construction and extractive occupations	100	311	95	308	4	(¹)
Helpers, construction trades	91	308	87	305	4	(¹)
Construction laborers	698	372	676	377	22	(¹)
Freight, stock, and material handlers	1,200	327	957	340	243	288
Stock handlers and baggers	551	282	399	292	152	262
Machine feeders and offbearers	58	328	30	(¹)	28	(¹)
Garage and service station related occupations	122	276	119	275	4	(¹)
Vehicle washers and equipment cleaners	201	292	180	296	21	(¹)
Hand packers and packagers	219	310	95	316	124	302
Laborers, except construction	1,136	342	922	360	214	298
Farming, forestry, and fishing	1,502	294	1,326	300	176	255
Farm operators and managers	83	442	72	461	11	(¹)
Farm managers	64	493	55	520	8	(¹)
Other agricultural and related occupations	1,353	285	1,190	291	163	249
Farm occupations, except managerial	636	271	562	278	73	229
Farm workers	591	265	527	271	63	221
Related agricultural occupations	717	298	627	303	90	271
Supervisors, related agricultural	69	417	68	418	–	–
Groundskeepers and gardeners, except farm	542	294	520	294	21	(¹)
Animal caretakers, except farm	55	292	19	(¹)	36	(¹)
Graders and sorters, agricultural products	51	257	20	(¹)	31	(¹)
Forestry and logging occupations	57	443	55	440	2	(¹)

¹ Data not shown where base is less than 50,000.   – Dash represents zero or rounds to zero

Appendix D

Industry Employment: 2005

EMPLOYMENT IN VARIOUS INDUSTRIES AND PROJECTED CHANGES BY 2005

Here are the numbers of workers employed in America's major industries and the number that will probably be employed in 2005, along with the percentage of change—up or down—each industry (numbers in thousands).

Industry	1994	2005	Change, 1994–2005	
			Number	Percent
Total, all industries	116,187	132,984	16,798	14
Agriculture, forestry, and fishing	1,881	1,999	118	6
Crops, livestock and livestock products	992	899	-93	-9
Agricultural services	837	1,050	213	25
Veterinary services	155	185	30	19
Animal services, except veterinary	47	50	3	7
Agricultural services, nec	635	815	180	28
Forestry	29	29	0	1
Fishing, hunting, and trapping	23	21	-2	-9
Mining	601	439	-162	-27
Metal mining	49	42	-7	-15
Coal mining	112	70	-43	-38
Oil and gas extraction	336	240	-96	-28
Crude petroleum, natural gas, and gas liquids	168	105	-63	-38
Oil and gas field services	168	136	-33	-19
Nonmetallic minerals, except fuels	104	88	-16	-15
Construction	5,010	5,500	490	10
General building contractors	1,200	1,234	33	3
Residential building construction	609	633	24	4
Operative builders	28	25	-3	-10
Nonresidential building construction	563	575	12	2
Heavy construction, except building	736	830	93	13
Highway and street construction	226	255	30	13
Heavy construction, except highway and street	511	574	64	12

Industry	1994	2005	Change, 1994–2005	
			Number	Percent
Special trade contractors	3,073	3,437	364	12
Plumbing, heating, and air-conditioning	687	754	67	10
Painting and paper hanging	173	200	27	15
Electrical work	566	648	82	14
Masonry, stonework, and plastering	430	479	49	11
Carpentering and floor work	210	231	21	10
Roofing, siding, and sheet metal work	206	229	23	11
Concrete work	244	272	28	11
Water well drilling	21	22	1	5
Miscellaneous special trade contractors	536	601	66	12
Manufacturing	18,304	16,990	-1,313	-7
Durable goods manufacturing	10,431	9,290	-1,141	-11
Lumber and wood products	752	685	-68	-9
Logging	82	74	-8	-9
Sawmills and planing mills	189	150	39	-20
Millwork, plywood, and structural members	271	250	-20	-8
Wood containers and miscellaneous wood products	138	138	0	0
Wood buildings and mobile homes	73	72	-1	-1
Furniture and fixtures	502	515	13	3
Household furniture	284	280	-4	-1
Partitions and fixtures	80	88	8	11
Office and miscellaneous furniture and fixtures	138	146	8	6
Stone, clay, and glass products	533	434	-99	-19
Flat glass and products of purchased glass	76	77	1	1
Glass and glassware, pressed or blown	77	48	-29	-38
Cement, hydraulic	18	14	-4	-22
Concrete, gypsum, and plaster products	198	172	-27	-14
Stone, clay, and miscellaneous mineral products	164	124	-40	-24
Primary metal industries	699	532	-168	-24
Blast furnaces and basic steel products	239	155	-84	-35
Iron and steel foundries	125	92	-32	-26
Primary nonferrous metals	41	36	-5	-13
Miscellaneous primary and secondary metals	44	40	-4	-8
Nonferrous rolling and drawing	167	135	-32	-19
Nonferrous foundries (castings)	84	74	-11	-13
Fabricated metal products	1,387	1,180	-207	-15
Metal cans and shipping containers	42	27	-15	36
Cutlery, handtools, and hardware	129	90	-39	-30
Plumbing and heating, except electric	60	48	-12	-19
Fabricated structural metal products	409	315	-94	-23
Screw machine products, bolts, etc.	96	78	-18	-18
Metal forgings and stampings	234	194	-40	-17
Metal services, nec	124	140	16	13
Ordnance and accessories, nec	54	51	-3	-6
Miscellaneous fabricated metal products	240	238	-3	-1
Industrial machinery and equipment	1,985	1,769	-216	-11
Engines and turbines	90	70	-19	-21
Farm and garden machinery	105	87	-18	-17
Construction and related machinery	210	188	-22	-10
Metalworking machinery	322	291	-31	-10
Special industry machinery	155	150	-5	-3
General industrial machinery	243	235	-8	-3
Computer and office equipment	351	263	-88	-25

Industry	1994	2005	Change, 1994–2005	
			Number	Percent
Refrigeration and service machinery	190	192	2	1
Industrial machinery, nec	319	292	-27	-9
Electronic and other electrical equipment	1,571	1,408	-163	-10
Electric distributing equipment	82	70	-12	-15
Electrical industrial apparatus	156	116	-40	-26
Household appliances	123	98	-26	-21
Electric lighting and wiring equipment	176	155	-21	-12
Household audio and video equipment	89	55	-34	-38
Communications equipment	244	210	-34	-14
Electronic components and accessories	544	553	8	2
Miscellaneous electrical equipment and supplies	156	151	-5	-3
Transportation equipment	1,749	1,567	-182	-10
Motor vehicles and equipment	899	775	-124	-14
Aircraft and parts	480	458	-22	-5
Ship and boat building and repairing	159	130	-29	-18
Railroad equipment	35	35	0	-1
Guided missiles, space vehicles, and parts	108	94	-14	-13
Miscellaneous transportation equipment	69	75	6	9
Instruments and related products	863	798	-66	-8
Search and navigation equipment	180	132	-48	-27
Measuring and controlling devices	284	248	-36	-13
Medical instruments and supplies	265	306	41	15
Ophthalmic goods	37	37	0	-1
Photographic equipment and supplies	89	70	-19	-21
Watches, clocks, watchcases and parts	8	5	-4	-45
Miscellaneous manufacturing industries	390	404	13	3
Jewelry, silverware, and plated ware	51	44	-8	-15
Toys and sporting goods	115	135	20	17
Manufactured products, nec	224	225	1	0
Nondurable goods manufacturing	7,872	7,700	-172	-2
Food and kindred products	1,680	1,696	17	1
Meat products	451	515	64	14
Dairy products	149	132	-16	-11
Preserved fruits and vegetables	245	260	15	6
Grain mill products and fats and oils	160	160	0	0
Bakery products	213	195	-18	-8
Sugar and confectionery products	99	90	-9	-9
Beverages	178	132	-46	-26
Miscellaneous foods and kindred products	185	211	26	14
Tobacco products	42	26	- 16	-38
Textile mill products	673	568	-105	-16
Weaving, finishing, yarn and thread mills	358	281	-77	-21
Knitting mills	199	173	-26	-13
Carpets and rugs	64	65	1	1
Miscellaneous textile goods	52	49	-3	-6
Apparel and other textile products	969	772	-198	-20
Apparel	755	547	-208	-28
Miscellaneous fabricated textile products	215	225	10	5
Paper and allied products	691	708	17	2
Pulp, paper and paperboard mills	232	218	-14	-6
Paperboard containers and boxes	213	230	17	8
Miscellaneous converted paper products	246	260	14	6
Printing and publishing	1,542	1,627	86	6
Newspapers	450	412	-38	-8
Periodicals	135	163	28	21
Books	120	130	10	9

Industry	1994	2005	Change, 1994–2005	
			Number	Percent
Miscellaneous publishing	84	85	1	1
Commercial printing and business forms	597	675	78	13
Greeting cards	29	32	3	12
Blankbooks and bookbinding	70	77	7	10
Printing trade services	57	52	-4	-7
Chemicals and allied products	1,061	1,067	6	1
Industrial inorganic chemicals	132	122	-10	-8
Plastics materials and synthetics	162	142	-19	-12
Drugs	263	325	62	23
Soap, cleaners, and toilet goods	153	165	12	8
Paints and allied products	58	48	-10	-16
Industrial organic chemicals	144	136	-8	-6
Agricultural chemicals	55	42	-12	-22
Miscellaneous chemical products	93	85	-8	-9
Petroleum and coal products	149	140	-9	-6
Petroleum refining	109	102	-6	-6
Miscellaneous petroleum and coal products	40	38	-2	-6
Rubber and miscellaneous plastics products	952	1,030	78	8
Tires and inner tubes	80	60	-20	-25
Rubber products and plastic hose and footwear	182	170	-12	-7
Miscellaneous plastics products	690	800	110	16
Leather and leather products	114	65	-48	-43
Footwear, except rubber and plastic	61	29	-32	-53
Luggage, handbags, and leather products, nec	53	36	-16	-31
Transportation and public utilities	6,006	6,431	425	7
Transportation	3,775	4,251	476	13
Railroad transportation	240	186	-55	-23
Local and interurban passenger transit	410	490	80	19
Local and suburban transportation	199	253	54	27
Taxicabs	32	35	4	12
Intercity buses, charter service, and terminals	54	60	6	12
School buses	126	142	16	13
Trucking and warehousing	1,797	2,000	203	11
Local and long distance trucking and terminals	1,658	1,840	182	11
Public warehousing and storage	140	160	20	15
Water transportation	169	165	-4	-2
Ocean, great lakes, and transportation of freight, nec	42	38	-4	-10
Water transportation of passengers	17	16	0	-2
Water transportation services	110	111	1	1
Transportation by air	748	870	122	16
Air carriers	643	740	97	15
Airports, flying fields, and services	105	130	25	24
Pipelines, except natural gas	18	15	-3	-16
Transportation services	392	525	133	34
Passenger transportation arrangement	197	255	58	29
Freight transportation arrangement	158	218	60	38
Transportation services, nec	38	53	15	39
Communications and utilities	2,231	2,180	-51	-2
Communications	1,304	1,235	-70	-5
Telephone communications	903	800	-103	-11
Telegraph and communication services, nec	22	10	-12	-54
Radio and television broadcasting	235	225	-10	-4
Cable and other pay TV services	145	200	55	38

Industry	1994	2005	Change, 1994–2005	
			Number	Percent
Electric, gas, and sanitary services	926	945	18	2
Electric services	417	400	-17	-4
Gas production and distribution	159	146	-14	-9
Combination utility services	178	169	-9	-5
Water supply and sanitary services	172	230	58	34
Wholesale and retail trade	26,577	29,653	3,075	12
Wholesale trade	6,140	6,558	419	7
Motor vehicles, parts, and supplies	472	500	29	6
Machinery, equipment, and supplies	751	822	71	9
Groceries and related products	868	911	43	5
Petroleum and petroleum products	163	174	12	4
Wholesale trade, other	3,887	4,151	264	7
Retail trade	20,438	23,094	2,657	13
Building materials and garden supplies	798	851	53	7
Lumber and other building materials	488	519	32	6
Paint, glass, and wallpaper stores	66	66	1	1
Hardware stores	159	161	2	1
Retail nurseries and garden stores	86	105	19	23
General merchandise stores	2,546	2,585	40	2
Department stores	2,212	2,281	69	3
General merchandise stores, nec	334	305	-29	-9
Food stores	3,289	3,930	641	19
Grocery stores	2,934	3,526	593	20
Meat and fish markets	46	47	0	0
Retail bakeries	175	195	20	11
Food stores, nec	134	162	28	21
Automotive dealers and service stations	2,153	2,252	99	5
Motor vehicle dealers	1,038	1,118	79	8
Auto and home supply stores	360	398	37	10
Gasoline service stations	632	623	-10	-2
Boat and miscellaneous vehicle dealers	121	114	-7	-6
Apparel and accessory stores	1,134	1,341	208	18
Clothing and accessories stores	843	993	151	18
Shoe stores	205	228	23	11
Miscellaneous apparel and accessory stores	86	120	34	39
Furniture and homefurnishings stores	890	1,034	144	16
Furniture and homefurnishings stores	473	501	28	6
Appliance, radio, TV, and music stores	417	533	116	28
Eating and drinking places	7,069	8,089	1,020	14
Miscellaneous retail stores	2,560	3,012	452	18
Drug stores and proprietary stores	601	672	71	12
Liquor stores	112	111	-1	-1
Miscellaneous shopping goods stores	901	1,172	271	30
Nonstore retailers	308	323	14	5
Fuel dealers	99	95	-4	-4
Used merchandise and retail stores, nec	538	639	101	19
Finance, insurance, and real estate	6,933	7,372	439	6
Depository institutions	2,076	1,886	-190	-9
Banking and closely related functions, nec	125	160	35	28
Commercial banks, savings institutions, and credit unions	1,950	1,726	-224	-12
Nondepository institutions	498	665	166	33
Federal and business credit institutions	108	141	33	31
Personal credit institutions	134	177	42	31
Mortgage bankers and brokers	256	348	91	36

Industry	1994	2005	Change, 1994–2005	
			Number	Percent
Security and commodity brokers	518	700	182	35
Security and commodity brokers and dealers	411	540	129	31
Security and commodity exchanges and services	107	160	53	50
Insurance carriers	1,551	1,633	82	5
Life insurance	578	595	17	3
Medical service and health insurance	295	324	29	10
Fire, marine, and casualty insurance	542	557	16	3
Pension funds and insurance, nec	136	157	20	15
Insurance agents, brokers, and service	686	702	16	2
Real estate	1,373	1,482	109	8
Real estate operators and lessors	575	606	32	6
Real estate agents and managers	651	725	74	11
Title abstract offices	35	36	1	3
Subdividers and developers	112	114	2	2
Holding and other investment offices	231	306	74	32
Services	41,204	54,700	13,496	33
Hotels and other lodging places	1,618	1,899	282	17
Personal services	1,139	1,374	235	21
Laundry, cleaning, and garment services	423	495	72	17
Photographic studios, portrait	75	95	21	28
Beauty shops	385	451	66	17
Barber shops	12	9	-3	-27
Shoe repair and shoeshine parlors	6	5	0	-9
Funeral service and crematories	89	100	11	13
Miscellaneous personal services	151	219	68	45
Business services	6,239	10,032	3,792	61
Advertising	224	250	26	12
Credit reporting and collection	116	159	43	37
Mailing, reproduction, and stenographic services	255	326	71	28
Services to buildings	854	1,350	496	58
Miscellaneous equipment rental and leasing	216	325	110	51
Personnel supply services	2,254	3,564	1,310	58
Computer and data processing services	950	1,610	660	70
Miscellaneous business services	1,370	2,447	1,077	79
Auto repair, services, and parking	970	1,345	375	39
Automotive rentals, no drivers	174	227	52	30
Automobile parking	62	80	18	28
Automotive repair shops	543	704	162	30
Automotive services, except repair	191	334	143	75
Miscellaneous repair services	334	400	66	20
Electrical repair shops	105	125	20	19
Watch, clock, and jewelry repair	5	5	0	-2
Reupholstery and furniture repair	21	20	-1	-6
Miscellaneous repair shops	202	250	48	24
Motion pictures	471	590	119	25
Motion picture production and distribution	220	307	87	40
Motion picture theaters	113	118	5	4
Video tape rental	138	165	27	20
Amusement and recreation services	1,344	1,844	500	37
Dance studios, schools, and halls	23	23	0	0
Producers, orchestras, and entertainers	148	200	52	36
Bowling centers	85	72	-13	-15
Commercial sports	106	137	31	29
Miscellaneous amusement and recreation services	983	1,411	429	44
Health services	10,082	13,165	3,083	31
Offices of physicians including osteopaths	1,592	2,158	566	36

Industry	1994	2005	Change, 1994–2005	
			Number	Percent
Offices and clinics of dentists		742	168	29
Offices of other health practitioners	379	625	246	65
Nursing and personal care facilities	1,649	2,400	751	46
Hospitals, public and private	4,855	5,340	485	10
Medical and dental laboratories	192	265	73	38
Home health care services	555	1,220	665	120
Health and allied services, nec	285	415	130	46
Legal services	927	1,270	343	37
Education, public and private	10,187	12,400	2,213	22
Social services	2,181	3,639	1,459	67
Individual and miscellaneous social services	779	1,314	536	69
Job training and related services	298	425	127	43
Child day care services		800	298	59
Residential care	602	1,100	498	83
Museums and botanical and zoological gardens	79	112	33	42
Membership organizations	1,059	2,336	277	13
Business and professional organizations	157	170	13	8
Labor organizations	141	147	6	4
Civic and social associations	413	459	46	11
Membership organizations, nec	110	142	32	29
Religious organizations	1,238	1,418	180	15
Engineering and management services	2,567	3,451	884	34
Engineering and architectural services	775	1,044	269	35
Accounting, auditing, and bookkeeping	513	613	100	19
Research and testing services	563	745	182	32
Management and public relations	716	1,049	333	47
Private households	966	800	-166	-17
Services, nec	40	43	3	6
Government	9,671	9,900	228	2
U.S. Postal Service	818	760	-58	-7
Federal Government	2,052	1,875	-178	-9
State government, except education and hospitals	2,282	2,376	95	4
Local government, except education and hospitals	4,520	4,888	369	8

Appendix E

Jobs and Education: 2005

The table on the following page indicates the number of workers employed in each type of major occupation in the United States and the number that will probably be employed in 2005, along with the percentage of change by then—up or down. Listed with each job are the current educational requirements for each—that is, the "most significant source of training: bachelor's degree, associate degree, on-the-job training, work experience etc.

Occupation	Employment		Employment change, 1994–2005		Total job openings due to growth and net replacements, 1994–2005[1]	Earnings quartile[2]	Most significant source of training
	1994	Projected, 2005	Percent	Number			
Total, all occupations	127,014	144,708	14	17,694	49,631		
Executive, administrative, and managerial occupations	12,903	15,071	17	2,168	4,844		
Managerial and administrative occupations	9,058	10,575	17	1,517	3,467		
Administrative services managers	279	307	10	28	87	1	Work experience, plus degree
Communication, transportation, and utilities operations managers	154	135	-12	-19	32	1	Work experience, plus degree
Construction managers	197	253	28	56	97	1	Bachelor's degree
Education administrators	393	459	17	66	176	1	Work experience, plus degree
Engineering, mathematical, and natural science managers	337	432	28	95	165	1	Work experience, plus degree
Financial managers	768	950	24	182	324	1	Work experience, plus degree
Food service and lodging managers	579	771	33	192	313	3	Work experience
Funeral directors and morticians	26	29	11	3	8		Long-term O-J-T
General managers and top executives	3,046	3,512	15	466	1,104	1	Work experience, plus degree
Government chief executives and legislators	91	94	4	4	26	1	Work experience, plus degree
Industrial production managers	206	191	-7	-15	43	1	Bachelor's degree
Marketing, advertising, and public relations managers	461	575	25	114	211	1	Work experience, plus degree
Personnel, training, and labor relations managers	206	252	22	46	104	1	Work experience, plus degree
Property and real estate managers	261	298	14	37	81	2	Bachelor's degree
Purchasing managers	226	235	4	9	55	1	Work experience, plus degree
All other managers and administrators	1,829	2,081	14	252	639	1	Work experience, plus degree
Management support occupations	3,845	4,496	17	651	1,377		
Accountants and auditors	962	1,083	13	121	312	1	Bachelor's degree
Budget analysts	66	74	12	8	19	1	Bachelor's degree
Claims examiner's, property and casualty insurance	56	65	15	9	14	2	Bachelor's degree
Construction and building inspectors	64	79	22	14	28	1	Work experience
Cost estimators	179	210	17	31	48	2	Work experience
Credit analysts	39	48	24	9	16	1	Bachelor's degree
Employment interviewers, private or public employment service	77	104	36	27	43	1	Bachelor's degree
Inspectors and compliance officers, except construction	157	175	12	18	50	1	Work experience
Loan officers and counselors	214	264	23	50	85	1	Bachelor's degree

Occupation	Employment		Employment change, 1994–2005		Total job openings due to growth and net replacements, 1994–2005[1]	Earnings quartile[2]	Most significant source of training
	1994	Projected, 2005	Percent	Number			
Management analysts	231	312	35	82	109	1	Masters's degree
Personnel, training, and labor relations specialists	307	374	22	57	129	1	Bachelor's degree
Purchasing agents, except wholesale, retail, and farm products	215	226	5	12	64	1	Bachelor's degree
Tax examiners, collectors, and revenue agents	63	63	0	0	14	1	Bachelor's degree
Underwriters	96	103	7	7	25	1	Bachelor's degree
Wholesale and retail buyers, except farm products	180	178	-2	-3	50	2	Bachelor's degree
All other management support workers	940	1,138	21	198	371	1	Bachelor's degree
Professional specialty occupations	17,314	22,387	29	5,073	8,376		
Engineers	1,327	1,573	19	246	581	1	Bachelor's degree
Aeronautical and astronautical engineers	56	59	6	3	16	1	Bachelor's degree
Chemical engineers	50	57	13	7	21	1	Bachelor's degree
Civil engineers, including traffic engineers	184	219	19	34	90	1	Bachelor's degree
Electrical and electronics engineers	349	417	20	69	157	1	Bachelor's degree
Industrial engineers, except safety engineers	115	131	13	15	47	1	Bachelor's degree
Mechanical engineers	231	276	19	45	98	1	Bachelor's degree
Metallurgists and metallurgical, ceramic, and materials engineers	19	20	5	1	6	1	Bachelor's degree
Mining engineers, including mine safety engineers	3	3	-18	-1	1	1	Bachelor's degree
Nuclear engineers	15	15	4	1	5	1	Bachelor's degree
Petroleum engineers	14	11	-21	-3	4	1	Bachelor's degree
All other engineers	292	367	26	75	136	1	Bachelor's degree
Architects and surveyors	200	215	7	14	70		
Architects, except landscape and marine	91	106	17	15	35	1	Bachelor's degree
Landscape architects	14	16	17	2	5	1	Bachelor's degree
Surveyors	96	92	-3	-3	30	2	Postsecondary vocational training
Life scientists	186	230	24	44	94		
Agricultural and food scientists	26	31	19	5	12	1	Bachelor's degree
Biological scientists	82	103	25	21	43	1	Doctor's degree
Foresters and conservation scientists	41	49	18	8	18	1	Bachelor's degree
Medical scientists	36	47	31	11	21	1	Doctor's degree

Occupation	Employment		Employment change, 1994–2005		Total job openings due to growth and net replacements, 1994–2005[1]	Earnings quartile[2]	Most significant source of training
	1994	Projected, 2005	Percent	Number			
All other life scientists	1	1	1	0	0	1	Doctor's degree
Computer, mathematical, and operations research occupations	917	1,696	85	779	863		
Actuaries	17	18	4	1	4	1	Bachelor's degree
Computer systems analysts, engineers, and scientists	828	1,583	91	755	819		
Computer engineers and scientists	345	655	90	310	338	1	Bachelor's degree
Computer engineers	195	372	90	177	191	1	Bachelor's degree
All other computer scientists	149	283	89	134	147	1	Bachelor's degree
Systems analysts	483	928	92	445	481	1	Bachelor's degree
Statisticians	14	15	3	0	3	1	Doctor's degree
Mathematicians and all other mathematical scientists	14	15	5	1	3	1	Doctor's degree
Operations research analysts	44	67	50	22	35	1	Master's degree
Physical scientists	209	250	19	41	104		
Chemists	97	115	19	18	45	1	Bachelor's degree
Geologists, geophysicists, and oceanographers	46	54	17	8	24	1	Bachelor's degree
Meteorologists	7	7	7	0	2	1	Bachelor's degree
Physicists and astronomers	20	18	-9	-2	5	1	Doctor's degree
All other physical scientists	40	56	41	16	27	1	Bachelor's degree
Social scientists	259	318	23	59	103		
Economists	48	59	25	12	30	1	Bachelor's degree
Psychologists	144	177	23	33	45	1	Master's degree
Urban and regional planners	29	35	24	7	13	1	Master's degree
All other social scientists	38	45	19	7	15	1	Master's degree
Social, recreational, and religious workers	1,387	1,924	39	536	810		
Clergy	195	234	20	38	77	2	First professional degree
Directors, religious activities and education	81	96	19	15	31	2	Bachelor's degree
Human services workers	168	293	75	125	170	4	Moderate-term O-J-T
Recreation workers	222	266	20	45	86	2	Bachelor's degree
Residential counselors	165	290	76	126	158	1	Bachelor's degree
Social workers	557	744	34	187	288	2	Bachelor's degree
Lawyers and judicial workers	735	918	25	183	279	2	Bachelor's degree

Occupation	Employment		Employment change, 1994-2005		Total job openings due to growth and net replacements, 1994-2005[1]	Earnings quartile[2]	Most significant source of training
	1994	Projected, 2005	Percent	Number			
Judges, magistrates, and other judicial workers	79	79	1	1	11	1	Work experience, plus degree
Lawyers	656	839	28	182	268	1	First professional degree
Teachers, librarians, and counselors	6,246	7,849	26	1,603	2,886		
Teachers, preschool and kindergarten	462	602	30	140	215	3	Bachelor's degree
Teachers, elementary	1,419	1,639	16	220	511	1	Bachelor's degree
Teachers, secondary school	1,340	1,726	29	386	782	1	Bachelor's degree
Teachers, special education	388	593	53	205	262	1	Bachelor's degree
College and university faculty	823	972	18	150	395	1	Doctor's degree
Other teachers and instructors	886	1,151	30	265	331	1	
Farm and home management advisors	14	14	-1	0	1	2	Bachelor's degree
Instructors and coaches, sports and physical training	282	381	35	98	119	2	Moderate-term O-J-T
Adult and vocational education teachers	590	757	28	167	211		
Instructors, adult (nonvocational) education	290	376	29	85	107	2	Work experience
Teachers and instructors, vocational education and training	299	381	27	81	104	2	Work experience
All other teachers and instructors	596	769	29	173	251	1	Master's degree
Librarians, archivists, curators, and related workers	168	182	8	14	56		
Curators, archivists, museum technicians, and restorers	19	23	19	4	9	1	Master's degree
Librarians, professional	148	159	7	10	47	1	Master's degree
Counselors	165	215	31	50	83	1	Master's degree
Health diagnosing occupations	850	1,003	18	153	312		
Chiropractors	42	54	29	12	20	1	First professional degree
Dentists	164	173	5	9	54	1	First professional degree
Optometrists	37	42	12	4	12	1	First professional degree
Physicians	539	659	22	120	205	1	First professional degree
Podiatrists	13	15	15	2	5	1	First professional degree
Veterinarians and veterinary inspectors	56	62	11	6	17	1	First professional degree
Health assessment and treating occupations	2,563	3,294	29	731	1,101		
Dietitians and nutritionists	53	63	19	10	24	2	Bachelor's degree
Pharmacists	168	196	17	28	54	1	Bachelor's degree
Physician assistants	56	69	23	13	22	1	Bachelor's degree

Occupation	Employment		Employment change, 1994–2005		Total job openings due to growth and net replacements, 1994–2005[1]	Earnings quartile[2]	Most significant source of training
	1994	Projected, 2005	Percent	Number			
Registered nurses	1,906	2,379	25	473	740	1	Associate degree
Therapists	380	586	54	207	262	1	Bachelor's degree
Occupational therapists	54	93	72	39	47	1	Bachelor's degree
Physical therapists	102	183	80	81	96	1	Bachelor's degree
Recreational therapists	31	37	22	7	11	1	Associate degree
Respiratory therapists	73	99	36	26	37	1	Master's degree
Speech-language pathologists and audiologists	85	125	46	39	52	1	Bachelor's degree
All other therapists	36	50	39	14	19	1	
Writers, artists, and entertainers	1,612	1,975	22	363	680		Work experience, plus degree
Artists and commercial artists	273	336	23	64	117	2	Long-term O-J-T
Athletes, coaches, umpires, and related workers	38	46	20	8	19	2	Postsecondary vocational training
Dancers and choreographers	24	30	24	6	11	2	
Designers	301	384	28	84	130		Bachelor's degree
Designers, except interior designers	238	314	32	76	113	1	Bachelor's degree
Interior designers	63	70	12	8	17	1	Long-term O-J-T
Musicians	256	317	24	62	105	3	
Photographers and camera operators	139	172	24	34	61		Moderate-term O-J-T
Camera operators, television, motion picture, video	18	19	6	1	5	2	Moderate-term O-J-T
Photographers	121	153	27	32	57	2	Long-term O-J-T
Producers, directors, actors, and entertainers	93	121	30	28	47	2	Bachelor's degree
Public relations specialists and publicity writers	107	128	20	21	44	2	Long-term O-J-T
Radio and TV announcers and newscasters	50	51	1	0	21	2	Bachelor's degree
Reporters and correspondents	59	57	-4	-2	13	1	Bachelor's degree
Writers and editors, including technical writers	272	332	22	59	111	1	Bachelor's degree
All other professional workers	822	1,142	39	319	494	2	Bachelor's degree
Technicians and related support occupations	4,439	5,316	20	876	1,798		
Health technicians and technologists	2,197	2,815	28	618	1,024		
Cardiology technologists	14	17	22	3	6	3	Associate degree
Clinical laboratory technologists and technicians	274	307	12	33	86	2	Bachelor's degree

Occupation	Employment		Employment change, 1994–2005		Total job openings due to growth and net replacements, 1994–2005[1]	Earnings quartile[2]	Most significant source of training
	1994	Projected, 2005	Percent	Number			
Dental hygienists	127	180	42	53	74	2	Associate degree
Electroneurodiagnostic technologists	6	8	28	2	3	3	Moderate-term O-J-T
EKG technicians	16	11	-30	-5	3	3	Moderate-term O-J-T
Emergency medical technicians	138	187	36	49	72	3	Postsecondary vocational training
Licensed practical nurses	702	899	28	197	341	2	Postsecondary vocational training
Medical records technicians	81	126	56	45	59	2	Associate degree
Nuclear medicine technologists	13	16	26	3	5	2	Associate degree
Opticians, dispensing and measuring	63	76	21	13	28	3	Long-term O-J-T
Pharmacy technicians	81	101	24	20	33	3	Moderate-term O-J-T
Psychiatric technicians	72	80	11	8	18	4	Associate degree
Radiologic technologists and technicians	167	226	35	59	82	2	Associate degree
Surgical technologists	46	65	43	19	27	3	Postsecondary vocational training
Veterinary technicians and technologists	22	26	18	4	8	2	Associate degree
All other health professionals and paraprofessionals	374	488	30	114	179	2	Associate degree
Engineering and science technicians and technologists	1,220	1,312	8	92	357		
Engineering technicians	685	746	9	61	207		
Electrical and electronic technicians and technologists	314	349	11	35	108	1	Associate degree
All other engineering technicians and technologists	371	397	7	26	99	2	Associate degree
Drafters	304	304	0	1	70	2	Postsecondary vocational training
Science and mathematics technicians	231	262	13	31	79	2	Associate degree
Technicians, except health and engineering and science	1,023	1,189	16	167	418		
Aircraft pilots and flight engineers	91	97	8	7	32	1	Long-term O-J-T
Air traffic controllers and airplane dispatchers	29	29	0	0	6	1	Long-term O-J-T
Broadcast technicians	42	40	-4	-2	9	1	Postsecondary vocational training
Computer programmers	537	601	12	65	228	1	Bachelor's degree
Legal assistants and technicians, except clerical	219	301	38	82	103	1	
Paralegals	110	175	58	64	74	2	Associate degree
Title examiners and searchers	28	28	0	0	3	2	Moderate-term O-J-T

Occupation	Employment		Employment change, 1994–2005		Total job openings due to growth and net replacements, 1994–2005[1]	Earnings quartile[2]	Most significant source of training
	1994	Projected, 2005	Percent	Number			
All other legal assistants, including law clerks	80	98	22	18	27	1	Associate degree
Programmers, numerical, tool, and process control	7	6	-9	-1	2	1	Work experience
Technical assistants, library	75	91	21	16	32	2	Short-term O-J-T
All other technicians	24	24	0	0	5	2	Moderate-term O-J-T
Marketing and sales occupations	13,990	16,502	18	2,512	6,706		
Cashiers	3,005	3,567	19	562	1,772	4	Short-term O-J-T
Counter and rental clerks	341	451	32	109	203	4	Short-term O-J-T
Insurance sales workers	418	436	4	18	88	1	Long-term O-J-T
Marketing and sales workers supervisors	2,293	2,673	17	380	788	2	Work experience
Real estate agents, brokers, and appraisers	374	407	9	33	113		Work experience
Brokers, real estate	67	75	12	8	22	1	Work experience
Real estate appraisers	47	53	13	6	16	1	Work experience
Sales agents, real estate	260	279	7	19	75	1	Postsecondary vocational training
Salespersons, retail	3,842	4,374	14	532	1,821	3	Short-term O-J-T
Securities and financial services sales workers	246	335	37	90	126	1	Long-term O-J-T
Travel agent	122	150	23	28	55	3	Postsecondary vocational training
All other sales and related workers	3,349	4,109	23	760	1,741	2	Moderate-term O-J-T
Administrative support occupations, including clerical	23,178	24,172	4	994	6,991		
Adjusters, investigators, and collectors	1,229	1,507	23	277	399		
Adjustment clerks	373	521	40	148	175	3	Short-term O-J-T
Bill and account collectors	250	342	36	91	112	3	Short-term O-J-T
Insurance claims and policy processing occupations	461	495	8	35	92		
Insurance adjusters, examiners, and investigators	162	192	19	30	45	2	Long-term O-J-T
Insurance claims clerks	119	135	13	16	27	2	Moderate-term O-J-T
Insurance policy processing clerks	179	168	-6	-12	20	3	Moderate-term O-J-T
Welfare eligibility workers and interviewers	104	108	4	4	16	2	Moderate-term O-J-T
All other adjusters and investigators	41	40	-1	0	4	2	Moderate-term O-J-T

Occupation	Employment		Employment change, 1994–2005		Total job openings due to growth and net replacements, 1994–2005[1]	Earnings quartile[2]	Most significant source of training
	1994	Projected, 2005	Percent	Number			
Communications equipment operators	319	266	-17	-53	83		
Telephone operators	310	260	-16	-50	81		
Central office operators	48	14	-70	-34	12	3	Moderate-term O-J-T
Directory assistance operators	33	10	-70	-24	8	3	Moderate-term O-J-T
Switchboard operators	228	236	3	7	62	3	Short-term O-J-T
All other communications equipment operators	9	6	-31	-3	2	3	Moderate-term O-J-T
Computer operators and peripheral equipment operators	289	175	-39	-114	62		
Computer operators, except peripheral equipment	259	162	-38	-98	56	3	Moderate-term O-J-T
Peripheral EDP equipment operators	30	13	-55	-16	6	3	Moderate-term O-J-T
Information clerks	1,477	1,832	24	355	699		
Hotel desk clerks	136	163	20	27	84	3	Short-term O-J-T
Interviewing clerks, except personnel and social welfare	69	83	20	14	36	3	Short-term O-J-T
New accounts clerks, banking	114	116	2	2	40	3	Work experience
Receptionists and information clerks	1,019	1,337	31	318	508	4	Short-term O-J-T
Reservation and transportation ticket agents and travel clerks	139	133	-4	-6	31	3	Short-term O-J-T
Mail clerks and messengers	260	256	-1	-4	70		
Mail clerks, except mail machine operators and postal service	127	116	-8	-10	35	4	Short-term O-J-T
Messengers	133	140	5	7	35	3	Short-term O-J-T
Postal clerks and mail carriers	474	481	1	7	126		
Postal mail carriers	320	320	0	-1	85	1	Short-term O-J-T
Postal service clerks	154	161	5	7	41	1	Short-term O-J-T
Material recording, scheduling, dispatching, and distributing occupations	3,556	3,688	4	132	863		
Dispatchers	224	258	15	34	65		
Dispatchers, except police, fire, and ambulance	141	168	19	27	46	3	Moderate-term O-J-T
Dispatchers, police, fire, and ambulance	83	90	8	7	18	3	Moderate-term O-J-T
Meter readers, utilities	57	46	-19	-11	13	3	Short-term O-J-T
Order fillers, wholesale and retail sales	215	231	8	16	63	2	Short-term O-J-T
Procurement clerks	57	52	-9	-5	13	3	Short-term O-J-T
Production, planning, and expediting clerks	239	251	5	12	56	2	Short-term O-J-T
Stock clerks	1,759	1,800	2	41	443	3	Short-term O-J-T
Traffic, shipping, and receiving clerks	798	827	4	29	150	3	Short-term O-J-T

Occupation	Employment		Employment change, 1994–2005		Total job openings due to growth and net replacements, 1994–2005[1]	Earnings quartile[2]	Most significant source of training
	1994	Projected, 2005	Percent	Number			
Weighers, measurers, and samplers, record keeping	45	46	3	1	12	3	Short-term O-J-T
All other material recording, scheduling, and distribution workers	161	177	10	16	47	3	Short-term O-J-T
Records processing occupations	3,733	3,438	-8	-294	877		
Advertising clerks	17	18	5	1	5	2	Short-term O-J-T
Brokerage clerks	73	73	1	1	9	3	Short-term O-J-T
Correspondence clerks	29	27	-8	-2	6	2	Short-term O-J-T
File clerks	278	236	-15	-42	102	4	Short-term O-J-T
Financial records processing occupations	2,757	2,506	-9	-250	573		
Billing, cost, and rate clerks	323	328	2	5	98	2	Short-term O-J-T
Billing, posting, and calculating machine operators	96	32	-67	-64	40	2	Short-term O-J-T
Bookkeeping, accounting, and auditing clerks	2,181	2,003	-8	-178	400	3	Moderate-term O-J-T
Payroll and timekeeping clerks	157	144	-9	-14	35	3	Short-term O-J-T
Library assistants and bookmobile drivers	121	127	5	7	57	3	Short-term O-J-T
Order clerks, materials, merchandise, and service	310	337	9	27	95	2	Short-term O-J-T
Personnel clerks, except payroll and timekeeping	123	98	-21	-26	27	2	Short-term O-J-T
Statement clerks	25	16	-38	-9	3	3	Short-term O-J-T
Secretaries stenographers, and typists	4,100	4,276	4	175	1,230		
Secretaries	3,349	3,739	12	390	1,102		
Legal secretaries	281	350	24	68	128	3	Postsecondary vocational training
Medical secretaries	226	281	24	55	103	3	Postsecondary vocational training
Secretaries, except legal and medical	2,842	3,109	9	267	871	3	Postsecondary vocational training
Stenographers	105	102	-3	-3	22	3	Postsecondary vocational training
Typists and word processors	646	434	-33	-212	106	3	Moderate-term O-J-T
Other clerical and administrative support workers	7,740	8,253	7	513	2,582		
Bank tellers	559	407	-27	-152	244	4	Short-term O-J-T
Clerical supervisors and managers	1,340	1,600	19	261	613	2	Work experience
Court clerks	51	59	15	8	12	2	Short-term O-J-T
Credit authorizers, credit checkers, and loan and credit clerks	258	267	4	9	49		Short-term O-J-T

Occupation	Employment		Employment change, 1994-2005		Total job openings due to growth and net replacements, 1994-2005[1]	Earnings quartile[2]	Most significant source of training
	1994	Projected, 2005	Percent	Number			
Credit authorizers	15	19	24	4	5	2	Short-term O-J-T
Credit checkers	40	35	-14	-6	3	3	Short-term O-J-T
Loan and credit clerks	187	196	5	10	37	3	Short-term O-J-T
Loan interviewers	16	17	10	2	4	3	Short-term O-J-T
Customer service representatives, utilities	150	179	19	29	61	2	Short-term O-J-T
Data entry keyers, except composing	395	370	-6	-25	17	3	Postsecondary vocational training
Data entry keyers, composing	19	6	-67	-13	1	3	Postsecondary vocational training
Duplicating, mail, and other office machine operators	222	166	-25	-56	99	2	Short-term O-J-T
General office clerks	2,946	3,071	4	126	908	3	Short-term O-J-T
Municipal clerks	22	21	-3	-1	2	2	Short-term O-J-T
Proofreaders and copy markers	26	20	-20	-5	7	3	Short-term O-J-T
Real estate clerks	24	25	5	1	8	3	Short-term O-J-T
Statistical clerks	75	68	-10	-7	11	3	Moderate-term O-J-T
Teacher aides and educational assistants	932	1,296	39	354	480	4	Short-term O-J-T
All other clerical and administrative support workers	721	698	-3	-23	69	2	Short-term O-J-T
Service occupations	20,239	24,832	23	4,593	9,813		
Cleaning and building service occupations, except private household	3,450	4,071	18	621	1,293	3	Work experience
Institutional cleaning supervisors	125	147	18	22	58	4	Short-term O-J-T
Janitors and cleaners, including maids and housekeeping cleaners	3,043	3,602	18	559	1,140	4	Moderate-term O-J-T
Pest controllers and assistants	56	76	36	20	31	4	Short-term O-J-T
All other cleaning and building service workers	226	245	8	19	63		Short-term O-J-T
Food preparation and service occupations	7,964	9,057	14	1,093	3,498		
Chefs, cooks, and other kitchen workers	3,237	3,739	16	502	1,102		Moderate-term O-J-T
Cooks, except short order	1,286	1,492	16	206	524		Long-term O-J-T
Bakers, bread and pastry	170	230	35	60	102	4	Long-term O-J-T
Cooks, institution or cafeteria	412	435	6	23	125	4	Long-term O-J-T
Cooks, restaurant	704	827	17	123	297	4	Short-term O-J-T
Cooks, short order and fast food	760	869	14	109	297	4	Short-term O-J-T
Food preparation workers	1,190	1,378	16	187	282	4	Short-term O-J-T

Occupation	Employment		Employment change, 1994–2005		Total job openings due to growth and net replacements, 1994–2005[1]	Earnings quartile[2]	Most significant source of training
	1994	Projected, 2005	Percent	Number			
Food and beverage service occupations	4,514	5,051	12	537	2,263	4	Short-term O-J-T
Bartenders	373	347	-7	-25	138	4	Short-term O-J-T
Dining room and cafeteria attendants and bar helpers	416	416	0	0	157	4	Short-term O-J-T
Food counter, fountain, and related workers	1,630	1,669	2	40	463	4	Short-term O-J-T
Hosts and hostesses, restaurant, lounge, or coffee shop	248	292	18	44	114	3	Short-term O-J-T
Waiters and waitresses	1,847	2,326	26	479	1,390	4	Short-term O-J-T
All other food preparation and service workers.	213	267	25	54	132	4	Short-term O-J-T
Health service occupations	2,086	2,846	36	759	1,131		
Ambulance drivers and attendants, except EMTs	18	21	15	3	8	4	Short-term O-J-T
Dental assistants	190	269	42	79	137	3	Moderate-term O-J-T
Medical assistants	206	327	59	121	155	3	Moderate-term O-J-T
Nursing aides and psychiatric aides	1,370	1,770	29	400	594		
Nursing aides, orderlies, and attendants	1,265	1,652	31	387	566	4	Short-term O-J-T
Psychiatric aides	105	118	12	13	28	4	Short-term O-J-T
Occupational therapy assistants and aides	16	29	82	13	16	3	Moderate-term O-J-T
Pharmacy assistants	52	64	23	12	22	3	Short-term O-J-T
Physical and corrective therapy assistants and aides	78	142	83	64	87	4	Moderate-term O-J-T
All other health service workers	157	224	43	67	112	4	Short-term O-J-T
Personal service occupations	2,530	3,719	47	1,189	1,670		
Amusement and recreation attendants	267	406	52	139	211	3	Short-term O-J-T
Baggage porters and bellhops	35	44	26	9	16	4	Short-term O-J-T
Barbers	64	60	-6	-4	20	4	Postsecondary vocational training
Child care workers	757	1,005	33	248	321	4	Short-term O-J-T
Cosmetologists and related workers	645	754	17	109	273	4	Postsecondary vocational training
Hairdressers, hairstylists, and cosmetologists	595	677	14	82	233	4	Postsecondary vocational training
Manicurists	38	64	69	26	36	4	Postsecondary vocational training
Shampooers	12	13	8	1	4	4	Short-term O-J-T
Flight attendants	105	135	28	30	49	2	Long-term O-J-T
Homemaker-home heath aides	598	1,238	107	640	747		

Occupation	Employment		Employment change, 1994–2005		Total job openings due to growth and net replacements, 1994–2005[1]	Earnings quartile[2]	Most significant source of training
	1994	Projected, 2005	Percent	Number			
Home health aides	420	848	102	428	488	4	Short-term O-J-T
Personal and home care aides	179	391	119	212	259	4	Short-term O-J-T
Ushers, lobby attendants, and ticket takers	59	77	29	17	33	3	Short-term O-J-T
Private household workers	808	682	-16	-125	245		Short-term O-J-T
Child care workers, private household	283	278	-2	-5	139	4	Short-term O-J-T
Cleaners and servants, private household	496	387	-22	-108	100	4	Short-term O-J-T
Cooks, private household	9	5	-49	-4	2	4	Moderate-term O-J-T
Housekeepers and butlers	20	12	-37	-7	4	4	Moderate-term O-J-T
Protective service occupations	2,381	3,199	34	818	1,514		
Fire fighting occupations	284	328	16	44	169		
Fire fighters	219	258	18	40	138	1	Long-term O-J-T
Fire fighting and prevention supervisors	52	56	7	4	24	1	Work experience
Fire inspection occupations	13	14	7	1	6	1	Work experience
Law enforcement occupations	992	1,316	33	324	610		
Correction officers	310	468	51	158	194	2	Long-term O-J-T
Police and detectives	682	848	24	166	416		
Police and detective supervisors	87	93	7	6	45	1	Work experience
Police detectives and investigators	66	80	20	13	40	1	Work experience
Police patrol officers	400	511	28	112	271	1	Long-term O-J-T
Sheriffs and deputy sheriffs	86	110	29	25	42	2	Long-term O-J-T
Other law enforcement occupations	43	54	25	11	19	2	Moderate-term O-J-T
Other protective service workers	1,106	1,554	41	449	735		
Detectives, except public	55	79	44	24	35	3	Moderate-term O-J-T
Guards	867	1,282	48	415	580	3	Short-term O-J-T
Crossing guards	58	60	3	2	17	3	Short-term O-J-T
All other protective service workers	126	133	6	8	104	4	Short-term O-J-T
All other service workers	1,020	1,259	23	240	462	3	Work experience
Agriculture, forestry, fishing, and related occupations	3,762	3,650	-3	-112	988	1	
Animal breeders and trainers	16	15	-5	-1	3	1	Bachelor's degree

Occupation	Employment		Employment change, 1994–2005		Total job openings due to growth and net replacements, 1994–2005[1]	Earnings quartile[2]	Most significant source of training
	1994	Projected, 2005	Percent	Number			
Animal caretakers, except farm	125	158	26	33	62	4	Short-term O-J-T
Farm workers	906	870	-4	-36	263	4	Short-term O-J-T
Gardening, nursery, and greenhouse and lawn service occupations	844	986	17	142	271		
Gardeners and groundskeepers, except farm	569	623	9	54	128	4	Short-term O-J-T
Lawn maintenance workers	96	127	32	31	43	4	Short-term O-J-T
Lawn service managers	36	47	33	12	18	3	Work experience
Nursery and greenhouse managers	19	26	37	7	11	3	Work experience
Nursery workers	83	109	31	26	50	4	Short-term O-J-T
Pruners	26	34	32	8	14	4	Short-term O-J-T
Sprayers/applicators	15	20	32	5	7	4	Moderate-term O-J-T
Farm operators and managers	1,327	1,050	-21	-277	221	4	Long-term O-J-T
Farmers	1,276	1,003	-21	-273	211	4	Work experience, plus degree
Farm managers	51	46	-9	-5	10	4	Short-term O-J-T
Fishers, hunters, and trappers	49	47	-4	-2	11		
Captains and other officers, fishing vessels	7	6	-11	-1	2	2	Work experience
Fishers, hunters, and trappers	42	41	-3	-1	9	2	Short-term O-J-T
Forestry and logging occupations	124	118	-5	-6	34		
Forest and conservation workers	42	42	1	1	12	3	Short-term O-J-T
Timber cutting and logging occupations	82	76	-8	-7	22		
Fallers and buckers	29	27	-9	-3	8	3	Short-term O-J-T
Logging tractor operators	20	20	-1	0	4	2	Short-term O-J-T
Log handling equipment operators	16	15	-9	-1	5	3	Short-term O-J-T
All other timber cutting and related logging workers	17	15	-13	-2	5	3	Short-term O-J-T
Supervisors, farming, forestry, and agricultural related occupations	85	91	7	6	22	3	Work experience
Veterinary assistants	31	37	19	6	13	4	Short-term O-J-T
All other agricultural, forestry, fishing, and related workers	255	278	9	23	87	4	Short-term O-J-T
Precision production, craft, and repair occupations	14,047	14,880	6	833	4,489		
Blue-collar worker supervisors	1,884	1,894	1	11	480	1	Work experience
Construction trades	3,616	3,956	9	340	1,183		

Occupation	Employment		Employment change, 1994–2005		Total job openings due to growth and net replacements, 1994–2005[1]	Earnings quartile[2]	Most significant source of training
	1994	Projected, 2005	Percent	Number			
Bricklayers and stone masons	147	162	10	15	43	2	Long-term O-J-T
Carpenters	992	1,074	8	82	290	2	Long-term O-J-T
Carpet installers	66	72	9	6	28	3	Moderate-term O-J-T
Ceiling tile installers and acoustical carpenters	16	14	-10	-2	3	3	Moderate-term O-J-T
Concrete and terrazzo finishers	126	141	12	15	41	3	Long-term O-J-T
Drywall installers and finishers	133	143	7	9	50	2	Moderate-term O-J-T
Electricians	528	554	5	25	152	2	Long-term O-J-T
Glaziers	34	34	2	1	9	2	Long-term O-J-T
Hard tile setters	27	28	1	0	7	2	Long-term O-J-T
Highway maintenance workers	167	182	9	15	62	3	Short-term O-J-T
Insulation workers	64	77	20	13	34	2	Moderate-term O-J-T
Painters and paperhangers, construction and maintenance	439	509	16	70	174	2	Moderate-term O-J-T
Paving, surfacing, and tamping equipment operators	73	93	26	19	37	2	Moderate-term O-J-T
Pipelayers and pipelaying fitters	57	63	12	7	23	3	Moderate-term O-J-T
Plasterers	30	33	11	3	11	2	Long-term O-J-T
Plumbers, pipefitters, and steamfitters	375	390	4	15	92	2	Long-term O-J-T
Roofers	126	143	13	17	42	3	Moderate-term O-J-T
Structural and reinforcing metal workers	61	64	5	3	19	2	Long-term O-J-T
All other construction trades workers	155	181	17	26	68	3	Moderate-term O-J-T
Extractive and related workers, including blasters	220	204	-7	-16	59		
Oil and gas extraction occupations	66	39	-41	-27	12		
Roustabouts	28	13	-55	-16	5	1	Short-term O-J-T
All other oil and gas extraction occupations	38	26	-30	-11	7	1	Moderate-term O-J-T
Mining, quarrying, and tunneling occupations	18	12	-34	-6	3	1	Long-term O-J-T
All other extraction and related workers	136	153	12	17	43	1	Moderate-term O-J-T
Mechanics, installers, and repairers	5,012	5,586	11	574	1,950		
Communications equipment mechanics, installers, and repairers	118	78	-34	-41	26	1	Postsecondary vocational training
Central office and PBX installers and repairers	84	51	-39	-33	17	1	Postsecondary vocational training
Radio mechanics	7	6	-16	-1	2	2	Postsecondary vocational training

Occupation	Employment		Employment change, 1994–2005		Total job openings due to growth and net replacements, 1994–2005[1]	Earnings quartile[2]	Most significant source of training
	1994	Projected, 2005	Percent	Number			
All other communications equipment mechanics, installers, and repairers	27	20	-25	-7	6	1	Postsecondary vocational training
Electrical and electronic equipment mechanics, installers, and repairers	554	555	0	1	175		
Data processing equipment repairers	75	104	38	29	49	2	Postsecondary vocational training
Electrical powerline installers and repairers	112	123	10	11	37	1	Long-term O-J-T
Electronic home entertainment equipment repairers	34	30	-10	-3	9	2	Postsecondary vocational training
Electronics repairers, commercial and industrial equipment	66	68	2	1	20	2	Postsecondary vocational training
Station installers and repairers, telephone	37	11	-70	- 26	7	1	Postsecondary vocational training
Telephone and cable TV line installers and repairers	191	181	-5	-9	43	1	Long-term O-J-T
All other electrical and electronic equipment mechanics, installers, and repairers	39	38	-3	-1	10	2	Postsecondary vocational training
Machinery and related mechanics, installers, and repairers	1,815	2,072	14	258	700		
Industrial machinery mechanics	464	502	8	38	173	2	Long-term O-J-T
Maintenance repairers, general utility	1,273	1,505	18	231	508	2	Long-term O-J-T
Millwrights	77	66	-15	-11	20	1	Long-term O-J-T
Vehicle and mobile equipment mechanics and repairers	1,502	1,736	16	234	655		
Aircraft mechanics, including engine specialists	119	134	13	15	49		
Aircraft engine specialists	23	25	8	2	8	1	Postsecondary vocational training
Aircraft mechanics	96	109	14	13	40	1	Postsecondary vocational training
Automotive body and related repairers	209	243	17	35	92	2	Long-term O-J-T
Automotive mechanics	736	862	17	126	347	2	Long-term O-J-T
Bus and truck mechanics and diesel engine specialists	250	293	17	42	100	2	Long-term O-J-T
Farm equipment mechanics	41	47	14	6	17	2	Long-term O-J-T
Mobile heavy equipment mechanics	101	110	9	9	37	2	Long-term O-J-T
Motorcycle, boat, and small engine mechanics	46	48	4	2	14		
Motorcycle repairers	11	12	4	0	4	2	Long-term O-J-T
Small engine specialists	35	36	4	1	11	2	Long-term O-J-T
Other mechanics, installers, and repairers	1,023	1,145	12	122	394		

Occupation	Employment		Employment change, 1994–2005		Total job openings due to growth and net replacements, 1994–2005[1]	Earnings quartile[2]	Most significant source of training
	1994	Projected, 2005	Percent	Number			
Bicycle repairers	40	44	10	4	13	2	Moderate-term O-J-T
Camera and photographic equipment repairers	11	12	9	1	4	2	Moderate-term O-J-T
Coin and vending machine servicers and repairers	19	17	-14	-3	4	2	Long-term O-J-T
Electric meter installers and repairers	12	10	-18	-2	3	2	Long-term O-J-T
Electromedical and biomedical equipment repairers	10	11	17	2	4	2	Long-term O-J-T
Elevator installers and repairers	24	28	15	4	10	2	Long-term O-J-T
Heat, air conditioning, and refrigeration mechanics and installers	233	299	29	66	125	2	Long-term O-J-T
Home appliance and power tool repairers	70	66	-6	-4	19	1	Long-term O-J-T
Locksmiths and safe repairers	20	21	10	2	7	2	Moderate-term O-J-T
Musical instrument repairers and tuners	10	11	15	1	4	2	Long-term O-J-T
Office machine and cash register servicers	59	63	6	4	29	2	Long-term O-J-T
Precision instrument repairers	40	40	0	0	10	2	Long-term O-J-T
Riggers	11	11	-4	0	2	2	Long-term O-J-T
Tire repairers and changers	89	95	7	6	42	4	Short-term O-J-T
Watchmakers	6	5	-15	-1	2	2	Long-term O-J-T
All other mechanics, installers, and repairers	371	412	11	42	116	2	Long-term O-J-T
Production occupations, precision	2,986	2,906	-3	-30	730		
Assemblers, precision	324	315	-3	-9	91		
Aircraft assemblers, precision	20	19	-8	-2	4	2	Work experience
Electrical and electronic equipment assemblers, precision	144	127	-12	-17	36	3	Work experience
Electromechanical equipment assemblers, precision	47	44	-6	-3	12	3	Work experience
Fitters, structural metal, precision	14	9	-35	-5	3	2	Work experience
Machine builders and other precision machine assemblers	58	65	11	6	18	2	Work experience
All other precision assemblers	40	50	26	11	18	2	Work experience
Food workers, precision	292	282	-4	-11	81		
Bakers, manufacturing	36	40	12	4	12	3	Moderate-term O-J-T
Butchers and meatcutters	219	202	-8	-17	58	3	Long-term O-J-T
All other precision food and tobacco workers	38	39	4	2	11	3	Long-term O-J-T
Inspectors, testers, and graders, precision	654	629	-4	-25	138	2	Work experience
Metal workers, precision	885	824	-7	-61	190		
Boilermakers	20	19	-4	-1	4	2	Long-term O-J-T

Occupation	Employment		Employment change, 1994–2005		Total job openings due to growth and net replacements, 1994–2005[1]	Earnings quartile[2]	Most significant source of training
	1994	Projected, 2005	Percent	Number			
Jewelers and silversmiths	30	32	6	2	8	2	Long-term O-J-T
Machinists	369	349	-5	-20	79	2	Long-term O-J-T
Sheet metal workers and duct installers	222	205	-8	-17	45	2	Moderate-term O-J-T
Shipfitters	12	11	-10	-1	2	2	Long-term O-J-T
Tool and die makers	142	127	-11	-15	34	1	Long-term O-J-T
All other precision metal workers	90	82	-9	-8	18	2	Long-term O-J-T
Printing workers, precision	150	157	4	7	53		Long-term O-J-T
Bookbinders	6	6	-4	0	1	3	Moderate-term O-J-T
Prepress printing workers, precision	131	132	1	1	43		Long-term O-J-T
Compositors and typesetters, precision	11	8	-23	-2	2	2	Long-term O-J-T
Job printers	14	11	-27	-4	3	2	Long-term O-J-T
Paste-up workers	22	16	-28	-6	4	2	Long-term O-J-T
Electronic pagination systems workers	18	33	83	15	19	2	Long-term O-J-T
Photoengravers	7	5	-20	-1	1	2	Long-term O-J-T
Camera operators	15	14	-6	-1	3	2	Long-term O-J-T
Strippers, printing	31	34	9	3	9	2	Long-term O-J-T
Platemakers	13	11	-15	-2	2	2	Long-term O-J-T
All other printing workers, precision	13	19	44	6	8	2	Long-term O-J-T
Textile, apparel, and furnishings workers, precision	240	219	-9	-21	40		Long-term O-J-T
Custom tailors and sewers	84	63	-25	-21	10	4	Work experience
Patternmakers and layout workers, fabric and apparel	17	23	31	5	7	4	Long-term O-J-T
Shoe and leather workers and repairers, precision	24	17	-28	-7	2	4	Long-term O-J-T
Upholsterers	63	64	1	1	9	4	Long-term O-J-T
All other precision textile, apparel, and furnishings workers	51	51	0	0	11	4	Long-term O-J-T
Woodworkers, precision	241	277	15	36	86		Long-term O-J-T
Cabinetmakers and bench carpenters	131	151	15	20	45	3	Long-term O-J-T
Furniture finishers	38	40	6	2	12	3	Long-term O-J-T
Wood machinists	50	59	19	10	19	3	Long-term O-J-T
All other precision woodworkers	22	26	19	4	10	3	Long-term O-J-T
Other precision workers	199	204	2	5	52	3	Long-term O-J-T

Occupation	Employment		Employment change, 1994–2005		Total job openings due to growth and net replacements, 1994–2005[1]	Earnings quartile[2]	Most significant source of training
	1994	Projected, 2005	Percent	Number			
Dental laboratory technicians, precision	49	47	-5	-2	11	3	Long-term O-J-T
Optical goods workers, precision	19	22	12	2	7	3	Long-term O-J-T
Photographic process workers, precision	14	16	15	2	6	4	Long-term O-J-T
All other precision workers	117	119	2	3	28	3	Long-term O-J-T
Plant and system occupations	330	334	1	4	87		
Chemical plant and system operators	37	36	-3	-1	8	1	Long-term O-J-T
Electric power generating plant operators, distributors, and dispatchers	43	42	-3	-1	10		
Power distributors and dispatchers	18	15	-14	-2	4	1	Long-term O-J-T
Power generating and reactor plant operators	26	26	4	1	6	1	Long-term O-J-T
Gas and petroleum plant and system occupations	31	28	-10	-3	7	1	Long-term O-J-T
Stationary engineers	30	27	-10	-3	7	1	Long-term O-J-T
Water and liquid waste treatment plant and system operators	95	104	9	9	30	1	Long-term O-J-T
All other plant and system operators	93	97	5	4	25	1	Long-term O-J-T
Operators, fabricators, and laborers	17,142	17,898	4	757	5,626		
Machine setters, set-up operators, operators, and tenders	4,779	4,505	-6	-274	1,353	3	
Numerical control machine tool operators and tenders, metal and plastic	75	94	26	20	34		Moderate-term O-J-T
Combination machine tool setters, set-up operators, operators, and tenders	106	123	16	17	38		Moderate-term O-J-T
Machine tool cut and form setters, operators, and tenders, metal and plastic	709	593	-16	-116	175	2	
Drilling and boring machine tool setters and set-up operators, metal and plastic	45	30	-35	-16	9	3	Moderate-term O-J-T
Grinding machine setters and set-up operators, metal and plastic	64	52	-18	-12	13	3	Moderate-term O-J-T
Lathe and turning machine tool setters and set-up operators, metal and plastic	71	50	-31	-22	14	3	Moderate-term O-J-T
Machine forming operators and tenders, metal and plastic	171	151	-11	-19	58	3	Moderate-term O-J-T
Machine tool cutting operators and tenders, metal and plastic	119	85	-29	-34	23	3	Moderate-term O-J-T
Punching machine setters and set-up operators, metal and plastic	48	37	-21	-10	12	3	Moderate-term O-J-T
All other machine tool cutting and forming etc.	191	188	-1	-2	46	3	Moderate-term O-J-T

Occupation	Employment		Employment change, 1994–2005		Total job openings due to growth and net replacements, 1994–2005[1]	Earnings quartile[2]	Most significant source of training
	1994	Projected, 2005	Percent	Number			
Metal fabricating machine setters, operators, and related workers	157	138	-12	-19	39	3	Moderate-term O-J-T
Metal fabricators, structural metal products	44	43	-3	-1	9	3	Moderate-term O-J-T
Soldering and brazing machine operators and tenders	10	8	-17	-2	3	3	Moderate-term O-J-T
Welding machine setters, operators, and tenders	103	87	-16	-16	28	2	Moderate-term O-J-T
Metal and plastic processing machine setters, operators, and related workers	425	444	4	19	152		
Electrolytic plating machine operators and tenders, setters and set-up operators, metal and plastic	42	45	6	2	14	3	Moderate-term O-J-T
Foundry mold assembly and shakeout workers	10	8	-23	-2	4	3	Moderate-term O-J-T
Furnace operators and tenders	20	19	-8	-2	4	2	Moderate-term O-J-T
Heat treating machine operators and tenders, metal and plastic	20	17	-12	-2	5	3	Moderate-term O-J-T
Metal molding machine operators and tenders, setters and set-up operators	40	40	0	0	14	3	Moderate-term O-J-T
Plastic molding machine operators and tenders, setters and set-up operators	165	177	7	12	68	3	Moderate-term O-J-T
All other metal and plastic machine setters, operators, and related workers	127	137	8	10	44	3	Moderate-term O-J-T
Printing, binding, and related workers	384	387	1	3	108		Moderate-term O-J-T
Bindery machine operators and set-up operators	72	77	7	5	18	2	Moderate-term O-J-T
Prepress printing workers, production	25	9	-64	-16	5		
Photoengraving and lithographic machine operators and tenders	5	3	-32	-2	1	2	Moderate-term O-J-T
Typesetting and composing machine operators and tenders	20	6	-71	-14	4	2	Moderate-term O-J-T
Printing press operators	218	223	2	5	62		
Letterpress operators	14	4	-71	-10	3	2	Moderate-term O-J-T
Offset lithographic press operators	79	84	7	5	22	2	Moderate-term O-J-T
Printing press machine setters, operators and tenders	113	119	6	6	31	2	Moderate-term O-J-T
All other printing press setters and set-up operators	13	16	24	3	6	2	Moderate-term O-J-T
Screen printing machine setters and set-up operators	26	30	16	4	10	2	Moderate-term O-J-T
All other printing, binding, and related workers	43	48	10	5	13	2	Moderate-term O-J-T
Textile and related setters, operators, and related workers	1,018	829	-19	-188	222	2	Moderate-term O-J-T

Occupation	Employment		Employment change, 1994–2005		Total job openings due to growth and net replacements, 1994–2005[1]	Earnings quartile[2]	Most significant source of training
	1994	Projected, 2005	Percent	Number			
Extruding and forming machine operators and tenders, synthetic or glass fibers	22	28	28	6	11	4	Moderate-term O-J-T
Pressing machine operators and tenders, textile, garment, and related materials	77	76	-1	-1	19	4	Moderate-term O-J-T
Sewing machine operators, garment	531	391	-26	-140	106	4	Moderate-term O-J-T
Sewing machine operators, non-garment	129	117	-9	-12	26	4	Moderate-term O-J-T
Textile bleaching and dyeing machine operators and tenders	30	37	24	7	14	4	Moderate-term O-J-T
Textile draw-out and winding machine operators and tenders	190	143	-25	-47	38	4	Moderate-term O-J-T
Textile machine setters and set-up operators	39	36	-6	-2	8	4	Moderate-term O-J-T
Woodworking machine setters, operators, and other related workers	126	97	-23	-29	32	4	Moderate-term O-J-T
Head sawyers and sewing machine operators and tenders, setters and set-up operators	62	47	-24	-15	16	4	Moderate-term O-J-T
Woodworking machine operators and tenders, setters and set-up operators	64	50	-22	-14	16	4	Moderate-term O-J-T
Other machine setters, set-up operators, operators, and tenders	1,779	1,799	1	20	554	1	Moderate-term O-J-T
Boiler operators and tenders, low pressure	18	12	-32	-6	4	3	Moderate-term O-J-T
Cement and gluing machine operators and tenders	36	25	-30	-11	9	1	Moderate-term O-J-T
Chemical equipment controllers, operators and tenders	75	67	-11	-8	28	3	Moderate-term O-J-T
Cooking and roasting machine operators and tenders, food and tobacco	28	30	8	2	9	3	Moderate-term O-J-T
Crushing and mixing machine operators and tenders	137	136	-1	-1	36	3	Moderate-term O-J-T
Cutting and slicing machine setters, operators and tenders	92	103	12	11	29	1	Moderate-term O-J-T
Dairy processing equipment operators, including setters	14	14	-1	0	5	3	Moderate-term O-J-T
Electronic semiconductor processors	33	34	4	1	10	3	Moderate-term O-J-T
Extruding and forming machine setters, operators and tenders	102	95	-8	-8	27	3	Moderate-term O-J-T
Furnace, kiln, or kettle operators and tenders	28	24	-13	-4	5	2	Moderate-term O-J-T
Laundry and drycleaning machine operators and tenders, except pressing	175	198	13	23	68	4	Moderate-term O-J-T
Motion picture projectionists	8	4	-47	-4	2	3	Short-term O-J-T
Packaging and filling machine operators and tenders	329	359	9	30	119	4	Moderate-term O-J-T
Painting and coating machine operators	155	159	2	3	47		Moderate-term O-J-T

Occupation	Employment		Employment change, 1994–2005		Total job openings due to growth and net replacements, 1994–2005[1]	Earnings quartile[2]	Most significant source of training
	1994	Projected, 2005	Percent	Number			
Coating, painting, and spraying machine operators, tenders, setters, and set-up operators	111	110	-1	-1	31	3	Moderate-term O-J-T
Painters, transportation equipment	45	49	9	4	16	3	Moderate-term O-J-T
Paper goods machine setters and set-up operators	51	42	-16	-8	13	3	Moderate-term O-J-T
Photographic processing machine operators and tenders	43	49	15	6	17	3	Short-term O-J-T
Separating and still machine operators and tenders	20	19	-6	-1	8	1	Moderate-term O-J-T
Shoe sewing machine operators and tenders	14	5	-64	-9	2	4	Moderate-term O-J-T
Tire building machine operators	14	13	-6	-1	4	3	Moderate-term O-J-T
All other machine operators, tenders, setters, and set-up operators	407	409	1	2	111	3	Moderate-term O-J-T
Hand workers, including assemblers and fabricators	2,605	2,665	2	60	784		
Cannery workers	73	82	12	9	29	4	Short-term O-J-T
Coil winders, tapers, and finishers	21	15	-26	-5	5	3	Short-term O-J-T
Cutters and trimmers, hand	51	47	-8	-4	14	3	Short-term O-J-T
Electrical and electronic assemblers	212	182	-14	-30	52	3	Short-term O-J-T
Grinders and polishers, hand	74	70	-6	-4	21	3	Short-term O-J-T
Machine assemblers	51	55	8	4	17	3	Short-term O-J-T
Meat, poultry, and fish cutters and trimmers, hand	132	168	28	36	74	3	Short-term O-J-T
Painting, coating, and decorating workers, hand	33	36	10	3	13	3	Short-term O-J-T
Pressers, hand	16	15	-4	-1	5	3	Short-term O-J-T
Sewers, hand	19	17	-9	-2	2	4	Short-term O-J-T
Solderers and brazers	27	31	17	5	12	3	Short-term O-J-T
Welders and cutters	314	316	1	3	88	2	Postsecondary vocational training
All other assemblers, fabricators, and hand workers	1,583	1,630	3	46	453	3	Short-term O-J-T
Transportation and material moving machine and vehicle operators	4,959	5,459	10	500	1,434		
Motor vehicle operators	3,620	4,045	12	425	1,066		
Bus drivers	568	663	17	95	193		
Bus drivers, except school	165	193	17	29	57	3	Moderate-term O-J-T
Bus drivers, school	404	470	16	66	136	3	Short-term O-J-T
Taxi drivers and chauffeurs	129	157	22	28	43	3	Short-term O-J-T

Occupation	Employment		Employment change, 1994–2005		Total job openings due to growth and net replacements, 1994–2005[1]	Earnings quartile[2]	Most significant source of training
	1994	Projected, 2005	Percent	Number			
Truck drivers	2,897	3,196	10	299	823	2	Short-term O-J-T
Driver/sales workers	331	359	8	28	122	2	Short-term O-J-T
Truck drivers light and heavy	2,565	2,837	11	271	701	2	Short-term O-J-T
All other motor vehicle operators	26	29	11	3[3]	8	2	Short-term O-J-T
Rail transportation workers	86	75	-12	-10	15	1	Work experience
Locomotive engineers	22	19	-14	-3	3	1	Work experience
Railroad brake, signal, and switch operators	19	13	-31	-5	3	1	Work experience
Railroad conductors and yardmasters	26	25	-6	-2	4	1	Work experience
Rail yard engineers, dinkey operators, and hostlers	6	4	-40	-2	1	1	Work experience
Subway and streetcar operators	12	15	23	3	5	1	Moderate-term O-J-T
Water transportation and related workers	48	48	0	0	10	1	Short-term O-J-T
Able seamen, ordinary seamen, and marine oilers	20	20	-3	-1	4	1	Work experience
Captains and pilots, ship	13	13	0	0	3	1	Work experience
Mates, ship, boat, and barge	7	8	6	0	2	1	Work experience
Ship engineers	8	8	3	0	2	1	Work experience
Material moving equipment operators	1,061	1,129	6	69	298		
Crane and tower operators	45	42	-6	-3	11	2	Moderate-term O-J-T
Excavation and loading machine operators	88	100	13	11	31	2	Moderate-term O-J-T
Grader, dozer, and scraper operators	108	113	5	6	27	2	Moderate-term O-J-T
Hoist and winch operators	9	9	-5	0	2	2	Moderate-term O-J-T
Industrial truck and tractor operators	464	493	6	29	132	2	Short-term O-J-T
Operating engineers	146	154	5	7	37	2	Moderate-term O-J-T
All other material moving equipment operators	201	219	9	18	59	2	Moderate-term O-J-T
All other transportation and material moving equipment operators	145	161	11	16	44	2	Moderate-term O-J-T
Helpers, laborers, and material movers, hand	4,799	5,270	10	471	2,056		
Freight, stock, and material movers, hand	765	728	-5	-36	306	4	Short-term O-J-T
Hand packers and packagers	942	1,102	17	160	429	4	Short-term O-J-T
Helpers, construction trades	513	581	13	68	240	4	Short-term O-J-T
Machine feeders and offbearers	262	242	-8	-20	80	3	Short-term O-J-T
Parking lot attendants	64	76	20	13	25	2	Short-term O-J-T

Occupation	Employment		Employment change, 1994–2005		Total job openings due to growth and net replacements, 1994–2005[1]	Earnings quartile[2]	Most significant source of training
	1994	Projected, 2005	Percent	Number			
Refuse collectors	111	115	4	4	31	3	Short-term O-J-T
Service station attendants	167	148	-12	-20	67	4	Short-term O-J-T
Vehicle washers and equipment cleaners	249	299	20	50	133	4	Short-term O-J-T
All other helpers, laborers, and material movers, hand	1,727	1,980	15	253	744	4	Short-term O-J-T

[1] Total job openings represent the sum of employment increases and net replacements. If employment change is negative, job openings due to growth are zero and total job openings equal net replacements.

[2] Codes for describing earnings quartiles are: 1 = Highest quartile, 2 = Second quartile, 3 = Third quartile, 4 = Lowest quartile.

Appendix F

Colleges Offering Cooperative Education Programs

Here is a list of more than 300 outstanding two- and four-year colleges that offer successful cooperative education programs that combine classroom study with paid, on-the-job training and experience. About 900 colleges offer such programs in the United States. Listed below are those that are members of the National Commission for Cooperative Education, which will happily send you more information about each college, if you write to them at 360 Huntington Avenue, Boston, MA 02115. The telephone number of the cooperative education office is provided for each institution, if you prefer to call them directly.

ALABAMA

Alabama State University
915 South Jackson Street
Montgomery, AL 36101-
0271
College Ph: 334/293-4200
Co-op Ph: 334/293-4156
Co-op Students: 387

**Auburn University
Main Campus**
Auburn University, AL
36849-5123
College Ph: 334/844-4000
Co-op Ph: 334/844-5410
Co-op Students: 593

**Auburn University at
Montgomery**
7300 University Drive
Montgomery, AL 36117-
3596
College Ph: 334/244-3000
Co-op Ph: 334/244-3342
Co-op Students: 39

**University of Alabama at
Birmingham**
917 11th Street South
Birmingham, AL
35294-4480
College Ph: 205/934-4011
Co-op Ph: 205/934-8252
Co-op Students: 33

**University of Alabama in
Huntsville**
Huntsville, AL 35899
College Ph: 205/895-6120
Co-op Ph: 205/895-6741
Co-op Students: 353

**University of South
Alabama**
307 University Boulevard
Mobile, AL 36688
College Ph: 334/675-5990
Co-op Ph: 334/460-6188
Co-op Students: 106

Wallace State College
P.O. Box 2000
Hanceville, AL
35077-9080
College Ph: 205/352-8000
Co-op Ph: 205/352-8178
Co-op Students: 314

ARIZONA

Cochise College
4190 West Highway 80
Douglas, AZ 85607
College Ph: 520/364-7943
Co-op Ph: 520/515-5460
Co-op Students: 345

Embry-Riddle Aeronautical
University
Prescott, AZ 86303
College Ph: 520/776-3800
Co-op Ph: 520/776-3820
Co-op Students: 91

Northern Arizona
University
Flagstaff, AZ 86011
College Ph: 520/523-9011
Co-op Ph: 520/523-5850
Co-op Students: 144

Scottsdale Community
College
9000 E. Chaparral Road
Scottsdale, AZ 85230
College Ph: 602/423-6000
Co-op Ph: 602/423-6375
Co-op Students: 140

University of Arizona
Tucson, AZ 85721
College Ph: 520/621-2211
Co-op Ph: 520/621-6736
Co-op Students: 296

ARKANSAS

University of Arkansas
411 Arkansas Union
Fayetteville, AR 72701
College Ph: 501/575-2000
Co-op Ph: 501/575-7379
Co-op Students: 502

University of Arkansas at
Little Rock
2801 South University
Little Rock, AR 72204
College Ph: 501/569-3000
Co-op Ph: 501/569-3584
Co-op Students: 86

CALIFORNIA

California Polytechnic State
University
San Luis Obispo, CA
93407
College Ph: 805/756-1111
Co-op Ph: 805/756-2502
Co-op Students: 474

California State Polytechnic
University
3801 West Temple Avenue
Pomona, CA 91768
College Ph: 909/869-2000
Co-op Ph: 909/869-3671
Co-op Students: 450

California State University
Dominquez Hills
1000 East Victoria Street
Carson, CA 90747
College Ph: 310/516-3300
Co-op Ph: 310/516-3735
Co-op Students: 100

California State University
Fresno
5241 North Maple Avenue
Fresno, CA 93740-0048
College Ph: 209/278-4240
Co-op Ph: 209/278-2381
Co-op Students: 550

California State University
Long Beach
1250 Bellflower Boulevard
Long Beach, CA
90840-0113
College Ph: 310/985-4111
Co-op Ph: 310/985-5554
Co-op Students: 302

California State University
Sacramento
6000 "J" Street
Sacramento, CA
95819-6023
Co-op Ph: 916/278-6011
Co-op Ph: 916/278-6231
Co-op Students: 510

Golden Gate University
536 Mission Street
San Francisco, CA
94105-2968
College Ph: 415/442-7000
Co-op Ph: 415/442-7868
Co-op Students: 20

Mira Costa College
One Branard Drive
Oceanside, CA
92056-3899
College Ph: 619/757-2121
Co-op Ph: 619/757-2121
Co-op Students: 55

Pacific Union College
Angwin, CA 94508
College Ph: 707/965-6311
Co-op Ph: 707/965-6409
Co-op Students: 10

Santa Clara University
Santa Clara, CA 95053
College Ph: 408/554-4764
Co-op Ph: 408/554-4423
Co-op Students: 45

Skyline College
3300 College Drive
San Bruno, CA 94066
College Ph: 415/738-4100
Co-op Ph: 415/738-4261
Co-op Students: 10

Victor Valley Community
College
18422 Bear Valley Road
Victorville, CA
92392-5849
College Ph: 619/245-4271
Co-op Ph: 619/245-4271
x283
Co-op Students: 190

COLORADO

Arapahoe Community College
2500 W. College Drive
Littleton, CO 80160
College Ph: 303/794-1550
Co-op Ph: 303/797-5725
Co-op Students: 116

Colorado State University
Administration Blvd. 108
Fort Collins, CO 80523
College Ph: 970/491-1101
Co-op Ph: 970/491-5709
Co-op Students: 0

Colorado Technical College
4435 North Chestnut St.
Colorado Springs, CO 80907
College Ph: 719/598-0200
Co-op Ph: 719/598-0200
Co-op Students: 35

Community College of Denver
P.O. Box 173363
Denver, CO 80217-3363
College Ph: 303/556-2600
Co-op Ph: 303/556-3607
Co-op Students: 310

Fort Lewis College
1000 Rim Drive
Durango, CO 81301-3999
College Ph: 303/247-7010
Co-op Ph: 303/247-7321
Co-op Students: 200

Trinidad State Junior College
600 Prospect Street
Trinidad, CO 81082
College Ph: 719/846-5621
Co-op Ph: 719/846-5552
Co-op Students: 30

University of Colorado at Boulder
Boulder, CO 80309
College Ph: 303/492-1411
Co-op Ph: 303/492-4122
Co-op Students: 1300

University of Northern Colorado
Greeley, CO 80639
College Ph: 303/351-1890
Co-op Ph: 303/351-2127
Co-op Students: 408

CONNECTICUT

Central Connecticut State University
1615 Stanley Street
New Britain, CT 06050
College Ph: 860/832-3200
Co-op Ph: 860/832-1633
Co-op Students: 366

Eastern Connecticut State University
83 Windham Street
Willimantic, CT 06226
College Ph: 860/465-5000
Co-op Ph: 860/465-5244
Co-op Students: 39

Manchester Community-Technical College
60 Bidwell Street
P.O. Box 1046
Manchester, CT 06045-1046
College Ph: 860/647-6000
Co-op Ph: 860/647-6077
Co-op Students: 143

Naugatuck Valley Community-Technical College
750 Chase Parkway
Waterbury, CT 06708
College Ph: 203/575-8044
Co-op Ph: 203/575-8069
Co-op Students: 275

Norwalk Community-Technical College
188 Richards Avenue
Norwalk, CT 06854
College Ph: 203/857-7000
Co-op Ph: 203/857-7281
Co-op Students: 20

Teikyo Post University
800 Country Club Road
Waterbury, CT 06723-2540
College Ph: 203/596-4500
Co-op Ph: 203/596-4506
Co-op Students: 100

University of Connecticut
233 Glenbrook Road
Storrs, CT 06268-4051
College Ph: 860/486-2000
Co-op Ph: 860/486-3013
Co-op Students: 220

DELAWARE

Delaware State University
1200 N. Dupont Highway
Dover, DE 19901
College Ph: 302/739-4924
Co-op Ph: 302/739-5141
Co-op Students: 22

Delaware Technical & Community College
P.O. Box 610
Georgetown, DE 19947
College Ph: 302/856-5400
Co-op Ph: 302/856-5400
Co-op Students: 85

University of Delaware
135 duPont Hall
Newark, DE 19716
College Ph: 302/831-2000
Co-op Ph: 302/831-4848
Co-op Students: 3

DISTRICT OF
COLUMBIA

Gallaudet University
800 Florida Avenue, NE
Washington, DC
20002-3695
College Ph: 202/651-5000
Co-op Ph: 202/651-5240
Co-op Students: 233

**George Washington
University**
801 22nd Street, NW
Washington, DC 20052
College Ph: 202/994-1000
Co-op Ph: 202/994-6495
Co-op Students: 638

Howard University
2400 Sixth Street, NW
Washington, DC 20059
College Ph: 202/806-6100
Co-op Ph: 202/806-5672
Co-op Students: 384

Southeastern University
501 "I" Street, SW
Washington, DC 20024
College Ph: 202/488-8162
Co-op Ph: 202/488-8162
x300
Co-op Students: 40

FLORIDA

**Central Florida
Community College**
P.O. Box 1388
Ocala, FL 34478
College Ph: 904/237-2111
Co-op Ph: 904/237-2111
x397
Co-op Students: 180

Florida A&M University
Orr Drive
Tallahassee, FL 32307
College Ph: 904/599-3000
Co-op Ph: 904/599-3044
Co-op Students: 50

**Gulf Coast Community
College**
5230 West Highway 98
Panama City, FL 32401
College Ph: 904/769-1551
Co-op Ph: 904/872-3874
Co-op Students: 200

**Miami-Dade Community
College**
11011 SW 104th Street
Room 6319
Miami, FL 33176-3393
College Ph: 305/237-3221
Co-op Ph: 305-237-2758
Co-op Students: 885

**Seminole Community
College**
100 Weldon Boulevard
Sanford, FL 32773-6199
College Ph: 407/328-4722
Co-op Ph: 407/328-2103
Co-op Students: 345

**University of Central
Florida**
P.O. Box 25000
Orlando, FL 32816
College Ph: 407/384-2000
Co-op Ph: 407/384-2667
Co-op Students: 769

University of Florida
Gainsville, FL 32611-2042
College Ph: 352/392-3261
Co-op Ph: 352/392-8242
Co-op Students: 245

University of West Florida
11000 University Parkway
Pensacola, FL 32514
College Ph: 904/474-2423
Co-op Ph: 904/474-2258
Co-op Students: 123

GEORGIA

**Armstrong Atlantic State
University**
11935 Abercorn Extension
Savannah, GA 31412
College Ph: 912/927-5275
Co-op Ph: 912/927-5269
Co-op Students: 8

**Atlanta Metropolitan
College**
1630 Stewart Avenue, SW
Atlanta, GA 30310
College Ph: 404/756-4441
Co-op Ph: 404/756-4491
Co-op Students: 150

Clayton State College
5900 N. Lee Street
Morrow, GA 30260
College Ph: 770/961-3400
Co-op Ph: 770/961-3518
Co-op Students: 102

Darton College
2400 Gillionville Road
Albany, GA 31707
College Ph: 912/888-8740
Co-op Ph: 912/430-6803
Co-op Students: 25

**Georgia Institute of
Technology**
225 North Avenue, NW
Atlanta, GA 30332-0260
College Ph: 404/894-2000
Co-op Ph: 404/894-3320
Co-op Students: 2363

**Georgia Southern
University**
P.O. Box 8033
Statesboro, GA
30460-8033
College Ph: 912/681-5611
Co-op Ph: 912/681-5197
Co-op Students: 118

Mercer University
1400 Coleman Avenue
Macon, GA 31207-0001
College Ph: 912/752-2700
Co-op Ph: 912/752-2862
Co-op Students: 47

State University of West
Georgia
Maple Street
Carrollton, GA
30118-0001
College Ph: 770/836-6500
Co-op Ph: 770/836-6431
Co-op Students: 100

University of Georgia
Athens, GA 30602-3332
College Ph: 706/542-3030
Co-op Ph: 706/542-3375
Co-op Students: 165

Valdosta State University
1500 N. Patterson Street
Valdosta, GA 31698
College Ph: 912/333-5800
Co-op Ph: 912/333-7172
Co-op Students: 200

HAWAII

Hawaii Pacific University
1132 Bishop Street
Suite 502
Honolulu, HI 96813
College Ph: 808/544-0200
Co-op Ph: 808/544-0230
Co-op Students: 360

University of Hawaii at
Manoa
2600 Campus Road
Honolulu, HI 96822
College Ph: 808/956-8111
Co-op Ph: 808/956-4399
Co-op Students: 125

IDAHO

University of Idaho
Moscow, ID 83844-3088
College Ph: 208/885-6111
Co-op Ph: 208/885-5822
Co-op Students: 265

ILLINOIS

Bradley University
Smith Career Center
Burgess Hall
Peoria, IL 61625
College Ph: 309/676-7611
Co-op Ph: 309/677-3040
Co-op Students: 216

College of DuPage
Lambert Road & 22nd
Street
Glen Ellyn, IL 60137
College Ph: 708/942-2800
Co-op Ph: 708/942-2610
Co-op Students: 331

DeVry Institute of
Technology
3300 North Campbell
Avenue
Chicago, IL 60618
College Ph: 773/929-8500
Co-op Ph: 773/929-7837
x2075
Co-op Students: 200

East-West University
816 South Michigan
Avenue
Chicago, IL 60605
College Ph: 312/939-
0111
Co-op Ph: 312/939-0111
x223
Co-op Students: 125

Elmhurst College
190 Prospect Avenue
Elmhurst, IL 60126
College Ph: 630/617-3500
Co-op Ph: 630/617-3186
Co-op Students: 30

Lewis & Clark Community
College
5800 Godfrey Road
Godfrey, IL 62035-2466
College Ph: 618/466-3411
Co-op Ph: 618/466-3411
Co-op Students: 25

Northern Illinois University
DeKalb, IL 60115
College Ph: 815/753-1000
Co-op Ph: 815/753-7204
Co-op Students: 850

Robert Morris College
180 N. LaSalle Street
Chicago, IL 60601
College Ph: 312/836-4805
Co-op Ph: 312/836-5467
Co-op Students: 350

Saint Xavier University
3700 West 103rd Street
Chicago, IL 60655
College Ph: 312/298-3000
Co-op Ph: 312/298-3133
Co-op Students: 100

Southern Illinois University
at Carbondale
Carbondale, IL 62901-
6603
College Ph: 618/453-2121
Co-op Ph: 618/453-7155
Co-op Students: 103

Southern Illinois University
at Edwardsville
Edwardsville, IL
62026-1620
College Ph: 618/692-2000
Co-op Ph: 618/692-3708
Co-op Students: 180

Triton College
2000 5th Avenue
River Grove, IL 60171
College Ph: 708/456-0300
Co-op Ph: 708/456-0300
Co-op Students: 120

University of Illinois at
Chicago
601 South Morgan–
M/C 102
Chicago, IL 60607-7128
College Ph: 312/996-7000
Co-op Ph: 312/996-0425
Co-op Students: 232

William Rainey Harper
College
1200 W. Algonquin Road
Palatine, IL 60067
College Ph: 847/925-6000
Co-op Ph: 847/925-6220
Co-op Students: 26

INDIANA

Indiana State University
567 North 5th Street
Terre Haute, IN 47809
College Ph: 812/237-4000
Co-op Ph: 812/237-5000
Co-op Students: 220

Indiana University-Purdue
University at Fort Wayne
2101 Coliseum Boulevard
East
Fort Wayne, IN
46805-1499
College Ph: 219/481-6100
Co-op Ph: 219/481-6918
Co-op Students: 98

Purdue University Calumet
Hammond, IN 46323
College Ph: 219/989-2993
Co-op Ph: 219/989-2419
Co-op Students: 45

University of Evansville
1800 Lincoln Avenue
Evansville, IN 47715
College Ph: 812/479-2000
Co-op Ph: 812/479-2663
Co-op Students: 25

IOWA

Clarke College
1550 Clarke Drive
Dubuque, IA 52001-9983
College Ph: 319/588-6300
Co-op Ph: 319/588-6302
Co-op Students: 53

University of Northern
Iowa
1222 West 27th Street
Cedar Falls, IA
50614-0002
College Ph: 319/273-2567
Co-op Ph: 319/273-6041
Co-op Students: 491

KANSAS

Butler County Community
College
901 South Haverhill Road
El Dorado, KS 67042
College Ph: 316/321-2222
Co-op Ph: 316/322-3133
Co-op Students: 108

Dodge City Community
College
2501 North 14th Avenue
Dodge City, KS 67801
College Ph: 316/225-1321
Co-op Ph: 316/227-9331
Co-op Students: 75

Kansas State University
Manhattan, KS 66506
College Ph: 913/532-6011
Co-op Ph: 913/532-6956
Co-op Students: 315

Wichita State University
1845 Fairmount
Wichita, KS 67208
College Ph: 978/689-3456
Co-op Ph: 978/689-3688
Co-op Students: 862

KENTUCKY

Eastern Kentucky
University
228 Beckham
Richmond, KY 40475
College Ph: 606/622-1000
Co-op Ph: 606/622-1296
Co-op Students: 595

Lexington Community
College
Cooper Drive
Lexington, KY
40506-0235
College Ph: 606/257-4831
Co-op Ph: 606/257-4735
Co-op Students: 60

Madisonville Community
College
2000 College Drive
Madisonville, KY 42431
College Ph: 502/821-2250
Co-op Ph: 502/821-2250
x2180
Co-op Students: 17

Murray State University
P.O. Box 9
Murray, KY 42071
College Ph: 502/762-3011
Co-op Ph: 502/762-2907
Co-op Students: 13

Northern Kentucky
University
Nunn Drive
Highland Heights, KY
41099-7205
College Ph: 606/572-5100
Co-op Ph: 606/572-5680
Co-op Students: 125

Somerset Community
College
808 Monticello Road
Somerset, KY 42501
College Ph: 606/679-8501
Co-op Ph: 606/679-8501
Co-op Students: 13

University of Kentucky
111 Administration
Building
Lexington, KY
40506-0046
College Ph: 606/257-8607
Co-op Ph: 606/257-8864
Co-op Students: 250

University of Louisville
South Third Street
Louisville, KY
40292-0103
College Ph: 502/852-5555
Co-op Ph: 502/852-6279
Co-op Students: 373

**Western Kentucky
University**
1 Big Red Way
Bowling Green, KY
42101-3576
College Ph: 502/745-0111
Co-op Ph: 502/745-2691
Co-op Students: 262

LOUISIANA

**Delgado Community
College**
501 City Park Avenue
New Orleans, LA
70119-4399
College Ph: 504/483-4114
Co-op Ph: 504/483-4366
Co-op Students: 50

**Southeastern Louisiana
University**
Western Avenue
Hammond, LA 70402
College Ph: 504/549-2000
Co-op Ph: 504/549-3767
Co-op Students: 65

**Southern University/A&M
at Baton Rouge**
P.O. Box 1098
Baton Rouge, LA 70813
College Ph: 504/771-4500
Co-op Ph: 504/771-4090
Co-op Students: 336

MAINE

**Kennebec Valley Technical
College**
92 Western Avenue
Fairfield, ME 04937
College Ph: 207/453-5000
Co-op Ph: 207/453-5169
Co-op Students: 25

**University of Maine at
Machias**
9 O'Brien Avenue
Machias, ME 04654
College Ph: 207/255-3313
Co-op Ph: 207/255-3313
x260
Co-op Students: 50

**University of Southern
Maine**
96 Falmouth Street,
P.O. Box 9300
Portland, ME 04104-9300
College Ph: 207/780-4141
Co-op Ph: 207/780-4199
Co-op Students: 100

MARYLAND

**Baltimore City Community
College**
2901 Liberty Heights
Avenue
Baltimore, MD 21215
College Ph: 410/462-7799
Co-op Ph: 410/986-5410
Co-op Students: 30

Bowie State University
14000 Jericho Park Road
Bowie, MD 20715
College Ph: 301/464-3000
Co-op Ph: 301/464-7260
Co-op Students: 87

Chesapeake College
P.O. Box 8
Wye Mills, MD 21679
College Ph: 410/822-5400
Co-op Ph: 410/822-5400
Co-op Students: 60

Essex Community College
7201 Rossville Boulevard
Baltimore, MD 21237
College Ph: 410/682-6000
Co-op Ph: 410/780-6728
Co-op Students: 100

Morgan State University
Cold Spring Lane &
Hillen Road
Baltimore, MD 21239
College Ph: 410/319-3333
Co-op Ph: 410/319-3110
Co-op Students: 20

University of Baltimore
Charles Street at Mt. Royal
Baltimore, MD
21201-5779
College Ph: 410/837-4200
Co-op Ph: 410/837-5440
Co-op Students: 255

**University of Maryland
Baltimore County**
1000 Hilltop Circle
Baltimore, MD 21250
College Ph: 410/455-1000
Co-op Ph: 410/455-2493
Co-op Students: 200

**University of Maryland-
Eastern Shore**
Princess Anne, MD 21853
College Ph: 410/651-2200
Co-op Ph: 410/651-6446
Co-op Students: 8

University of Maryland
University College
University Boulevard
at Adelphi Road
College Park, MD
20742-1662
College Ph: 301/985-7000
Co-op Ph: 301/985-7780
Co-op Students: 100

Villa Julie College
Green Spring Valley Road
Baltimore, MD 21153
College Ph: 410/486-7000
Co-op Ph: 410/653-6403
Co-op Students: 94

MASSACHUSETTS

Boston University
147 Bay State Road
Boston, MA 02215
College Ph: 617/353-2000
Co-op Ph: 617/353-5731
Co-op Students: 135

Bristol Community College
777 Elsbree Street
Fall River, MA 02720
College Ph: 508/678-2811
Co-op Ph: 508/678-2811
x2471
Co-op Students: 200

Gordon College
255 Grapevine Road
Wenham, MA
01984-1899
College Ph: 508/927-2300
Co-op Ph: 508/927-2306
x4275
Co-op Students: 45

Holyoke Community
College
303 Homestead Avenue
Holyoke, MA 01040
College Ph: 413/538-7000
Co-op Ph: 413/538-7000
x299
Co-op Students: 325

Merrimack College
315 Turnpike Street
North Andover, MA
01845
College Ph: 508/837-5000
Co-op Ph: 508/837-5184
Co-op Students: 230

Mt. Wachusett Community
College
444 Green Street
Gardner, MA 01440
College Ph: 508/632-6600
Co-op Ph: 508/632-6600
Co-op Students: 20

Newbury College
129 Fisher Avenue
Brookline, MA 02146
College Ph: 617/730-7000
Co-op Ph: 617/730-7221
Co-op Students: 50

North Shore Community
College
1 Ferncroft Road
Danvers, MA 01923
College Ph: 508/762-4000
Co-op Ph: 508/762-4000
Co-op Students: 50

Northeastern University
360 Huntington Avenue
Boston, MA 02115
College Ph: 617/373-2000
Co-op Ph: 617/373-3400
Co-op Students: 5808

Northern Essex
Community College
Elliott Way
Haverhill, MA 01830
College Ph: 508/374-3900
Co-op Ph: 508/374-5805
Co-op Students: 216

Springfield College
263 Alden Street
Springfield, MA 01109
College Ph: 413/748-3000
Co-op Ph: 413/748-3110
Co-op Students: 100

Suffolk University
8 Ashburton Place
Boston, MA 02108
College Ph: 617/573-8000
Co-op Ph: 617/573-8312
Co-op Students: 180

University of Massachusetts
Amherst
Amherst, MA 01003
College Ph: 413/545-0111
Co-op Ph: 413/545-6253
Co-op Students: 435

University of Massachusetts
Boston
1000 Morrissey Boulevard
Boston, MA 02125-3393
College Ph: 617/287-5000
Co-op Ph: 617/287-7931
Co-op Students: 227

University of Massachusetts
Dartmouth
Old Westport Road
Dartmouth, MA 02747
College Ph: 508/999-8000
Co-op Ph: 508/999-8596
Co-op Students: 0

Wentworth Institute of
Technology
550 Huntington Avenue
Boston, MA 02115
College Ph: 617/442-9010
Co-op Ph: 617/442-9010
x267
Co-op Students: 687

Worcester Polytechnic
Institute
100 Institute Road
Worcester, MA 01609
College Ph: 508/831-5000
Co-op Ph: 508/831-5549
Co-op Students: 151

MICHIGAN

Aquinas College
1607 Robinson Road, SE
Grand Rapids, MI
49506-1799
College Ph: 616/459-8281
Co-op Ph: 616/459-8181
x5550
Co-op Students: 55

**GMI Engineering &
Management Institute**
1700 W. 3rd Avenue
Flint, MI 48502
College Ph: 810/762-9500
Co-op Ph: 810/762-9760
Co-op Students: 2450

**Kellogg Community
College**
450 North Avenue
Battle Creek, MI 49017
College Ph: 616/965-3931
Co-op Ph: 616/965-3931
x2500
Co-op Students: 125

**Macomb Community
College**
14500 Twelve Mile Road
Warren, MI 48093-3896
College Ph: 810/455-7000
Co-op Ph: 810/286-2217
Co-op Students: 581

Madonna University
36600 Schoolcraft Road
Livonia, MI 48150-1173
College Ph: 313/591-5000
Co-op Ph: 313/432-5620
Co-op Students: 123

Marygrove College
8425 W. McNichols Road
Detroit, MI 48221
College Ph: 313/862-8000
Co-op Ph: 313/862-8000
x321
Co-op Students: 52

Michigan State University
East Lansing, MI
48824-1226
College Ph: 517/355-1855
Co-op Ph: 517/355-5163
Co-op Students: 416

**Michigan Technological
University**
1400 Townsend Drive
Houghton, MI 49931
College Ph: 906/487-1885
Co-op Ph: 906/487-2313
Co-op Students: 321

**Northwestern Michigan
College**
1701 East Front Street
Traverse City, MI 49686
College Ph: 616/922-1000
Co-op Ph: 616/922-1170
x72
Co-op Students: 36

**Saginaw Valley State
University**
4700 Bay Road
University Center, MI
48710
College Ph: 517/790-4000
Co-op Ph: 517/790-4288
Co-op Students: 192

University of Detroit Mercy
4001 West McNichols Rd.
Detroit, MI 48221
College Ph: 313/993-1000
Co-op Ph: 313/993-1446
Co-op Students: 395

University of Michigan
Fleming Building
Ann Arbor, MI
48109-2126
College Ph: 313/764-1817
Co-op Ph: 313/763-6134
Co-op Students: 300

**Washtenaw Community
College**
4800 East Huron River
Drive
Ann Arbor, MI
48106-0978
College Ph: 313/973-3300
Co-op Ph: 313/973-3421
Co-op Students: 185

**Wayne County Community
College**
801 West Fort Street
Detroit, MI 48226
College Ph: 313/496-2500
Co-op Ph: 313/496-2500
Co-op Students: 20

**Western Michigan
University**
Seibert Administration
Building
Kalamazoo, MI 49008
College Ph: 616/387-1000
Co-op Ph: 616/387-3723
Co-op Students: 107

MINNESOTA

**University of Minnesota-
Twin Cities**
Minneapolis, MN 55455
College Ph: 612/625-5000
Co-op Ph: 612/625-5000
Co-op Students: 270

MISSISSIPPI

Alcorn State University
Lorman, MS 39096
College Ph: 601/877-6100
Co-op Ph: 601/877-6324
Co-op Students: 112

Mississippi State University
P.O. Box 6046
Mississippi State, MS
39762
College Ph: 601/325-2131
Co-op Ph: 601/325-3823
Co-op Students: 1138

University of Southern
Mississippi
Box 5014
Hattiesburg, MS
39406-5014
College Ph: 601/266-4111
Co-op Ph: 601/266-4844
Co-op Students: 100

MISSOURI

Maryville University of
St. Louis
13550 Conway Road
St. Louis, MO 63141
College Ph: 314/529-9300
Co-op Ph: 314/529-9375
Co-op Students: 63

University of Missouri at
St. Louis
8001 Natural Bridge Road
St. Louis, MO
63121-4499
College Ph: 314/516-5000
Co-op Ph: 314/516-5002
Co-op Students: 275

Washington University
One Brookings Drive
St. Louis, MO 63130
College Ph: 314/935-5000
Co-op Ph: 314/935-6130
Co-op Students: 105

MONTANA

Montana State University
Billings
1500 North 30th
Billings, MT 59101-0298
College Ph: 406/657-2011
Co-op Ph: 406/657-2168
Co-op Students: 51

Montana State University
Northern
P.O. Box 7751
Havre, MT 59501
College Ph: 406/265-3700
Co-op Ph: 406/265-3708
Co-op Students: 147

University of Montana
Missoula, MT 59812
College Ph: 406/243-0211
Co-op Ph: 406/243-2815
Co-op Students: 439

NEBRASKA

Peru State College
P.O. Box 10
Peru, NE 68421
College Ph: 402/872-3815
Co-op Ph: 402/872-2420
Co-op Students: 143

University of Nebraska at
Kearney
25th Street & 9th Avenue
Kearney, NE 68849-0601
College Ph: 308/865-8441
Co-op Ph: 308/865-8327
Co-op Students: 325

University of Nebraska at
Lincoln
Lincoln, NE 68588-0495
College Ph: 402/472-2111
Co-op Ph: 402/472-7094
Co-op Students: 25

NEVADA

University of Nevada Reno
VPAA, Mailstop 005
Reno, NV 89557
College Ph: 702/784-1110
Co-op Ph: 702/784-1110
Co-op Students: 1006

NEW HAMPSHIRE

New Hampshire College
2500 North River Road
Manchester, NH 03106
College Ph: 603/668-2211
Co-op Ph: 603/645-9630
Co-op Students: 100

New Hampshire
Community Technical
College
Prescott Hill, Rte. 106
Laconia, NH 03246
College Ph: 603/524-3207
Co-op Ph: 603/524-3207
x62
Co-op Students: 137

NEW JERSEY

Atlantic Community
College
5100 Black Horse Pike
Mays Landings, NJ 08330
College Ph: 609/343-4900
Co-op Ph: 609/343-4900
Co-op Students: 200

Bergen Community College
400 Paramus Road
Paramus, NJ 07652
College Ph: 201/447-7100
Co-op Ph: 201/447-7171
Co-op Students: 292

Berkeley College
44 Rifle Camp Road
West Paterson, NJ 07424
College Ph: 201/278-5400
Co-op Ph: 201/278-5400
Co-op Students: 50

Brookdale Community
College
765 Newman Springs
Road
Lincroft, NJ 07738
College Ph: 908/842-1900
Co-op Ph: 908/224-2574
Co-op Students: 500

Caldwell College
9 Ryerson Avenue
Caldwell, NJ 07006-6195
College Ph: 201/228-4424
Co-op Ph: 201/228-4424
x290
Co-op Students: 93

County College of Morris
214 Center Grove Road
Randolph, NJ 07869
College Ph: 201/328-5000
Co-op Ph: 201/328-5245
Co-op Students: 275

Fairleigh Dickinson University
1000 River Road
Teaneck, NJ 07666
College Ph: 201/692-2000
Co-op Ph: 201/443-8940
Co-op Students: 235

Jersey City State College
2039 Kennedy Boulevard
Jersey City, NJ 07305
College Ph: 201/200-6000
Co-op Ph: 201/200-2181
Co-op Students: 485

Kean College of New Jersey
Morris Avenue
Union, NJ 07083
College Ph: 908/527-2000
Co-op Ph: 908/527-2357
Co-op Students: 257

Middlesex County College
155 Mill Road, Box 3050
Edison, NJ 08818-3050
College Ph: 908/548-6000
Co-op Ph: 908/906-2595
Co-op Students: 400

Monmouth University
Cedar Avenue
West Long Branch, NJ
07764
College Ph: 908/571-3400
Co-op Ph: 908/571-3458
Co-op Students: 82

Montclair State University
Upper Montclair, NJ
07043
College Ph: 201/655-4000
Co-op Ph: 201/655-7553
Co-op Students: 470

New Jersey Institute of Technology
University Heights
Newark, NJ 07102-1982
College Ph: 201/596-3000
Co-op Ph: 201/596-5745
Co-op Students: 323

Raritan Valley Community College
P.O. Box 3300
Somerville, NJ
08876-1265
College Ph: 908/526-1200
Co-op Ph: 908/231-8804
Co-op Students: 150

Rutgers, The State University of New Jersey, Cook College
P.O. Box 231
New Brunswick, NJ
08903-0231
College Ph: 908/932-9465
Co-op Ph: 908/932-9149
Co-op Students: 300

Saint Peter's College
2641 Kennedy Boulevard
Jersey City, NJ 07306
College Ph: 201/915-9000
Co-op Ph: 201/915-9302
Co-op Students: 352

Seton Hall University
400 South Orange Avenue
South Orange, NJ 07079
College Ph: 201/761-9000
Co-op Ph: 201/761-9355
Co-op Students: 200

Stevens Institute of Technology
Castle Point
Hoboken, NJ 07030
College Ph: 201/216-5000
Co-op Ph: 201/216-8228
Co-op Students: 304

NEW MEXICO

San Juan College
4601 College Boulevard
Farmington, NM 87402
College Ph: 505/326-3311
Co-op Ph: 505/599-0245
Co-op Students: 64

NEW YORK

Alfred University
26 North Main Street
Alfred, NY 14802
College Ph: 607/871-2111
Co-op Ph: 607/871-2426
Co-op Students: 42

Clarkson University
P.O. Box 5500
Potsdam, NY 13699
College Ph: 315/268-6400
Co-op Ph: 315/268-6578
Co-op Students: 70

Cornell University
Ithaca, NY 14853
College Ph: 607/255-2000
Co-op Ph: 607/255-3512
Co-op Students: 445

CUNY/City College
140 Street & Covent
Avenue
New York, NY 10031
College Ph: 212/650-7000
Co-op Ph: 212/650-8040
Co-op Students: 190

CUNY/LaGuardia
Community College
31-10 Thomson Avenue
Long Island City, NY
11101
College Ph: 718/482-7200
Co-op Ph: 718/482-5200
Co-op Students: 1995

Daemen College
4380 Main Street
Amherst, NY 14226
College Ph: 716/839-3600
Co-op Ph: 716/839-8334
Co-op Students: 78

Dowling College
Idle Hour Boulevard
Oakdale, NY 11768
College Ph: 516/244-3000
Co-op Ph: 516/244-3391
Co-op Students: 175

Laboratory Institute of
Merchandising
12 East 53rd Street
New York, NY
10022-5268
College Ph: 212/752-1530
Co-op Ph: 212/752-1530
Co-op Students: 50

Long Island University/
Brooklyn Campus
1 University Plaza
Brooklyn, NY 11201
College Ph: 718/488-1000
Co-op Ph: 718/488-1039
Co-op Students: 210

Long Island University/
C. W. Post Campus
720 Northern Boulevard
Greenvale, NY
11548-1300
College Ph: 516/299-0200
Co-op Ph: 516/299-2435
Co-op Students: 234

Long Island University/
Southampton Campus
Montauk Highway
Southampton, NY 11968
College Ph: 516/283-4000
Co-op Ph: 516/287-8272
Co-op Students: 195

Manhattan College
4513 Manhattan College
Parkway
Bronx, NY 10471
College Ph: 718/862-8000
Co-op Ph: 718/862-7421
Co-op Students: 133

Marist College
North Road,
Poughkeepsie, NY
12601-1387
College Ph: 914/575-3000
Co-op Ph: 914/575-3543
Co-op Students: 59

Mercy College
555 Broadway
Dobbs Ferry, NY 10522
College Ph: 914/693-4500
Co-op Ph: 914/674-7203
Co-op Students: 150

Monroe College
29 East Fordham Road
Bronx, NY 10468
College Ph: 718/933-6700
Co-op Ph: 718/933-7065
Co-op Students: 150

Nassau Community College
1 Education Drive
Garden City, NY 11530
College Ph: 516/572-7501
Co-op Ph: 516/572-7832
Co-op Students: 250

Niagara University
P.O. Box 2015
Niagara, NY 14109-1946
College Ph: 716/285-1212
Co-op Ph: 716/286-8539
Co-op Students: 286

Onondaga Community
College
Rte. 175
Syracuse, NY 13215
College Ph: 315/469-7741
Co-op Ph: 315/469-2488
Co-op Students: 182

Pace University
1 Pace Plaza
New York, NY 10038
College Ph: 212/346-1200
Co-op Ph: 212/346-1950
Co-op Students: 1094

Polytechnic University
6 Metrotech Center
Brooklyn, NY 11201
College Ph: 718/260-3600
Co-op Ph: 718/260-3650
Co-op Students: 40

Rensselaer Polytechnic
Institute
Troy, NY 12180
College Ph: 518/276-6000
Co-op Ph: 518/276-6243
Co-op Students: 434

Rochester Institute of
Technology
51 Lomb Memorial Drive
Rochester, NY 14623
College Ph: 716/475-2400
Co-op Ph: 716/475-2301
Co-op Students: 2529

Russell Sage College
45 Ferry Street
Troy, NY 12180
College Ph: 518/270-2000
Co-op Ph: 518/270-2272
Co-op Students: 160

Suffolk Community
College
533 College Road
Selden, NY 11784
College Ph: 516/451-4110
Co-op Ph: 516/451-4760
Co-op Students: 330

SUNY/College at
Brockport
350 New Campus Drive
Brockport, NY
14420-2974
College Ph: 716/395-2211
Co-op Ph: 716/395-5417
Co-op Students: 50

Syracuse University
Syracuse, NY 13244
College Ph: 315/443-1870
Co-op Ph: 315/443-4345
Co-op Students: 106

The College of Insurance
101 Murray Street
New York, NY
10007-2165
College Ph: 212/962-4111
Co-op Ph: 212/815-9292
Co-op Students: 45

U.S. Merchant Marine
Academy
Steamboat Road
Kings Point, NY 11024
College Ph: 516/773-5000
Co-op Ph: 516/773-5518
Co-op Students: 800

Utica College of Syracuse
University
1600 Burrstone Road
Utica, NY 13502
College Ph: 315/792-3111
Co-op Ph: 315/792-3027
Co-op Students: 136

NORTH CAROLINA

Alamance Community
College
P.O. Box 8000
Graham, NC 27253-8000
College Ph: 910/578-2002
Co-op Ph: 910/578-2002
Co-op Students: 251

Appalachian State
University
Boone, NC 28608
College Ph: 704/262-2000
Co-op Ph: 704/262-2382
Co-op Students: 81

Central Piedmont
Community College
P.O. Box 35009
Charlotte, NC 28235
College Ph: 704/330-6633
Co-op Ph: 704/330-6217
Co-op Students: 450

East Carolina University
Greenville, NC 27858
College Ph: 919/328-6131
Co-op Ph: 919/328-6979
Co-op Students: 762

Elizabeth City State
University
1704 Weeksville Road
Elizabeth City, NC 27909
College Ph: 919/335-3230
Co-op Ph: 919/335-3287
Co-op Students: 100

Guilford Technical
Community College
Box 309
Jamestown, NC 27282
College Ph: 910/334-4822
Co-op Ph:
910/334-4822x2429
Co-op Students: 200

Haywood Community
College
Freedlander Drive
Clyde, NC 28721
College Ph: 704/627-2821
Co-op Ph: 704/627-4523
Co-op Students: 20

North Carolina A&T State
University
1601 East Market Street
Greensboro, NC 27411
College Ph: 910/334-7500
Co-op Ph: 910/334-7755
Co-op Students: 136

North Carolina Central
University
1801 Fayetteville Street
Durham, NC 27707
College Ph: 919/560-6100
Co-op Ph: 919/560-6198
Co-op Students: 60

North Carolina State
University
P.O. Box 71110
Raleigh, NC 27695
College Ph: 919/515-2011
Co-op Ph: 919/515-2300
Co-op Students: 1269

University of North
Carolina Charlotte
132 King Building
Charlotte, NC 28223
College Ph: 704/547-2000
Co-op Ph: 704/547-2231
Co-op Students: 283

Wake Technical
Community College
9101 Fayetteville Road
Raleigh, NC 27603-5696
College Ph: 919/662-3400
Co-op Ph: 919/662-3377
Co-op Students: 307

Western Carolina
University
Cullowhee, NC 28723
College Ph: 704/227-
7211
Co-op Ph: 704/227-7133
Co-op Students: 143

NORTH DAKOTA

Mayville State University
330 Third Street NE
Mayville, ND 58257
College Ph: 701/786-2301
Co-op Ph: 701/786-4899
Co-op Students: 100

Minot State University-Bottineau Campus
105 Simrall Blvd.
Bottineau, ND 58318
College Ph: 701/858-3000
Co-op Ph: 701/228-5454
Co-op Students: 75

North Dakota State University
Bottineau, ND 58318
College Ph: 701/231-8011
Co-op Ph: 701/231-7188
Co-op Students: 616

University of North Dakota
Box 9014
Grand Forks, ND 58202
College Ph: 701/777-2011
Co-op Ph: 701/777-4104
Co-op Students: 500

Valley City State University
101 College Street
Valley City, ND 58257
College Ph: 701/845-7102
Co-op Ph: 701/845-7428
Co-op Students: 100

OHIO

Bowling Green State University
Bowling Green, OH
43403
College Ph: 419/372-2531
Co-op Ph: 419/372-2452
Co-op Students: 890

Cincinnati State Technical and Community College
3520 Central Parkway
Cincinnati, OH 45223
College Ph: 513/569-1599
Co-op Ph: 513/569-1738
Co-op Students: 1940

Cleveland State University
2344 Euclid Avenue
Cleveland, OH 44115
College Ph: 216/687-2000
Co-op Ph: 216/687-2246
Co-op Students: 1380

College of Mount Saint Joseph
5701 Delhi Road
Cincinnati, OH
45223-1672
College Ph: 513/224-4888
Co-op Ph: 513/244-4888
Co-op Students: 146

Hocking College
3301 Hocking Parkway
Nelsonville, OH
45764-9704
College Ph: 614/753-3591
Co-op Ph: 614/753-3591
Co-op Students: 20

John Carroll University
20700 North Park Blvd.
Cleveland, OH 44118
College Ph: 216/397-1886
Co-op Ph: 216/397-4237
Co-op Students: 650

Mount Union College
1972 Clark Avenue
Alliance, OH 44601
College Ph: 330/821-5320
Co-op Ph: 330/823-2889
Co-op Students: 75

Notre Dame College of Ohio
4545 College Road
South Euclid, OH 44121
College Ph: 216/381-1680
Co-op Ph: 216/381-1680
Co-op Students: 45

Ohio University
Athens, OH 45701
College Ph: 614/593-1000
Co-op Ph: 614/593-1618
Co-op Students: 216

Sinclair Community College
444 West Third Street
Dayton, OH 45402
College Ph: 513/226-2500
Co-op Ph: 513/226-2769
Co-op Students: 600

University of Akron
Akron, OH 44325-6212
College Ph: 330/972-7111
Co-op Ph: 330/972-7827
Co-op Students: 180

University of Cincinnati
P.O. Box 210063
Cincinnati, OH
45221-0063
College Ph: 513/556-6000
Co-op Ph: 513/556-6571
Co-op Students: 3,021

University of Toledo
2801 West Bancroft Street
Toledo, OH 43606-3390
College Ph: 419/530-4242
Co-op Ph: 419/530-3600
Co-op Students: 326

Ursuline College
2550 Lander Road
Pepper Pike, OH 44124
College Ph: 216/449-4200
Co-op Ph: 216/646-8322
Co-op Students: 25

Wilberforce University
1055 No. Bickett Road
Wilberforce, OH 45384
College Ph: 513/376-2911
Co-op Ph: 513/376-2911
x737
Co-op Students: 200

Wright State University
364 Colonel Glenn
Highway
Dayton, OH 45431
College Ph: 937/775-3333
Co-op Ph: 937/775-2556
Co-op Students: 231

**Youngstown State
University**
One University Plaza
Youngstown, OH 44555
College Ph: 330/742-2000
Co-op Ph: 330/742-1405
Co-op Students: 167

OKLAHOMA

**Northeastern State
University**
Tahlequah, OK
74464-7098
College Ph: 918/456-5511
Co-op Ph: 918/456-5511
x3111
Co-op Students: 20

Oklahoma State University
Stillwater, OK
74078-0535
College Ph: 405/744-5000
Co-op Ph: 405/744-6188
Co-op Students: 72

OREGON

**Clackamas Community
College**
19600 South Molalla
Avenue
Oregon City, OR 97045
College Ph: 503/657-6958
Co-op Ph: 503/657-6958
Co-op Students: 350

Lane Community College
4000 E. 30th Avenue
Eugene, OR 97405
College Ph: 541/747-4501
Co-op Ph: 541/726-2203
Co-op Students: 1887

**Mount Hood Community
College**
26000 SE Stark Street
Gresham, OR 97030
College Ph: 503/667-6422
Co-op Ph: 503/667-7223
Co-op Students: 950

PENNSYLVANIA

Beaver College
450 South Easton Road
Glenside, PA 19038
College Ph: 215/572-2900
Co-op Ph: 215/572-2972
Co-op Students: 5

Cabrini College
610 King of Prussia Road
Radnor, PA 19087
College Ph: 610/902-8100
Co-op Ph: 610/902-8305
Co-op Students: 162

Drexel University
3141 Chestnut Street
Philadelphia, PA 19104
College Ph: 215/895-2000
Co-op Ph: 215/895-1630
Co-op Students: 2245

Holy Family College
Grant & Frankford
Avenues
Philadelphia, PA 19114-
2094
College Ph: 215/637-7700
Co-op Ph: 215/637-7330
Co-op Students: 81

**Indiana University of
Pennsylvania**
201 Sutton Hall
Indiana, PA 15705-1082
College Ph: 412/357-2100
Co-op Ph: 412/357-2487
Co-op Students: 100

Neumann College
One Neumann Drive
Aston, PA 19014
College Ph: 610/459-0905
Co-op Ph: 610/558-5527
Co-op Students: 47

Peirce College
1420 Pine Street
Philadelphia, PA 19102
College Ph: 215/545-6400
Co-op Ph: 215/545-6400
Co-op Students: 77

**Pennsylvania Institute of
Technology**
800 Manchester Avenue
Media, PA 19063
College Ph: 610/565-7900
Co-op Ph: 610/565-7900
Co-op Students: 195

Pennsylvania State
University
201 Old Main
University Park, PA 16801
College Ph: 814/865-4700
Science Co-op
Ph: 814/865-5000
Engineering Co-op
Ph: 814/863-1032
Science Co-op
Students: 111
Engineering Co-op
Students: 687

Philadelphia College of
Textiles & Science
4201 Henry Avenue
Philadelphia, PA 19114
College Ph: 215/951-2700
Co-op Ph: 215/951-2825
Co-op Students: 128

Temple University
Broad Street & Burks Mall
Philadelphia, PA 19122
College Ph: 215/204-7000
Co-op Ph: 215/204-7981
Co-op Students: 500

Thiel College
75 College Avenue
Greenville, PA 16125
College Ph: 412/589-2000
Co-op Ph: 412/589-2015
Co-op Students: 73

University of Pittsburgh
Pittsburg, PA 15260
College Ph: 412/624-4141
Co-op Ph: 412/624-9892
Co-op Students: 419

Wilkes University
P.O. Box 111
Wilkes-Barre, PA 18766
College Ph: 717/831-5000
Co-op Ph: 717/831-4645
Co-op Students: 175

NORTHERN MARIANAS

Northern Marianas College
Box 1250
Saipan, CM 96950
College Ph: 670/234-7642
Co-op Ph: 670/234-5498
x1511
Co-op Students: 28

PUERTO RICO

Inter American Univ. of
P.R., Ponce Campus
Bo Sabanetas Carr 1
Mercedita, PR 00715
College Ph: 809/840-9090
Co-op Ph: 809/840-9090
Co-op Students: 23

University of Puerto Rico,
Mayaguez Campus
P.O. Box 5000
Mayaguez, PR
00709-5000
College Ph: 787/832-4040
Co-op Ph: 787/832-4040
Co-op Students: 30

RHODE ISLAND

Community College of
Rhode Island
1762 Louisquissett Pike
Lincoln, RI 02865
College Ph: 401/825-1000
Co-op Ph: 401/333-7254
Co-op Students: 330

Johnson & Wales
University
8 Abbott Park Place
Providence, RI 02903
College Ph: 401/598-1000
Co-op Ph: 401/456-4659
Co-op Students: 700

SOUTH CAROLINA

Clemson University
321 Brackett Hall
Clemson, SC 29634
College Ph: 864/656-3311
Co-op Ph: 864/656-3150
Co-op Students: 720

Morris College
100 West College Street
Sumter, SC 29150
College Ph: 803/775-9371
Co-op Ph: 803/775-9371
Co-op Students: 50

South Carolina State
University
300 College Street, NE
Orangeburg, SC
29117-0001
College Ph: 803/536-7000
Co-op Ph: 803/536-8572
Co-op Students: 150

TENNESSEE

Chattanooga State
Technical Community
College
4501 Amnicola Highway
Chattanooga, TN 37406
College Ph: 423/697-4400
Co-op Ph: 423/697-4720
Co-op Students: 37

Middle Tennessee State
University
P.O. Box 31
Murfreesboro, TN 37132
College Ph: 615/898-2300
Co-op Ph: 615/898-2225
Co-op Students: 67

Motlow State Community
College
P.O. Box 88100
Tullahoma, TN
37388-8100
College Ph: 615/393-1500
Co-op Ph: 615/393-1764
Co-op Students: 30

Nashville State Technical
Institute
120 White Bridge Road
Nashville, TN 37209
College Ph: 615/353-3333
Co-op Ph: 615-353-3248
Co-op Students: 100

Tennessee State University
3500 John A. Merrit Blvd.
Nashville, TN
37209-1561
College Ph: 615/963-5000
Co-op Ph: 615/963-7465
Co-op Students: 125

TEXAS

Collin County Community
College
4800 Preston Park Blvd.
Plano, TX 75073
College Ph: 972/548-6790
Co-op Ph: 972/881-5735
Co-op Students: 253

El Centro College
Main & Lamar Streets
Dallas, TX 75202-2202
College Ph: 214/746-2200
Co-op Ph: 214/746-2202
Co-op Students: 364

El Paso Community
College
P.O. Box 20500
El Paso, TX 79998
College Ph: 915/594-2638
Co-op Ph: 915/594-2638
Co-op Students: 410

Houston Community
College
Houston, TX 77270
College Ph: 713/718-5000
Co-op Ph: 713/718-7589
Co-op Students: 319

Jarvis Christian College
Highway 80 West
P.O. Drawer G
Hawkins, TX 75765-9989
College Ph: 903/769-5700
Co-op Ph: 903/769-5739
Co-op Students: 100

Paris Junior College
2400 Clarksville Street
Paris, TX 75460
College Ph: 903/785-7661
Co-op Ph: 903/784-9366
Co-op Students: 22

Prairie View A&M
University
P.O. Box 66
Prairie View, TX 77446
College Ph: 409/857-3311
Co-op Ph: 409/857-2120
Co-op Students: 900

Richland College
12800 Abrams Road
Dallas, TX 75243-2199
College Ph: 214/238-6194
Co-op Ph: 214/238-6190
Co-op Students: 20

Southern Methodist
University
P.O. Box 750335
Dallas, TX 75275-0335
College Ph: 214/768-2000
Co-op Ph: 214/768-3033
Co-op Students: 93

Texas A&M University
College Station, TX
77843-1476
College Ph: 409/845-3211
Co-op Ph: 409/845-7725
Co-op Students: 501

Texas State Technical
College
3801 Campus Drive
Waco, TX 76705
College Ph: 817/867-4891
Co-op Ph: 817/867-4860
Co-op Students: 266

University of Houston
Clear Lake
2700 Bay Area Boulevard
Houston, TX 77058
College Ph: 281/283-7600
Co-op Ph: 281/283-2600
Co-op Students: 150

University of Houston
University Park
4800 Calhoun
Houston, TX 77204
College Ph: 713/743-1000
Co-op Ph: 713/743-4232
Co-op Students: 300

University of North Texas
P.O. Box 13737
Denton, TX 76203-3737
College Ph: 817/565-3200
Co-op Ph: 817/565-2865
Co-op Students: 703

University of Texas at
Austin
Austin, TX 78712
College Ph: 512/471-3434
Co-op Ph: 512/471-5954
Co-op Students: 353

University of Texas at El Paso
500 West University
Avenue
El Paso, Tx 79968-0512
College Ph: 915/747-5000
Co-op Ph: 915/747-5640
Co-op Students: 388

University of Texas at
San Antonio
6900 Northwest Loop,
#1604
San Antonio, TX 78249
College Ph: 210/458-4011
Co-op Ph: 210/691-4596
Co-op Students: 290

University of the Incarnate
Word
4301 Broadway, Box 36
San Antonio, TX
78209-6397
College Ph: 210/829-6000
Co-op Ph: 210/829-3931
Co-op Students: 29

UTAH

Brigham Young University
110 FOB
Provo, UT 84602
College Ph: 801/378-1211
Co-op Ph: 801/378-3337
Co-op Students: 3992

Snow College
150 East College Avenue
Ephraim, UT 84627
College Ph: 801/283-4021
Co-op Ph: 801/283-4021
Co-op Students: 225

University of Utah
Salt Lake City, UT 24112
College Ph: 801/581-7200
Co-op Ph: 801/581-6186
Co-op Students: 1000

Utah Valley State College
800 West 1200 South
Orem, UT 84058-5999
College Ph: 801/222-8000
Co-op Ph: 801/222-8123
Co-op Students: 450

Weber State University
University Circle
Ogden, UT 84408
College Ph: 801/626-6000
Co-op Ph: 801/626-6393
Co-op Students: 4180

VERMONT

Sterling College
Main Street
Craftsbury Common, VT
05827
College Ph: 802/586-7711
Co-op Ph: 802/586-7711
Co-op Students: 25

Vermont Law School
P.O. Box 96
South Royalton, VT
05068
College Ph: 802/763-8303
Co-op Ph: 802/763-8303
Co-op Students: 25

VIRGINIA

Hampton University
Hampton, VA 23668
College Ph: 804/727-5000
Co-op Ph: 804/727-5331
Co-op Students: 267

Norfolk State University
2401 Corprew Avenue
Norfolk, VA 23504
College Ph: 804/683-8600
Co-op Ph: 804/683-8629
Co-op Students: 50

Old Dominion University
5215 Hampton Blvd.
Norfolk, VA 23529-0013
College Ph: 757/683-3000
Co-op Ph: 757/683-4388
Co-op Students: 350

Virginia State University
Petersburg, VA
23806-2099
College Ph: 804/524-5000
Co-op Ph: 804/524-5211
Co-op Students: 35

WASHINGTON

**Eastern Washington
University**
Cheney, WA 99004
College Ph: 509/359-6200
Co-op Ph: 509/359-2329
Co-op Students: 350

Olympic College
1600 Chester Avenue
Bremerton, WA
98337-1699
College Ph: 360/792-6050
Co-op Ph: 360/478-7197
Co-op Students: 150

Seattle Central Community
College
1701 Broadway
Seattle, WA 98122
College Ph: 206/587-3800
Co-op Ph: 206/587-6996
Co-op Students: 500

Skagit Valley College
2405 College Way
Mount Vernon, WA
98273
College Ph: 360/428-1261
Co-op Ph: 360/416-7630
Co-op Students: 200

Spokane Falls Community
College
West 3410 Fort George
Wright Drive
Spokane, WA 99204-5288
College Ph: 509/533-3500
Co-op Ph: 509/533-3415
Co-op Students: 21

University of Puget Sound
1500 North Warner
Tacoma, WA 98416
College Ph: 206/756-3337
Co-op Ph: 206/756-3433
Co-op Students: 21

Walla Walla Community
College
500 Tausick Way
Walla, Walla, WA 99362
College Ph: 509/527-2615
Co-op Ph: 509/527-4253
Co-op Students: 316

WEST VIRGINIA

West Virginia State College
P.O. Box 1000
Institute, WV 25112
College Ph: 304/766-3000
Co-op Ph: 304/766-3134
Co-op Students: 51

West Virginia University
Institute of Technology
Old Main Boulevard
Box 31
Montgomery, WV 25136
College Ph: 304/442-3071
Co-op Ph: 304/442-3185
Co-op Students: 140

WISCONSIN

Fox Valley Technical
College
1825 N. Bluemound Dr.
Appleton, WI 54913-2277
College Ph: 414/735-5600
Co-op Ph: 414/735-5678
Co-op Students: 607

Marian College of Fond
Du Lac
45 South National Avenue
Fond Du Lac, WI
54935-4699
College Ph: 414/923-7600
Co-op Ph: 414/923-8097
Co-op Students: 103

Milwaukee Area Technical
College
700 W. State Street
Milwaukee, WI 53233
College Ph: 414/297-6600
Co-op Ph: 414/297-6644
Co-op Students: 30

University of Wisconsin,
Madison
1415 Johnson Drive
Madison, WI 53706
College Ph: 608/262-1234
Co-op Ph: 608/262-8883
Co-op Students: 475

University of Wisconsin,
Oshkosh
800 Algoma Boulevard
Oshkosh, WI 54901-8601
College Ph: 414/424-1234
Co-op Ph: 414/424-1137
Co-op Students: 100

University of Wisconsin,
Platteville
One University Plaza
Platteville, WI
53818-3099
College Ph: 608/342-1491
Co-op Ph: 608/342-1686
Co-op Students: 120

University of Wisconsin,
River Falls
410 S. 3rd Street
River Falls, WI 54022
College Ph: 715/425-3911
Co-op Ph: 715/425-0683
Co-op Students: 150

University of Wisconsin,
Stout
Menomonie, WI 54751
College Ph: 715/232-1123
Co-op Ph: 715/232-1129
Co-op Students: 455

Waukesha County
Technical College
800 Main Street
Pewaukee, WI 53072
College Ph: 414/691-5566
Co-op Ph: 414/695-7801
Co-op Students: 863

WYOMING

Central Wyoming College
2660 Peck Avenue
Riverton, WY 82501
College Ph: 307/856-9291
Co-op Ph: 397/856-9291
Co-op Students: 41

University of Wyoming
Box 3434, University
Station
Laramie, WY 82071
College Ph: 307/766-1121
Co-op Ph: 307/766-2398
Co-op Students: 27

Western Wyoming
Community
College
2500 College Drive, E-572
Rock Springs, WY
82902-0428
College Ph: 307/382-1600
Co-op Ph: 307/382-1761
Co-op Students: 78

Index

Job Index

(Listings limited to jobs employing 500,000 people and not requiring a four-year college degree. See Appendix C for alphabetical listing of median weekly pay for 600 different jobs.)